THE FIRST TIME

THE FIRST TIME

Initial Sexual Experiences in Fiction

Lawrence Broer

Herb Karl

Charles Weingartner

The Bobbs-Merrill Company, Inc.
Indianapolis

once
before free love
and apartments
and mind drugs

there was my first car
and cheap whiskey

and a little-used country road
that meandered along the river
to a secluded field
where we made love
THE FIRST TIME

Copyright © 1975 by The Bobbs-Merrill Company, Inc.
Printed in the United States of America
All rights reserved. No part of this book shall be
reproduced or transmitted in any form or by any means,
electronic or mechanical, including photocopying, recording,
or by any information or retrieval system, without written
permission from the Publisher:

The Bobbs-Merrill Company, Inc.
4300 West 62nd Street
Indianapolis, Indiana 46268

First Edition
First Printing 1975
Design and photo research by Anita Duncan
The poem on page iii, by Pete Pages, an undergraduate student at the
University of South Florida, is used by permission.

All photographs courtesy of Photo Researchers, Inc.:

p. ii   Rock concert patrons, Michael Gamer.
p. 4   Couple's shadows on water, Howard Earl Vible.
p. 40   Couple on parkbench, Richard Frieman.
p. 104   Couple in tall grass, Dean Hollyman.
p. 182   Couple silhouetted on bench, Jerry Cooke.
p. 220   Couple with bouquet, Richard Frieman.
p. 264   Couple in mist, F. B. Grunzweig.

Library of Congress Cataloging in Publication Data

Broer, Lawrence R. comp.

The first time; initial sexual experiences in fiction.
1. Sex—Fiction. 2. American fiction—20th century.
3. English fiction—20th century. I. Karl, Herb, joint
comp. II. Weingartner, Charles, joint comp.
III. Title.
PZ1.B778Fi   [PS648.S47]   823'.01   74-9903
ISBN 0-672-61355-7 (pbk)

CONTENTS

INTRODUCTION

What is pornography to one man is
the laughter of genius to another.
  D. H. Lawrence
Pornography a matter of geography.
  Sakini in "Teahouse of the August Moon"

Humankind's attempt to understand the nature of its own sexuality has always been one of its most basic, if elusive, drives. Carl Jung explains that like such compelling and universal experiences as the human desire for ritual, for purification, for belief in a godhead, our sexual desire constitutes an "archetype" equally rich in mythic power and deeply reflective of our essential, innermost needs. It is a recurring pattern which persists amid minor variations from age to age, and we are stirred by its presence in life and in art because it is something that has happened to our ancestors countless times, in generation after generation.

It is not difficult to understand, then, why something as unchanging, as universal, as our sexual experience has always been a primary subject for writers seeking some form of permanence in the face of life's changing currents and circumstances. But the prominence of sexual themes in literature in all times and places has practical implications as well. Initial sexual relationships are frequently associated with loss of innocence and the baptism or initiation into adulthood, and intrinsically embody the basic ingredients of the writer's craft: emotional stress, intensity, conflict, climactic development, the gaining of insight, and, finally, the growth or stunting of personality.

Long before the time of Freud writers appreciated the element of crisis inherent in man or woman's initial sexual experience, and the potential for such experience to nurture or thwart the growth of human character. It is an experience which can create emotional reverberations that follow us all the days of our lives—which can cripple or foster our ability to develop healthy and constructive relationships with members of the opposite sex. It is a time which can be as terrifying as it can be exhilarating, as profound as it can be profane, as ugly as it can be beautiful.

Yet, until recently, the serious writer's struggle to explore this crucial aspect of human development freely and frankly has been severely curtailed by social taboos and deep prohibitions against the expression or acknowledgment of the kind of sexual realities which are a daily part of the human condition. Convention has required that writers regard sex solely as a mystery or a hallowed, sentimentalized, idealized experience never to be indulged in except after marriage. But the recent so-called "sex revolution" has changed that, and changed it drastically. During the decade of the 1960s a great many young men and women have simply refused to accept a view of sex as something inherently sinful if engaged in before marriage or with more than one partner, rather than as a natural human process to be equally shared by men and women.

There has been more than a decade of unprecedented liberation from traditional restraints and notions of propriety in sexual matters, and it has permitted an almost radically frank and more honest treatment of sexual themes in literature.

What recent literature means in this regard has been misunderstood or misinterpreted by many people. It is true that sex has been the target of the so-called Black Humorists, especially in stripping away its pretentions to holiness, love, mystery, and galactic significance. Yet, ironically, the majority of current writers look upon sex with almost religious solemnity—not as a target, but as a sanctuary, a source of salvation or, at least, of emotional nourishment in a mechanical and depersonalized world. Despite various differences of vision, these writers generally view sex as an absolute good—as an act that is sufficient to dispel, for a time at least, the knowledge that life is essentially absurd. Gore Vidal summed up the predominantly spiritual attitude of his contemporaries toward sex when he said: "The art of love, like the creation of a work of art, is our one small 'yes' at the center of a vast 'No.' In the act of love, man can forget his fate—that cold drowning which awaits us all."

So the collective story told in this anthology is as urgent as it is historic. But even more important, for the prospective reader who must suddenly learn to live in a society whose traditional morality is being redefined, it has an educational, even a therapeutic, value. One of the greatest ironies of the changing moral and sexual phenomenon brought about by such developments as the pill, increasing leisure, and modified religious restraints, is that instant "liberation" has not proven to be the great balm to the human spirit that many thought it would be. Rather, it has created as many problems as it has solved. As a case in point, one need only examine recent studies of experiments in communal living, and radical forms of group sex, to note the array of emotional disturbances that have resulted. More often than not, it is not the salubrious aspects of the sex revolution which have caught the attention of the serious writer, but rather the inability of society (particularly Western society) to permit itself to freely express liberated sexual appetites without going through the old-fashioned pattern of nagging middle-class guilt and spiritual confusion. In short, these writers show that having sex, liberated or otherwise, can be as frustrating and demoralizing as not having it.

What this anthology obviously does *not* pretend to do, then, is to provide the kind of rigid, formulistic descriptions of sexual "normality" found in the various sex manuals which abound today. Nor does it provide mechanical or statistical gauges for determining sexual adequacy or inadequacy, nor promote a program for instant sexual happiness. Such an absolutist approach to sex can not only rob it of its important emotional and spiritual resonance by dehumanizing it, but can also foster absurdly idealistic and guilt-generating notions of what is desirable in sex. To the contrary, while sex is usually viewed in these stories as an assertion of the ultimate potential in our lives for beauty and joy, it is recognized too as something that can be agonizingly and unwittingly unfulfilling.

Because these writers are not dealing with the simple and sterile "coupling" of machines or computers, but rather with infinitely complicated human beings brought together in an act as delicate and intimate as any in human experience, their characters experience sex as a source of joy and of trauma, of hope and of frustration. And while their conflicts seem strikingly contemporary, we see finally that they are those that have always attended humankind's attempt to fulfill its sexual nature to the utmost: between instinct and law, biology and society, flesh and spirit, vague ideals and uncontrolled desires. It is in the creation of just such a saving awareness as this that these writers do what great writers have always done. They allow us to put our personal experience into a universal perspective that can help to restore balance and sanity to our lives, and they make us not only more understanding and tolerant of others, but of ourselves as well.

THE FIRST TIME

PROLOGUE

This anthology begins with the most famous and consequential seduction in the history of Western man: that of Adam and Eve, as
described in chapter 3 of the King James version of Genesis. We will
see from many of the selections that follow that our Judeo-Christian
parable of the introduction of sin and misery into the world has
profoundly influenced our view of sexual intercourse. The story of
man's fall from grace and expulsion from the Garden of Eden is
loaded down with associations of wrongdoing (such as the loss of
innocence, guilt and shame, eternal damnation of soul, and death
itself) that continue to taint, for many people, the most beneficial and
communionable act known to man. The great irony which many
people find in the story of Adam and Eve is that rather than appearing inherently sinful through the imposition of an arbitrary morality,
the act is really shown to be pleasant, practical, and instructive. Man
does not so much fall as he does rise above a mindless and amoral
condition to acquire those qualities that render him basically human:
self-awareness, a knowledge of good and evil, and the ability to
exercise intelligence and moral choice.

Now the serpent was more subtil than any beast of the field which the
LORD God had made. And he said unto the woman, Yea, hath God said,
Ye shall not eat of every tree of the garden?

And the woman said unto the serpent, We may eat of the fruit of the
trees of the garden:

But of the fruit of the tree which *is* in the midst of the garden, God hath
said, Ye shall not eat of it, neither shall ye touch it, lest ye die.

And the serpent said unto the woman, Ye shall not surely die:

For God doth know that in the day ye eat thereof, then your eyes shall be opened, and ye shall be as gods, knowing good and evil.

And when the woman saw that the tree *was* good for food, and that it *was* pleasant to the eyes, and a tree to be desired to make *one* wise, she took of the fruit thereof, and did eat, and gave also unto her husband with her; and he did eat.

And the eyes of them both were opened, and they knew that they *were* naked; and they sewed fig leaves together, and made themselves aprons.

And they heard the voice of the LORD God walking in the garden in the cool of the day: and Adam and his wife hid themselves from the presence of the LORD God amongst the trees of the garden.

And the LORD God called unto Adam, and said unto him, Where *art* thou?

And he said, I heard thy voice in the garden, and I was afraid, because I *was* naked; and I hid myself.

And he said, Who told thee that thou *wast* naked? Hast thou eaten of the tree, whereof I commanded thee that thou shouldest not eat?

And the man said, The woman whom thou gavest *to be* with me, she gave me of the tree, and I did eat.

And the LORD God said unto the woman, What *is* this *that* thou hast done? And the woman said, The serpent beguiled me, and I did eat.

And the LORD God said unto the serpent, Because thou hast done this, thou *art* cursed above all cattle, and above every beast of the field; upon thy belly shalt thou go, and dust shalt thou eat all the days of thy life:

And I will put enmity between thee and the woman, and between thy seed and her seed; it shall bruise thy head, and thou shalt bruise his heel.

Unto the woman he said, I will greatly multiply thy sorrow and thy conception; in sorrow thou shalt bring forth children; and thy desire *shall be* to thy husband, and he shall rule over thee.

And unto Adam he said, Because thou hast hearkened unto the voice of thy wife, and hast eaten of the tree, of which I commanded thee, saying, Thou shalt not eat of it: cursed *is* the ground for thy sake; in sorrow shalt thou eat *of* it all the days of thy life;

Thorns also and thistles shall it bring forth to thee; and thou shalt eat the herb of the field;

In the sweat of thy face shalt thou eat bread, till thou return unto the ground; for out of it wast thou taken: for dust thou *art*, and unto dust shalt thou return.

And Adam called his wife's name Eve; because she was the mother of all living.

Unto Adam also and to his wife did the LORD God make coats of skins, and clothed them.

And the LORD God said, Behold, the man is become as one of us, to know good and evil: and now, lest he put forth his hand, and take also of the tree of life, and eat, and live for ever:

Therefore the LORD God sent him forth from the garden of Eden, to till the ground from whence he was taken.

So he drove out the man; and he placed at the east of the garden of Eden Cher'-u-bims, and a flaming sword which turned every way, to keep the way of the tree of life.

ONE
Nothing Personal

There are sins it may be to discover,
There are deeds it may be to delight.
What new work wilt thou find for thy lover,
What new passions for daytime or night?
What spells that they know not a word of
Whose lives are as leaves overblown?
What tortures undreamt of, unheard of,
    Unwritten, unknown?

DOLORES, OUR LADY OF SENSUAL PAIN
A. C. Swinburne

NOBODY KNOWS

Sherwood Anderson

In this study of machismo, Sherwood Anderson reveals to the reader the thoughts of young George Willard as he anticipates and later consummates a sexual encounter with Louise Trunnion (about whom there were "whispered tales"). We see George as he agonizes with self-doubt: "He was afraid the adventure on which he had set out would be spoiled, that he would lose courage and turn back." Abruptly, the self-doubt turns into an inflated self-confidence: "He became wholly the male, bold and aggressive. In his heart there was no sympathy for her." Anxiously priding himself on his stereotypic male victory, George concludes: "She hasn't got anything on me. Nobody knows." And so reveals the real meaning of the experience for him.

Looking cautiously about, George Willard arose from his desk in the office of the *Winesburg Eagle* and went hurriedly out at the back door. The night was warm and cloudy and although it was not yet eight o'clock, the alleyway back of the *Eagle* office was pitch dark. A team of horses tied to a post somewhere in the darkness stamped on the hard-baked ground. A cat sprang from under George Willard's feet and ran away into the night. The young man was nervous. All day he had gone about his work like one dazed by a blow. In the alleyway he trembled as though with fright.

In the darkness George Willard walked along the alleyway, going carefully and cautiously. The back doors of the Winesburg stores were open and he could see men sitting about under the store lamps. In Myerbaum's Notion Store Mrs. Willy the saloon keeper's wife stood by the counter with a basket on her arm. Sid Green the clerk was waiting on her. He leaned over the counter and talked earnestly.

George Willard crouched and then jumped through the path of light that came out at the door. He began to run forward in the darkness. Behind Ed Griffith's saloon old Jerry Bird the town drunkard lay asleep on the ground. The runner stumbled over the sprawling legs. He laughed brokenly.

George Willard had set forth upon an adventure. All day he had been trying to make up his mind to go through with the adventure and now he was acting. In the office of the *Winesburg Eagle* he had been sitting since six o'clock trying to think.

There had been no decision. He had just jumped to his feet, hurried past Will Henderson who was reading proof in the print shop and started to run along the alleyway.

Through street after street went George Willard, avoiding the people who passed. He crossed and recrossed the road. When he passed a street lamp he pulled his hat down over his face. He did not dare think. In his mind there was a fear but it was a new kind of fear. He was afraid the adventure on which he had set out would be spoiled, that he would lose courage and turn back.

George Willard found Louise Trunnion in the kitchen of her father's house. She was washing dishes by the light of a kerosene lamp. There she stood behind the screen door in the little shed-like kitchen at the back of the house. George Willard stopped by a picket fence and tried to control the shaking of his body. Only a narrow potato patch separated him from the adventure. Five minutes passed before he felt sure enough of himself to call to her. "Louise! Oh Louise!" he called. The cry stuck in his throat. His voice became a hoarse whisper.

Louise Trunnion came out across the potato patch holding the dish cloth in her hand. "How do you know I want to go out with you," she said sulkily. "What makes you so sure?"

George Willard did not answer. In silence the two stood in the darkness with the fence between them. "You go on along," she said. "Pa's in there. I'll come along. You wait by William's barn."

The young newspaper reporter had received a letter from Louise Trunnion. It had come that morning to the office of the *Winesburg Eagle*. The letter was brief. "I'm yours if you want me," it said. He thought it annoying that in the darkness by the fence she had pretended there was nothing between them. "She has a nerve!

Well, gracious sakes, she has a nerve," he muttered as he went along the street and passed a row of vacant lots where corn grew. The corn was shoulder high and had been planted right down to the sidewalk.

When Louise Trunnion came out of the front door of her house she still wore the gingham dress in which she had been washing dishes. There was no hat on her head. The boy could see her standing with the doorknob in her hand talking to someone within, no doubt to old Jake Trunnion, her father. Old Jake was half deaf and she shouted. The door closed and everything was dark and silent in the little side street. George Willard trembled more violently than ever.

In the shadows by William's barn George and Louise stood, not daring to talk. She was not particularly comely and there was a black smudge on the side of her nose. George thought she must have rubbed her nose with her finger after she had been handling some of the kitchen pots.

The young man began to laugh nervously. "It's warm," he said. He wanted to touch her with his hand. "I'm not very bold," he thought. Just to touch the folds of the soiled gingham dress would, he decided, be an exquisite pleasure. She began to quibble. "You think you're better than I am. Don't tell me, I guess I know," she said drawing closer to him.

A flood of words burst from George Willard. He remembered the look that had lurked in the girl's eyes when they had met on the streets and thought of the note she had written. Doubt left him. The whispered tales concerning her that had gone about town gave him confidence. He became wholly the male, bold and aggressive. In his heart there was no sympathy for her. "Ah, come on, it'll be all right. There won't be anyone know anything. How can they know?" he urged.

They began to walk along a narrow brick sidewalk between the cracks of which tall weeds grew. Some of the bricks were missing and the sidewalk was rough and irregular. He took hold of her hand that was also rough and thought it delightfully small. "I can't go far," she said and her voice was quiet, unperturbed.

They crossed a bridge that ran over a tiny stream and passed another vacant lot in which corn grew. The street ended. In the path at the side of the road they were compelled to walk one behind the other. Will Overton's berry field lay beside the road and there was a pile of boards. "Will is going to build a shed to store berry crates here," said George and they sat down upon the boards.

When George Willard got back into Main Street it was past ten o'clock and had begun to rain. Three times he walked up and down the length of Main Street. Sylvester West's Drug Store was still open and he went in and bought a cigar. When Shorty Crandall the clerk came out at the door with him he was pleased. For five minutes the two stood in the shelter of the store awning and talked. George Willard felt satisfied. He had wanted more than anything else to talk to some man. Around a corner toward the New Willard House he went whistling softly.

On the sidewalk at the side of Winny's Dry Goods Store where there was a high board fence covered with circus pictures, he stopped whistling and stood perfectly still in the darkness, attentive, listening as though for a voice calling his name. Then again he laughed nervously. "She hasn't got anything on me. Nobody knows," he muttered doggedly and went on his way.

CORRUPTERS OF CHASTITY

Thomas Wolfe

It is not a matter of burning desire or curiosity that sends Eugene Gant to end his virginity with Lily, a crude, country, middle-aged woman, but rather one of saving face—of establishing the fact of his manhood. This insistent goading of his college pals is as much a challenge to his sense of manly honor, pride, and courage as it is to his virility; in fact, both are inseparably bound together in his mind and in the minds of his friends. Eugene's conspirators do little to set him at ease during his visit to the local brothel. Instead, they assume an air of worldliness and shared secret knowledge that augments the suffering of their young initiate. For Eugene, there is far more torment than joy to the experience. The fun that is poked at his raw-boned physical awkwardness, and his predictable tenseness, leaves him unnerved, trembling, and impotent. But his inability to rise is equally the result of his disgust with "bought, unlovely loves" that offends his youthful idealism and taints his long-sought loss of innocence. He finds the experience so sordid and mechanical that he vomits in the street afterwards, believing himself branded with sin. Only later does he achieve consummation.

Eugene lived in a small world, but its ruins for him were actual. His misfortunes were trifling, but their effect upon his spirit was deep and calamitous. He withdrew deeply and scornfully into his cell. He was friendless, whipped with scorn and pride. He set his face blindly against all the common united life around him.

It was during this bitter and desperate autumn that Eugene first met Jim Trivett.

Jim Trivett, the son of a rich tobacco farmer in the eastern part of the State, was a good tempered young tough of twenty years. He was a strong, rather foul-looking boy, with a coarse, protruding mouth, full-meated and slightly ajar, constantly rayed with a faint loose smile and blotted at the corner with a brown smear of tobacco juice. He had bad teeth. His hair was light-brown, dry, and unruly: it stuck out in large untidy mats. He was dressed in the last cheap extreme of the dreadful fashion of the time: skin-tight trousers that ended an inch above his oxford shoes exposing an inch of clocked hose, a bobtailed coat belted in across his kidneys, large striped collars of silk. Under his coat he wore a big sweater with high-school numerals.

Jim Trivett lived with several other students from his community in a lodging-house near Mrs. Bradley's but closer to the west gate of the university. There were four young men banded together for security and companionship in two untidy rooms heated to a baking dryness by small cast-iron stoves. They made constant preparations for study, but they never studied: one would enter sternly, announcing that he had "a hell of a day tomorrow," and begin the most minute preparations for a long contest with his books: he would sharpen his pencils carefully and deliberately, adjust his lamp, replenish the red-hot stove, move his chair, put on an eyeshade, clean his pipe, stuff it carefully with tobacco, light, relight, and empty it, then, with an expression of profound relief, hear a rapping on his door.

"Come in the house, Goddamn it!" he would roar hospitably.

"Hello, 'Gene! Pull up a chair, son, and sit down," said Tom Grant. He was a thickly built boy, gaudily dressed; he had a low forehead, black hair, and a kind, stupid, indolent temper.

"Have you been working?"

"Hell, yes!" shouted Jim Trivett. "I've been working like a son-of-a-bitch."

"God!" said Tom Grant, turning slowly to look at him. "Boy, you're going to choke to death on one of those some day." He shook his head slowly and sadly, then continued with a rough laugh: "If old man Trivett knew what you were doing with his money, damn if he wouldn't bust a gut."

" 'Gene!" said Jim Trivett, "what the hell do you know about this damned English, anyway?"

"What he doesn't know about it," said Tom Grant, "you could write out on the back of a postage stamp. Old man Sanford thinks you're hell, 'Gene."

"I thought you had Torrington," said Jim Trivett.

"No," said Eugene, "I wasn't English enough. Young and crude. I changed, thank God! What is it you want, Jim?" he asked.

"I've got a long paper to write. I don't know what to write about," said Jim Trivett.

"What do you want me to do? Write it for you?"

"Yes," said Jim Trivett.

"Write your own damn paper," said Eugene with mimic toughness, "I won't do it for you. I'll help you if I can."

"When are you going to let Hard Boy take you to Exeter?" said Tom Grant, winking at Jim Trivett.

Eugene flushed, making a defensive answer.

"I'm ready to go any time he is," he said uneasily.

"Look here, Legs!" said Jim Trivett, grinning loosely. "Do you really want to go with me or are you just bluffing?"

"I'll go with you! I've told you I'd go with you!" Eugene said angrily. He trembled a little.

Tom Grant grinned slyly at Jim Trivett.

"It'll make a man of you, 'Gene," he said. "Boy, it'll sure put hair on your chest." He laughed, not loudly, but uncontrollably, shaking his head as at some secret thought.

Jim Trivett's loose smile widened. He spat into the woodbox.

"Gawd!" he said. "They'll think Spring is here when they see old Legs. They'll need a stepladder to git at him."

Tom Grant was shaken with hard fat laughter.

"They sure God will!" he said.

"Well, what about it, 'Gene?" Jim Trivett demanded suddenly. "Is it a go? Saturday?"

"Suits me!" said Eugene.

When he had gone, they grinned thirstily at each other for a moment, the pleased corrupters of chastity.

"Pshaw!" said Tom Grant. "You oughtn't to do that, Hard Boy. You're leading the boy astray."

"It's not going to hurt him," said Jim Trivett. "It'll be good for him."

He wiped his mouth with the back of his hand, grinning.

"Wait a minute!" whispered Jim Trivett. "I think this is the place."

They had turned away from the centre of the dreary tobacco town. For a quarter of an hour they had walked briskly through drab autumnal streets, descending finally a long rutted hill that led them, past a thinning squalor of cheap houses, almost to the outskirts. It was three weeks before Christmas: the foggy air was full of chill menace. There was a brooding quietness, broken by far small sounds. They turned into a sordid little road, unpaved, littered on both sides with negro shacks and the dwellings of poor whites. It was a world of rickets. The road was unlighted. Their feet stirred dryly through fallen leaves.

They paused before a two-storey frame house. A lamp burned dimly behind lowered yellow shades, casting a murky pollen out upon the smoky air.

"Wait a minute," said Jim Trivett, in a low voice, "I'll find out."

They heard scuffling steps through the leaves. In a moment a negro man prowled up.

"Hello, John," said Jim Trivett, almost inaudibly.

"Evenin', boss!" the negro answered wearily, but in the same tone.

"We're looking for Lily Jones' house," said Jim Trivett. "Is this it?"

"Yes, suh," said the negro, "dis is it."

Eugene leaned against a tree, listening to their quiet con-spiratorial talk. The night, vast and listening, gathered about him its evil attentive consciousness. His lips were cold and trembled. He thrust a cigarette between them and, shivering, turned up the thick collar of his overcoat.

"Does Miss Lily know you're comin'?" the negro asked.

"No," said Jim Trivett. "Do you know her?"

"Yes, suh," said the negro. "I'll go up dar wid yo'."

Eugene waited in the shadow of the tree while the two men went up to the house. They avoided the front veranda, and went around to the side. The negro rapped gently at a latticed door. There were always latticed doors. Why?

He waited, saying farewell to himself. He stood over his life, he felt, with lifted assassin blade. He was mired to his neck, inextricably, in complication. There was no escape.

There had been a faint closed noise from the house: voices and laughter, and the cracked hoarse tone of an old phonograph. The sound stopped quickly as the negro rapped: the shabby house seemed to listen. In a moment, a hinge creaked stealthily: he caught the low startled blur of a woman's voice. Who is it? Who?

In another moment Jim Trivett returned to him, and said quietly:

"It's all right, 'Gene. Come on."

He slipped a coin into the negro's hand, thanking him. Eugene looked for a moment into the black broad friendliness of the man's face. He had a flash of warmth through his cold limbs. The black bawd had done his work eagerly and kindly: over their bought unlovely loves lay the warm shadow of his affection.

They ascended the path quietly and, mounting two or three steps, went in under the latticed door. A woman stood beside it, holding it open. When they had entered, she closed it securely. Then they crossed the little porch and entered the house.

They found themselves in a little hall which cleft the width of the house. A smoky lamp, wicked low, cast its dim circle into the dark. An uncarpeted stair mounted to the second floor. There were two doors both to left and right, and an accordion hat-rack, on which hung a man's battered felt hat.

Jim Trivett embraced the woman immediately, grinning, and fumbling in her breast.

"Hello, Lily," he said.

"Gawd!" She smiled crudely, and continued to peer at Eugene, curious at what the maw of night had thrown in to her. Then, turning to Jim Trivett with a coarse laugh, she said:

"Lord a' mercy! Any woman that gits him will have to cut off some of them legs."

"I'd like to see him with Thelma," said Jim Trivett, grinning.

Lily Jones laughed hoarsely. The door to the right opened and Thelma, a small woman, slightly built, came out, followed by high empty yokel laughter. Jim Trivett embraced her affectionately.

"My Gawd!" said Thelma, in a tinny voice. "What've we got here?" She thrust out her sharp wrenny face, and studied Eugene insolently.

"I brought you a new beau, Thelma," said Jim Trivett.

"Ain't he the lankiest feller you ever seen?" said Lily Jones impersonally. "How tall are you, son?" she added, addressing him in a kind drawl.

He winced a little.

"I don't know," he said. "I think about six three."

"He's more than that!" said Thelma positively. "He's seven foot tall or I'm a liar."

"He's hasn't measured since last week," said Jim Trivett. "He can't be sure about it."

"He's young, too," said Lily, staring at him intently. "How old are you, son?"

Eugene turned his pallid face away, indefinitely.

"Why,"he croaked, "I'm about——"

"He's going on eighteen," said Jim Trivett loyally. "Don't you worry about him. Old Legs knows all the ropes, all right. He's a bearcat. I wouldn't kid you. He's been there."

"He don't look that old," said Lily doubtfully. "I wouldn't call him more'n fifteen, to look at his face. Ain't he got a little face, though?" she demanded in a slow puzzled voice.

"It's the only one I've got," said Eugene angrily. "Sorry I can't change it for a larger one."

"It looks so funny stickin' way up there above you," she went on patiently.

Thelma nudged her sharply.

"That's because he's got a big frame," she said. "Legs is all right. When he begins to fill out an' put some meat on them bones he's goin' to make a big man. You'll be a heartbreaker sure, Legs," she said harshly, taking his cold hand and squeezing it. In him the ghost, his stranger, turned grievously away. O God! I shall remember, he thought.

"Well," said Jim Trivett, "let's git goin'." He embraced Thelma again. They fumbled amorously.

"You go on upstairs, son," said Lily. "I'll be up in a minute. The door's open."

"See you later, 'Gene," said Jim Trivett. "Stay with them, son."

He hugged the boy roughly with one arm, and went into the room to the left with Thelma.

Eugene mounted the creaking stairs slowly and entered the room with the open door. A hot mass of coals glowed flamelessly in the hearth. He took off his hat and overcoat and threw them across a wooden bed. Then he sat down tensely in a rocker and leaned forward, holding his trembling fingers to the heat. There was no light save that of the coals; but, by their dim steady glow, he could make out the old and ugly wall-paper, stained with long streaks of water rust, and scaling, in dry tattered scrolls, here and there. He sat quietly, bent forward, but he shook violently, as with an ague, from time to time. Why am I here? This is not I, he thought.

Presently he heard the woman's slow heavy tread upon the stairs: she entered in a swimming tide of light, bearing a lamp before her. She put the lamp down on a table and turned the wick. He could see her now more plainly. Lily was a middle-aged country woman, with a broad heavy figure, unhealthily soft. Her smooth peasant face was mapped with fine little traceries of wrinkles at the corners of mouth and eyes, as if she had worked much in the sun. She had black hair, coarse and abundant. She was whitely plastered with talcum powder. She was dressed shapelessly in a fresh loose dress of gingham, unbelted. She was dressed like a housewife, but she conceded to her profession stockings of red silk, and slippers of red felt, trimmed with fur, in which she walked with a flat-footed tread.

The woman fastened the door, and returned to the hearth where the boy was now standing. He embraced her with feverish desire, fondling her with his long nervous hands. Indecisively, he sat in the rocker and drew her down clumsily on his knee. She yielded her kisses with the coy and frigid modesty of the provincial harlot, turning her mouth away. She shivered as his cold hands touched her.

"You're cold as ice, son," she said. "What's the matter?"

She chafed him with rough embarrassed professionalism. In a moment she rose impatiently.

"Let's git started," she said. "Where's my money?"

He thrust two crumpled bills into her hand.

Then he lay down beside her. He trembled, unnerved and impotent. Passion was extinct in him.

The massed coals caved in the hearth. The lost bright wonder died.

When he went down stairs, he found Jim Trivett waiting in the hall, holding Thelma by the hand. Lily led them out quietly, after peering through the lattice into the fog, and listening for a moment.

"Be quiet," she whispered, "there's a man across the street. They've been watching us lately."

"Come again, Slats," Thelma murmured, pressing his hand.

They went out softly, treading gently until they reached the road. The fog had thickened: the air was saturated with fine stinging moisture.

At the corner, in the glare of the street-lamp, Jim Trivett released his breath with loud relief, and stepped forward boldly.

"Damn!" he said. "I thought you were never coming. What were you trying to do with the woman, Legs?" Then, noting the boy's face, he added quickly, with warm concern: "What's the matter, 'Gene? Don't you feel good?"

"Wait a minute!" said Eugene thickly. "Be all right!"

He went to the curb, and vomited into the gutter. Then he straightened, mopping his mouth with a handkerchief.

"How do you feel?" asked Jim Trivett. "Better?"

"Yes," said Eugene, "I'm all right now."

"Why didn't you tell me you were sick?" said Jim Trivett chidingly.

"It came on all of a sudden," said Eugene. He added presently: "I think it was something I ate at that damn Greek's to-night."

"I felt all right," said Jim Trivett. "A cup of coffee will fix you up," he added with cheerful conviction.

They mounted the hill slowly. The light from winking corner-lamps fell with a livid stare across the fronts of the squalid houses.

"Jim," said Eugene, after a moment's pause.

"Yes. What is it?"

"Don't say anything about my getting sick," he said awkwardly.

Surprised, Jim Trivett stared at him.

"Why not? There's nothing in that," he said. "Pshaw, boy, any one's likely to get sick."

"Yes, I know. But I'd rather you wouldn't."

"Oh, all right. I won't. Why should I?" said Jim Trivett.

Eugene was haunted by his own lost ghost; he knew it to be irrecoverable. For three days he avoided every one: the brand of his sin, he felt, was on him. He was published by every gesture, by every word. His manner grew more defiant, his greeting to life more unfriendly. He clung more closely to Jim Trivett, drawing a sad pleasure from his coarse loyal praise. His unappeased desire began to burn anew: it conquered his bodily disgust and made new pictures. At the end of the week he went again, alone, to Exeter. No more of him, he felt, could be lost. This time he sought out Thelma.

THE GRADUATION OF AUGIE MARCH

Saul Bellow

Unlike the visit to a prostitute by Thomas Wolfe's protagonist, the post-graduation ceremony of Augie March has no searing or profound effect on him. His loss of virginity is told about in unemotional, reportorial tones, tinged with a mild, Jewish reflectiveness. The act is more cerebral than sensual, analytical than emotional. Rather than leaving him sin-ridden, angry, or fearful, Augie ponders that the relative tenderness he has been shown has been lucky for him, issuing him across the threshold into manhood in a merciful fashion. "I knew later I had been lucky with her that she had tried not to be dry with me, or satirical, and had done it mercifully." Augie's emotions are more engaged by feelings of responsibility for his corrupt, lusting friend than by the act itself.

What I was particularly bidden to recall in this talk was the night of my graduation from high school. The Einhorns had been extremely kind to me. A wallet with ten dollars in it was my present from the three of them, and Mrs. Einhorn came to the graduation exercises with Mama and the Kleins and Tambows that February night. Afterward there was a party at the Kleins', where I was expected. I drove Mama home from the assembly—I didn't have my name in the evening program, like Simon, but Mama was pleased and smoothed my hand as I was leading her upstairs.

19

Tillie Einhorn waited below in the car. "You go to your party," she said as I was taking her back to the poolroom. My having finished high school was of immense importance in her eyes, and she honored me extraordinarily, in the tone she took. She was a warm woman, in most matters very simple, she wanted to give me some sort of blessing, and my "education" had, I think, suddenly made her timid of me. So we drove in the black and wet cold to the poolroom, and she said several times over, "Willie says you got a good head. You'll be a teacher yourself." And then she crushed up against me in her sealskin coat, belonging to the good days, to kiss me on the cheek, and had the happy tears of terribly deep feeling to wipe from her face before we went into the poolroom. Behind this, probably, was my "orphancy," and the occasion woke it up. We were dressed in our best; Mrs. Einhorn even gave off a perfume, in the car, from her silk scarf and dress established with silver buttons on her breast. We crossed the wide sidewalk to the poolroom. Below, the windows, as required by law, were curtained, and above, the rods of the signs writhed in their colors in the wet. The crowd in the poolroom was small tonight because of graduation. So you could hear the kissing of the balls from the farthest cavelike lights and soft roaring of green tables, and the fat of wieners on the grill. Dingbat came from the back, holding the wooden triangle ball rack, to shake hands.

"Augie is going to a party by Klein," said Mrs. Einhorn.

"Congratulations, son," said Einhorn with state manners. "He's going, Tillie, but not right away. I have a treat for him first. I'm taking him to a show."

"Willie," she said, disturbed, "let him go. Tonight it's his night."

"Not just a neighborhood movie, but to McVicker's, a stage show with little girls, trained animals, and a Frenchman from the Bal Tabarin who stands on his head on a pop bottle. How does that sound to you, Augie? Like a good thing? I planned it out a week ago."

"Sure, that's all right. Jimmy said the party would run late, and I can go after midnight."

"But Dingbat can take you, Willie. Augie wants to be with young people tonight, not with you."

"If I'm going out Dingbat is needed here and will stay here," said Einhorn and shook off her arguments.

I wasn't so intoxicated with its being *my* night that I couldn't see a reason for Einhorn's insistence, a small darkness of a reason no bigger than a field mouse yet and very swift.

Mrs. Einhorn dropped her hands to her sides. "Willie, when he *wants—*" she apologized to me. But I was practically one of the family, now that no inheritances were in the way. I tied on his cloak and carried him to the car. My face was red in the night air, and I was annoyed. For it was a chore to take Einhorn to the theater, and there were many steps and negotiations necessary. First to park the car, and then to find the manager and explain that two seats had to be found near the exit; next to arrange to have the steel firedoors opened, to drive down the alley, tote Einhorn into the theater, back out of the alley, and find another parking space. And at that, once in the theater, you sat at a bad angle to the stage. He had to be right next to the emergency exit. "Imagine me in the middle of a stampede in case of fire," he said. Hence we saw things to the side of the main confrontation of the big dramatic shell, powder and paint on the faces, and voices muffled, then loud, or glenny silver, and frequently didn't know what made the audience laugh.

"Don't speed," said Einhorn to me on Washington Boulevard. "Take it slow here." I suddenly observed that he had an address in his hand.

"It's near Sacramento. You didn't think I really was going to drag you to McVicker's tonight, did you, Augie? No, we're not going downtown. This place I'm taking you to, I've never been in before. It's a back entrance, I understand, and on the third floor."

I stopped the car and went out to scout, came back when I had found the joint, and got him on my back. He used to talk about himself as the Old Man of the Sea riding Sinbad. But there was Aeneas too, who carried his old dad Anchises in the burning of Troy, and *that* old man had been picked by Venus to be her lover; which strikes me as the better comparison. Except that there was no fire or war cry around us, but dead-of-night silence on the boulevard, and ice. I went down the narrow cement walk, below sleeping windows, with Einhorn telling me, clear and loud, to watch my step. Luckily I had cleared out my locker that day and was wearing the rubbers that had lain at the bottom of it the better part of a year, and so my feet didn't slip. But it was difficult work all the same, up the wooden stairs and under the short clotheslines on the porches. "This better be it," he said when I rang the bell on the third floor, "or they'll be asking me what the hell I'm doing." It always was he who was principally present in a place.

But we hadn't rung the wrong bell. A woman opened the door, and I said, "Where?" out of wind. "Go on, go on," said Einhorn. "This is only the kitchen." Which it was; a beery place. I walked with him carefully into the parlor and put him down before the astonished people there, on the couch. Seated, he felt equal to them all and looked at all the women. I stood beside him and looked too, in great eagerness and excitement. I always felt, in taking him somewhere, a great sense of responsibility; and here, far more than ever, I sensed how heavy his dependence on me was. And I didn't want to have to worry about it now. Though he didn't look at a disadvantage, only imperious and imperturbable, with no uneasy flinch of disgrace at being a man of importance seen helpless before terrible needs. "I heard the girls were nice here," he said, "and they are nice. Pick one out."

"Me?"

"Of course you. Which one of you girls is going to entertain this handsome boy who graduated from high school tonight? Look around, kid, and keep your head," he said to me.

The madam came to the parlor from one of the rooms. Her peculiarity was in the paint of her face, the insect dust or lamp-black of colors and moth's wing red of the cheek pigment.

"Mister," she began to say.

But it was all right. Einhorn had a card from someone, and it had been prearranged, as she recalled. Only she hadn't been told, I could see, that Einhorn would be carried in. He wouldn't have trusted himself here without an introduction.

Nevertheless there was embarrassment, and Einhorn sat shoe to shoe and in the banker's trousers covering his immovable legs. When I think of it with a collected mind, Einhorn, asking who would entertain me, might well have been voicing anticipation of the aversion of the girl *he* chose. Even here, where he was paying. But perhaps it wasn't so. My head was a long way from being clear in this lionish place, the paltry, ritzy den of a parlor, and he maybe was not as bold and easy as he sounded.

At last Einhorn said to the girl he had called over to chat with, "Which is your room, kid?" and with perfect calm, ignoring the effect of it, had me carry him there. A pink coverlet was on the bed (this was a better-class place as I was later to know by contrast), and she skimmed it off. I laid him down. As the girl, in a corner of the room, began to take off her clothes, he beckoned me to bend to him again and whispered, "Take my wallet," and I took out the heavy leather article and put it in my pocket. "Hang on to it," he said. The look of his eye was bold, full, even resentful. Resentful of this posture, I think, not of me. There was a pressure in his face, and his hair spread on the pillow. He began to talk to the woman in a tone of instruction. "Take off my shoes," he said. She did. He watched in that active way; along the line of his entire body his glance went, to the woman in her wrapper who bent over his feet, this woman of strong neck and red fingernails, standing in a pair of felt slippers by the bed. "Just a thing or two more I have to tell you," he said. "There's my back; I have to go easy till I'm set right, miss, and take everything step by step."

"Haven't you gone yet?" He saw me by the door. "Go on, do you have to be told what to do? I'll send them for you after."

I didn't have to be told, but as long as he didn't send me from him I'd have delayed.

I went back to the parlor, where there was someone waiting for me; the rest had gone, so the choice had been made for me. As always with strangers, I behaved as if I knew exactly what I was doing and from an idea that at a critical time it was best and most decent to have my own momentum. She did not take this away from me. She whose business or burden it was to be calm in the primal thing, where no one else is, and have an advantage of the strong. She wasn't young—the women had made the right choice for me—and she had sort of a crude face; but she encouraged me to treat her loverlike. Undressing, she had playful frills or pointed edges on her underthings—these gewgaws that go with the imposing female fact, the brilliant, profound thing. My clothes were off and I waited. She approached and took me round the body. She even set me on the bed. As if, it being her bed, she'd show me how to use it. And she pressed up her breasts against me, she curved her shoulders back, she closed her eyes and held me by the sides. So that I didn't lack kindness of person and wasn't pushed off when done. I knew later I had been lucky with her, that she had tried not to be dry with me, or satirical, and done it mercifully.

Yet when the thrill went off, like lightning smashed and dispersed into the ground, I knew it was basically only a transaction. But that didn't matter so much. Nor did the bed; nor did the room; nor the thought that the woman would have been amused—with as much amusement as could make headway against other considerations—at Einhorn and me, the great sensationalist riding into the place on my back with bloodshot eyes and voracious in heart but looking perfectly calm and superior. Paying didn't matter. Nor using what other people used. That's what city life is. And so it *didn't* have the luster it should have had, and there *wasn't* any epithalamium of gentle lovers. . . .

I had to wait for Einhorn in the kitchen, and to think of him, close by, having this violence done to him for his pleasure. The madam didn't look pleased about it. Other men were coming in, and she was mixing drinks in the kitchen, and I came in for peevish glances until Einhorn's girl came in dressed again to have me fetch him. The madam went along with me for the money, and Einhorn paid with finesse and gave tips, and as I carried him through the parlor where my partner was with another man, smoking a cigarette. Einhorn said to me for my private ear, "Don't look at anybody, understand?" Was he afraid to be recognized, or was this order simply about the best composure for passing through the parlor again with him clinging to my back in his dark garments?

"You'll have to be careful as hell about the way you go down," he said on the porch. "It was stupid not to bring a flashlight. All we need now is a spill." And he laughed; with irony, but laughed. The house was thoughtful though, and a whore came out, in a coat like any ordinary woman, to light our way down to the yard, where we thanked her and all politely said good night.

I brought him home and took him into the house, though the poolroom was still open; and he said, "Never mind putting me to bed. Go on to your party. You can take the car, but don't go getting drunk and joy-riding, that's all I ask."

UP IN MICHIGAN

Ernest Hemingway

In "Up in Michigan," Hemingway writes about the potential of sexual instinct to be blind and cruel. The story occurs in a naturalistic setting—that is, against a primitive background where hunting, fishing, eating, drinking, and sex are the primal pleasures, and feeling and instinct, rather than thought, determine the course of individual lives. Jim Gilmore "loved the *taste* and *feel* of whiskey," Hemingway writes. Love, as an abstract, civilized value, becomes questionable in such an environment. Neither love nor tenderness attend Gilmore's ruthless assault of Liz Coates; nor does he consciously wish to harm her. The sexual force which he is helpless to control, and she is unable to understand, is flatly indifferent and, in a sense, victimizes them both. But Liz comes away the loser. The brutishness of the assault rudely disillusions her, and spoils her romantic expectations forever. The affectionate gesture of covering the drunk, snoring Gilmore with a coat is pathetic in light of the unfeeling thing that has just happened to her.

Jim Gilmore came to Hortons Bay from Canada. He bought the blacksmith shop from old man Horton. Jim was short and dark with big mustaches and big hands. He was a good horseshoer and did not look much like a blacksmith even with his leather apron on. He lived upstairs above the blacksmith shop and took his meals at D. J. Smith's.

Liz Coates worked for Smith's. Mrs. Smith, who was a very large clean woman, said Liz Coates was the neatest girl she'd ever seen. Liz had good legs and always wore clean gingham aprons and Jim noticed that her hair was always neat behind. He liked her face because it was so jolly but he never thought about her.

Liz liked Jim very much. She liked it the way he walked over from the shop and often went to the kitchen door to watch for him to start down the road. She liked it about his mustache. She liked it about how white his teeth were when he smiled. She liked it very much that he didn't look like a blacksmith. She liked it how much D. J. Smith and Mrs. Smith liked Jim. One day she found that she liked it the way the hair was black on his arms and how white they were above the tanned line when he washed up in the washbasin outside the house. Liking that made her feel funny.

Hortons Bay, the town, was only five houses on the main road between Boyne City and Charlevoix. There was the general store and post office with a high false front and maybe a wagon hitched out in front, Smith's house, Stroud's house, Dillworth's house, Horton's house and Van Hoosen's house. The houses were in a big grove of elm trees and the road was very sandy. There was farming country and timber each way up the road. Up the road a ways was the Methodist church and down the road the other direction was the township school. The blacksmith shop was painted red and faced the school.

A steep sandy road ran down the hill to the bay through the timber. From Smith's back door you could look out across the woods that ran down to the lake and across the bay. It was very beautiful in the spring and summer, the bay blue and bright and usually white-caps on the lake out beyond the point from the breeze blowing from Charlevoix and Lake Michigan. From Smith's back door Liz could see ore barges way out in the lake going toward Boyne City. When she looked at them they didn't seem to be moving at all but if she went in and dried some more dishes and then came out again they would be out of sight beyond the point.

All the time now Liz was thinking about Jim Gilmore. He didn't seem to notice her much. He talked about the shop to D. J. Smith and about the Republican Party and about James G. Blaine. In the evenings he read *The Toledo Blade* and the Grand Rapids paper by the lamp in the front room or went out spearing fish in the bay with a jacklight with D. J. Smith. In the fall he and Smith and Charley Wyman took a wagon and tent, grub, axes, their rifles and two dogs and went on a trip to the pine plains beyond Vanderbilt deer hunting. Liz and Mrs. Smith were cooking for four days for them before they started. Liz wanted to make something special for Jim to take but she didn't finally because she was afraid to ask Mrs. Smith for the eggs and flour and afraid if she bought them Mrs. Smith would catch her cooking. It would have been all right with Mrs. Smith but Liz was afraid.

All the time Jim was gone on the deer hunting trip Liz thought about him. It was awful while he was gone. She couldn't sleep well from thinking about him but she discovered it was fun to think about him too. If she let herself go it was better. The night before they were to come back she didn't sleep at all, that is she didn't think she slept because it was all mixed up in a dream about not sleeping and really not sleeping. When she saw the wagon coming down the road she felt weak and sick sort of inside. She couldn't wait till she saw Jim and it seemed as though everything would be all right when he came. The wagon stopped outside under the big elm and Mrs. Smith and Liz went out. All the men had beards and there were three deer in the back of the wagon, their thin legs sticking stiff over the edge of the wagon box. Mrs. Smith kissed D. J. and he hugged her. Jim said "Hello, Liz," and grinned. Liz hadn't known just what would happen when Jim got back but she was sure it would be something. Nothing had happened. The men were just home, that was all. Jim pulled the burlap sacks off the deer and Liz looked at them. One was a big buck. It was stiff and hard to lift out of the wagon.

"Did you shoot it, Jim?" Liz asked.

"Yeah. Ain't it a beauty?" Jim got it onto his back to carry to the smokehouse.

That night Charley Wyman stayed to supper at Smith's. It was too late to get back to Charlevoix. The men washed up and waited in the front room for supper.

"Ain't there something left in that crock, Jimmy?" D. J. Smith asked, and Jim went out to the wagon in the barn and fetched in the jug of whiskey the men had taken hunting with them. It was a four-gallon jug and there was quite a little slopped back and forth in the bottom. Jim took a long pull on his way back to the house. It was hard to lift such a big jug up to drink out of it. Some of the whiskey ran down on his shirt front. The two men smiled when Jim came in with the jug. D. J. Smith sent for glasses and Liz brought them. D. J. poured out three big shots.

"Well, here's looking at you, D. J.," said Charley Wyman.

"That damn big buck, Jimmy," said D. J.

"Here's all the ones we missed, D. J.," said Jim, and downed his liquor.

"Tastes good to a man."

"Nothing like it this time of year for what ails you."

"How about another, boys?"

"Here's how, D. J."

"Down the creek, boys."

"Here's to next year."

Jim began to feel great. He loved the taste and the feel of whiskey. He was glad to be back to a comfortable bed and warm food and the shop. He had another drink. The men came in to supper feeling hilarious but acting very respectable. Liz sat at the table after she put on the food and ate with the family. It was a good dinner. The men ate seriously. After supper they went into the front room again and Liz cleaned off with Mrs. Smith. Then Mrs. Smith went upstairs and pretty soon Smith came out and went upstairs too. Jim and Charley were still in the front room. Liz was sitting in the kitchen next to the stove pretending to read a book and thinking about Jim. She didn't want to go to bed yet because she knew Jim would be coming out and she wanted to see him as he went out so she could take the way he looked up to bed with her.

She was thinking about him hard and then Jim came out. His eyes were shining and his hair was a little rumpled. Liz looked down at her book. Jim came over back of her chair and stood there and she could feel him breathing and then he put his arms around her. Her breasts felt plump and firm and the nipples were erect under his hands. Liz was terribly frightened, no one had ever touched her, but she thought, "He's come to me finally. He's really come."

She held herself stiff because she was so frightened and did not know anything else to do and then Jim held her tight against the chair and kissed her. It was such a sharp, aching, hurting feeling that she thought she couldn't stand it. She felt Jim right through the back of the chair and she couldn't stand it and then something clicked inside of her and the feeling was warmer and softer. Jim held her tight, hard against the chair and she wanted it now and Jim whispered, "Come on for a walk."

Liz took her coat off the peg on the kitchen wall and they went out the door. Jim had his arm around her and every little way they stopped and pressed against each other and Jim kissed her. There was no moon and they walked ankle-deep in the sandy road through the trees down to the dock and the warehouse on the bay. The water was lapping in the piles and the point was dark across the bay. It was cold but Liz was hot all over from being with Jim. They sat down in the shelter of the warehouse and Jim pulled Liz close to him. She was frightened. One of Jim's hands went inside her dress and stroked over her breast and the other hand was in her lap. She was very frightened and didn't know how he was going to go about things but she snuggled close to him. Then the hand that felt so big in her lap went away and was on her leg and started to move up it.

"Don't, Jim," Liz said. Jim slid the hand further up.

"You mustn't, Jim. You mustn't." Neither Jim nor Jim's big hand paid any attention to her.

The boards were hard. Jim had her dress up and was trying to do something to her. She was frightened but she wanted it. She had to have it but it frightened her.

"You mustn't do it, Jim. You mustn't."

"I got to. I'm going to. You know we got to."

"No we haven't, Jim. We ain't got to. Oh, it isn't right. Oh, it's so big and it hurts so. You can't. Oh, Jim. Jim. Oh."

The hemlock planks of the dock were hard and splintery and cold and Jim was heavy on her and he had hurt her. Liz pushed him, she was so uncomfortable and cramped. Jim was asleep. He wouldn't move. She worked out from under him and sat up and straighted her skirt and coat and tried to do something with her hair. Jim was sleeping with his mouth a little open. Liz leaned over and kissed him on the cheek. He was still asleep. She lifted his head a little and shook it. He rolled his head over and swallowed. Liz started to cry. She walked over to the edge of the dock and looked down to the water. There was a mist coming up from the bay. She was cold and miserable and everything felt gone. She walked back to where Jim was lying and shook him once more to make sure. She was crying.

"Jim," she said, "Jim. Please, Jim."

Jim stirred and curled a little tighter. Liz took off her coat and leaned over and covered him with it. She tucked it around him neatly and carefully. Then she walked across the dock and up the steep sandy road to go to bed. A cold mist was coming up through the woods from the bay.

THE FLATTERERS

LeRoi Jones

In *The System of Dante's Hell,* LeRoi Jones explores extremes of spiritual and physical dissolution and torment bred by conditions in the black ghetto in America. We find in the stream-of-consciousness reverie that follows, that even the relatively innocent time of Jones's childhood was brutalized by fearful rumors of murderers loose in his apartment house, extreme poverty, and sexual perversion. Yet the montage of astonishingly poignant images that here comprise the author's memory of childhood consists of gentler recollections as well, those of athletic prowess, batting averages, boyhood pals, and tentative sexual adventures. It is a time, Jones recalls, of "childish sun" and "secret fruit," the essence of which was his first sexual episode with a girl called Beverly. The experience proves as natural a part of boyish adventure as learning to play a pinball machine or to smoothly field a hard hit grounder.

.284, a good season. In the sun. In hell, my head
so much sun, and cold for this month. Cars too,
squealing at the clocks. Gone past. These hands,
the metal burning night / are pictures, dreams, cousins.

A good season. Lost, the dust settling. On water, cobblestones, porches. We sat there staring at the blue street. The restaurant. My lovers' drums. Heaps of night. "You are a young man & soon will be off to college." They knew then, and walked around me for it.

Tough fat poet hung in the custard store. A marine. The silent brothers. Huge slick hands. They all had. Except fat awkward William / eyes were flowers. Bellbottom pants. Slate buildings.

"The woman that ran the place was a grouch, & you had to stand up with the cold wind blowing on your back. Her husband, I think, was a postman . . . like my father . . . but darker & more from the south."

Down low for the dirt. For the hands touch. The backs of the hands, dug in the dirt. Straight at you. On tar, in those low fences. Murderers loose in the buildings. A severed head, bloody in the winter. Near anthony's house & those other guys . . . The Buccaneers. But later, summer, it bounced right & he swept it up, wheeling in the air to throw it towards first. They were tough.

Or, the air, again, cold sun, wheeling, with hands strained, sun full in the eyes, up & around, the ball leaving, towards the squat shade homes, they yelled. They yelled, at me. The ball rolling out. Amazed, they loved it. Even the weather. Our sweatshirts, and Ginger strolling on the tar towards the jews. (Who got locked in the bread box. With the cakes? The same place used to stink the windows up. Frozen bums peeing through the windows. For cupcakes. Jelly donuts. Adventure. We laughed about it.)

She looked at my legs. They had grease on them then, when I wasn't at the clock. The quick fingers & fear at cripple tommy, the hero of the projects. William cd beat me, for sure. In that big big gym I hid from my thighs. Too long. Strong gripping fingers.

What else. Lefty? You cd catch him in that park. More days strung out. Time & sun. He laughed about it himself, when those two bears waited outside the stadium. "Lenora sd that you were hers. Is that true?" Jo Anne. She got pregnant & somber. Like today, near father's hotel. Divine. The doctors lived near there & one of my dianes. Diana, really, & her tall dark mother & drunken aunts. That was like cellars. That smell, & big cars to boot. Her father was white & died old with a big mustache. She wanted to make it with him, & was afraid I did too. She wouldn't fix the phonograph where my picture was. What did that photo look like? (I think I had a german bush then.) Not as large as that time in Orange watching the fags dance. His hair was red & mine stylish. My mother sat close to me watching my sister die. She really did later, when I was away. She sent me letters begging me to help her. Help her.

Beverly was my size & that started it. In the slums. Even we called them that, but all my later friends lived there. Behind those metal fences, for the playground. I never went there much, or only at night, to dance, & walk that fat girl home. They were all hip & beautiful. Even now, coming to strange things. Like this mist pushing off the day, Strange. These strangers, are beautiful. Be wary of them.

The woman liked me. Smart kid, she told everybody. I was fucking Beverly a little bit. The head of my dick went in, but I learned later to put my legs between hers, & that made it easier. She smiled when she found out. In that wet cellar.

Spots. She never really was happy. Maybe / at the proctors with me because it was dark & she could laugh at stupid things. I killed her. She let me do anything because of it. Eat her years later when I learned. Too late then, she kept calling. Believed me dead or in "Porto Rico." I came back furious with her chimneys. Her father was right. After all.

Can you plunge into the woods? Lying by the stoop. Sell those gas heaters. Cook that food. Clean that building. Go to church.

Do you really think you were sane always. What about that powder-blue suit. Or dry-fucking Dolores Dean in your grandmother's house. Dolores Dean, and her less fortunate baby, Morgan. Big belly. Calvin Lewis did it.

He cdn't really play, I bet. I know pinball cdn't. Garmoney loved me. He got fat & forgot who I was. Hauling boxes. Bowling.

Playmaker. Strange for him to say it. At Robert Treat? The Boys' Club. Some obscure move with the hands. Across from Diane. Blacker, less desirable earlier. Grew huge in my eyes after all that killing. (Murdered my mother, father, sister, all the grandparents & uncles. Stepped out of their bloody flesh, a sinister shadow waiting for hardons.) She thought she could handle it, but it drove her crazy. She got educated & learned to make artificial birds. Another father for me, then. Blacker, too, less desirable. He walked her, on his wedding day, to the roof, & made her take off her skirt. He told me later drugged & dying.

"Anything you want Miss Sweeney. Bigeyed Miss Sweeney." "She Got Some bigass eyes." Ora Matthews. William Knowles (after he climbed the gaspipes & began drumming like Elks on the desk), Murray Jackson. The Geeks. Miss Mawer, also, but better. Crippled lady. What wd she say now. Suck my pussy, hero. Eat me up.

You left that. But the cold is back. The hard gravel. Dorothy Bowman. Donald Pegram. Don't limit the world. It grows. It bulges. It is bleeding with your names, your soft fingers.

Who do you think you are on that couch with the lights off? Her father? Her porch? Her long street behind the railroad tracks? You are a train. Her father's noise in his sleep, of the south, from his eyes, under the weather, for you. Separate, again. These radios.

In the dark, she was soft. In the cellar. In the bedrooms. On the couch. Even with my mother's voice. My mother. My aunt frightened of the girl because they were both ugly. My aunt Gottlieb. Oh what an ugly church that ugly girl goes to. My grandfather had died in a warehouse full of election machines. Does that mean it was Autumn? Or that I wore badges or made it with Aubry at Belmar. Aubry who?

They all turn out good. I did. The way this is going. Who? Go back. Turn. The door will swing open into sun. Into Autumn. Into the cold. Into loud arguments at night with the door open. Small children die. I kill everything . . . I can. This is This. I am left only with my small words . . . against the day. Against you. Against. My self.

The corner is old. Headlight, bubbles. Now. Look for the lies. Them now. They go away, these lovers. For my running. Those soft flies over the shortstop's head. Please. Not as a dead man. Even Diane. A fair second baseman. You let him die. No. The lies. No.

(Have they moved out of the city? I mean her tall beautiful mother & no good boyfriend)

Good field

No Hit!

TO THOSE TO COME

William Goldman

Raymond Euripides Trevitt is sixteen and a junior in high school. Miss Twilly, Raymond's former piano teacher, is just a couple of years older; she has just graduated from high school. This selection, distinctively light and humorous, is set in the 1950s in a small midwestern college town—Athens, Illinois. The "initiation" function of a first sexual experience is again a focal point, and the earthy Miss Twilly takes on archetypal proportions as the initiator. Since Raymond is the narrator, the meaning of it for him is relatively clear. What is left unclear is the meaning of it for Miss Twilly.

I have to start this with Helen Twilly.

Who was a freshman in the college when I first knew her, and a very easy person to describe. Helen Twilly had huge cans. Now ordinarily, in this day and age, that should be enough to make a girl reasonably popular. But not Helen. For her face wasn't much and neither was her figure, her butt also being very large. Her cans were so big, though, that it made you forget most of the rest. Zock and I used to refer to other girls' with her name. "Twillies," we called them. But that was later.

The reason I met her at all was because of my mother. I was in the seventh grade at the time, when, out of the blue, my mother decided that I should have piano lessons. It was, I suppose, a last-ditch attempt on her part to bring some culture into my life. Culture, even today, is not one of my strongest points and I had less of it then. Anyway, my mother had a long talk with me one night at supper, beating around the bush, going on about the importance of the arts, especially music. Finally, she came out with it: I was to take piano lessons. My father had asked at the college for someone who might give them to me and had come up with Miss Twilly. So, in spite of anything I could do, the lessons began.

The first one was the worst. Mainly because my mother insisted on staying in the room while Miss Twilly gave me the business about scales. They were as far as I ever got, scales, but nobody knew it then. I sat there, sweating, pounding away on our little upright piano with Miss Twilly beside me, smiling over at my mother who smiled back, and I don't know how. For my ear has never been very good as far as music is concerned. The reason I stopped taking piano was because it turned out I was tone deaf. This has never been a heavy cross for me to bear, but it did come as a blow to my mother who, I think, honestly had visions of me being a child prodigy and knocking them dead at Carnegie Hall.

"You must cup your hands, Raymond," Miss Twilly said to me that day. "Cup them over the keyboard."

"Sure thing," I said, doing as I was told. Which didn't make the scales sound any better since, being tone deaf, I was never sure when I did something right or not.

"Do, re, mi, fa, sol, la, ti, do," Miss Twilly sang along. "No, Raymond. La. La." And she hit the correct note.

"La," I said. "La, la, la." And I pounded away on that poor key.

"Not so hard, Raymond," Miss Twilly pleaded, smiling at my mother. "Gently. We must learn to caress the keys. As though they were our friends."

And that was how it went for the first lesson. I wasn't as unhappy about it as I might have been, for I knew from the start that I was never going to play at Carnegie Hall or any place else. Some things you take to right away, but to the piano I never did. It was all a joke, my only worry being that the news might spread around school. Which never happened, since Zock was always a good man at keeping a secret.

I told him right after it was over. Mother and Miss Twilly were having a whispered conversation so I slipped on by them to Zock's house. He was waiting to hear, but what I talked about was not so much the music as Miss Twilly's cans. I was so expressive that he asked if he could see them.

And the next time she came, the following Tuesday, he was there, waiting. She walked in and smiled at me. He just stared. Then, before the lesson started, he got up to go.

"They're big all right," Zock said, and he took off.

Which threw Miss Twilly. "What are big?" she asked me.

"I don't know," I answered. "Sometimes it's very hard to figure just what he's talking about."

But all the same, she knew. She was a little flustered during the lesson. Not really embarrassed, just flustered. She kind of hunched her shoulders forward, trying to make them seem not so noticeable, which in her case was an impossibility.

After that, I began to like her. I think she knew about my being tone deaf from the start but said nothing of it to anyone because she needed the money. At any rate, from then on we played the piano less and talked more, about all kinds of things. She had a way of patting me on top of the head which, with most people, you don't like, seeing as it makes you feel as though you are a dog and they are petting you. But with Miss Twilly it was all right. She was such a sweet girl. Very shy and kind, with a soft, gentle voice. She was so shy she blushed all the time, even in front of me, which should show the kind of person she was.

But the music part never got anywhere. I stayed with those scales the whole eight weeks I took piano lessons. And I did try. Each time before she came I'd practice half an hour, trying to cup my hands and sit up straight, trying to make those notes come out right. But some people can do some things and others can't, and playing the piano was not my forte, a pun Zock thought up one day.

So, finally, Miss Twilly had a long talk with my mother and told her the truth. About my being tone deaf and how this kind of hurts your chances of ever making it as a piano player. And my mother stopped the lessons right after. At the last one, Miss Twilly and I talked and laughed, having a gay old time. But when she got up to go, I think we both felt sad.

"Well good-by, Raymond," she said, patting me on the head.

"So long, Miss Twilly," I answered, walking her to the door. "I sure hope you can make it to Carnegie Hall." Which of course she never did, but just the same it was what she wanted more than anything else in the world. "Maybe I'll see you around sometime."

"Maybe," she said, patting my head once more. "Let's hope so."

And I did see her. Often, during the next couple of years. Uptown or around the campus I'd see her walking alone or with some other girls. Whenever that happened, I'd wave and shout: "Hello there, Miss Twilly." And she'd blush and wave back. She was never with a boy, at least none I ever saw. And that was a shame, her being such a fine girl, shy and gentle and all.

Then, in June of my sophomore year in high school, her class graduated, her along with it. Graduation day at Athens was something I never cared for. All those caps and gowns and crying mothers. I had already made up my mind that when I graduated from college, I was going to skip the whole business. But of course, the way things worked out, I never had to miss much sleep on that score.

Anyhow, I was puttering around the house, waiting for it to get over. Zock used to like to watch, so he was up by the college auditorium taking it in. My father was there, too, being as he was such a big deal at the school he had to go. And my mother wouldn't have missed it for the world. About the time I figured it was done, I started getting ready for the trip to Zock's house, when there was a buzz at the front door. I went down to answer. It was her.

"Hi, Miss Twilly," I said, opening it.

"Hello, Raymond," she said, walking in. It was a hot day and she was perspiring so she took off her cap and gown, smiling at me. She was wearing a big skirt and a very thin white blouse you could see through. "I thought I'd come over and say good-by," she told me. "I'm leaving this afternoon."

"That was real nice of you, Miss Twilly," I said. "I'm glad you did." She put her hand on my shoulder and we walked into the living-room where the little upright piano was. We started laughing.

"I suppose," she began. "You don't. I mean. Any more, do you?" She was very nervous on account of just having graduated, but I got what she meant.

"Practice?" I answered. "I'd rather be strung up by my thumbs."

It was very hot and stuffy and we both laughed at what I said, even though it wasn't funny. That is something I'm not much good at. Being funny. Once in a while, alone with Zock, I could do all right, but not often. He said not to worry about it since I had a fine sense of humor and could appreciate a joke as well as anyone. And that, he explained, was every bit as important, for if there was nobody around to laugh, where would the funny men be? True enough, I suppose, although I suspect he was just trying to make me feel better at the time. Which he did.

So we laughed at my joke, standing there in that stuffy room. We laughed for a long time, giggling away, and the next thing I knew she had her arms around me and was kissing me on the mouth, something that had never happened to me before. She pulled me in close and held me tight, kissing me over and over. First I tried to get away. But I stopped that quick.

Then she turned my head and began blowing in my ear, which
has never made me turn cartwheels. Actually, I believe it really
doesn't do anything to anybody, but long ago the idea started that
it did, and it's kept on ever since because no one has had the guts
to stop it. Well, she was blowing away at my ear, tickling me, though
I never in this world would have laughed, as it would have hurt her
feelings. Then she started to talk.

"Raymond," she said."Raymond. Raymond. Raymond."

"What?" I asked her.

She didn't answer but just kept saying my name again and again
as she horsed with my ear. And I knew that sure as God made green
apples, I wasn't keeping my part of the bargain.

So finally, I suppose by instinct, I started doing something which
I now know was a good thing, being what she wanted. Except then
it was pure luck that I did it.

I started unbuttoning her blouse. It took me about an hour, since
my hands were shaking, but I finally managed it. After which I pulled
her blouse out from her skirt. A woman's brassière is something I can
now work with my eyes closed, and frequently have. But right then,
I couldn't find the handle. I tugged and pulled and sweated over it,
but the goddam thing stayed put. I tried lifting it up, pushing it down,
yanking on it every which way, getting no place. Then she gave that
soft laugh of hers, put her hands behind her back for just a second,
and it was loose. I lifted it, gently I think, and there they were.

"My God, Miss Twilly," I said. "They're huge."

She blushed, tried to cover herself. "I know," she whispered.
"I'm sorry."

"No," I told her, pushing her hands away. "It's O.K. with me."

She put her arm around me and began walking me toward the
stairs. "Come on, Raymond," she said. "Come on." And she started
up with me following.

I have walked those stairs many times in my life, both before
and since, but never has it seemed as hard or taken as long. Because
halfway up I started sweating and shivering so that I could barely
move. We got to my bedroom where she pulled down all the shades,
one by one, and when she did that I could tell her hands were none
too steady either. Then she closed the door. It wasn't very dark; we
could still see each other plain. As I watched, Miss Twilly started
taking off her clothes.

"You too, Raymond," she said.

But I didn't move. I couldn't. So when she was done she came
over and tried pulling off my shirt.

"I can do it," I whispered, my throat very dry.

"All right," she said. "Show me you can."

I turned my back and she laughed softly at that, so I turned to face her again. I took off my shirt and pants. Finally I stood there, wearing just my sneakers.

"Finish it up," she said.

"Even my shoes?"

"Even your shoes."

I kicked them off. She sat down on the bed, smiling, and then she lay all the way back, stretching her arms toward me. I didn't move. She sat up again, reached out her hands, taking me gently, guiding me over to the bed. Pretty soon everything was warm and soft and neither of us was shaking any more.

Anyway, that was the first time.

After we'd said good-by at the front door, her patting me on the head, sort of crying, I ran over to Zock's house and told him all about it. Not in a boasting way but mainly because I was confused and him, being older, knew more of such things than I did.

He listened very carefully, pulling at his lower lip, a way he had when he was concentrating.

"That's it," I finished up. "She was crying and we went downstairs to say good-by. What do you think?"

"You bastard," Zock said, laughing.

"Come on," I said. "Don't kid around."

"A toast," he shouted. "A toast is definitely called for," and he took off, running to Old Crowe's liquor cabinet, me in hot pursuit. I watched as he filled two glasses, handed me one, smiling.

"And now we need a toast," he said. "But to what?"

"To Miss Twilly," I suggested, raising my glass.

"No," he said. "No good. She's over and done with. A thing of the past." He pulled at his lip awhile. "Wait. How about this? How about: a toast to those to come."

Which sounded fine to me and we drank to it.

So, at the age of sixteen, I had lost my virginity but had never been out with a girl.

TWO
Discovery

Abstinence sows sand all over
The ruddy limbs and flaming hair,
But Desire Gratified
Plants fruits of life and beauty there.

ETERNITY
William Blake

FROM THE JOURNAL
OF HARRY SCHACHT

Robert H. Rimmer

Harry Schacht, a freshman at Harrad College, is six feet tall, gangly, and bookish. His "roommate" is Beth Hillyer, the most beautiful of the fifty girls at Harrad. After three weeks of sharing an apartment, they make love in a pile of leaves. It's Harry's first time. Here, in his journal, is the account of that mellifluent experience. Harrad is not a real college, Beth and Harry are not real people, the journal entries which comprise the structure of the book in which this selection appears are all part of Robert Rimmer's imagination. Nothing remotely resembling the Harrad experiment could ever take place in America's colleges or universities, of course. This selection depicts, perhaps more so than in some of the others, the crucial role that prior experience plays in determining the meaning of an immediate experience.

They call a day like yesterday Indian Summer. A blue-sky placid day, soft and balmy, with the temperature climbing almost to eighty degrees. Harrad was deserted. Most of the kids had gone to football games. A gang of them were going over to "A" College stadium. They had invited Beth and me to go along. When I asked Beth why she hadn't gone with them, she said: "You didn't invite me. I didn't want to go alone."

"I'm sorry," I said. "See, I told you that I was an odd-ball. I guess I don't really like football. But I would have gone if you wanted to."

"Harry," Beth said, "I'm the cheerleader type . . . didn't you know? Rah . . . rah . . . har . . . rah . . . Harrad! Go, Team! Go! Dopey, if I had wanted to see a football game, I would have twisted you around my little finger. But don't think I haven't got ulterior motives. You and I, Harry, are going exploring!" Beth's smile was mischievous, a blonde pixie. "See this box. In it are two ham and cheese sandwiches . . . by tomorrow you may be dead mixing *milchik* and *fleischik*. In this thermos bottle is some dago red wine that cost me one dollar. See, I have all the ingredients and I'm proposing: 'A loaf of bread, a jug of wine' " . . .

"I'm thou," I said fervently.

"No, I am Thou," Beth said. "You're Omar, the Tentmaker."

So we went exploring. Beth held my hand, and I carried the sandwiches and the wine. She brought a book of Dylan Thomas' poems which she promised to read to me with my head in her lap.

"That's the way it's done in all the romantic movies," she said, smiling happily. "I'll bet you don't know it, but I found a book about the first John Carnsworth. It tells of the days he lived here in Cambridge. Somewhere in the middle of these grounds, running right through them, is a brook. Years ago they had a fish hatchery, Carnsworth kept it stocked for his millionaire friends. The Tenhausens have been so busy teaching us about love and life, they've overlooked the pastoral things."

Beth, dressed in a green skirt and white V-necked blouse, skipped along like a six-year old, her blonde hair flying, her face flushed with excitement. She, hastening me along a wooded path, was a reincarnation of Rima, transplanted from a South American jungle . . . but now quite real and tangible. I measured my ordinary pedestrian steps to her rhythm and soon I, too, was buoyant as the leaves floating unhurriedly as they glided down from the nearly naked maples and elms.

"Isn't this our day, Harry?" she asked me. "For a moment we are the only two humans in the world."

And it was our day. It held us in its sunny hands and filled our nostrils with the dry musty odor of millions of leaves, earthy and crumbling beneath our feet. And then we found the brook, about twenty feet across, studded with alluvial rocks and running rapidly with clear bubbly water flowing over a mulch of soft black muck and slippery leaves.

Near the brook on a dirt road two gardeners who took care of the Harrad grounds were unloading a Ford pick-up truck piled high with leaves. They waved at us good-naturedly.

"We've found other humans," I suggested to Beth.

"Not really humans." Beth took off her shoes and paddled in the water. "Just a picturesque back-drop to the stage we are acting on."

We sat on a rock near the edge of the brook and dangled our feet in the water. The gardeners drove away in their truck and then came back with more leaves. We watched them while we ate our sandwiches and took swigs of wine from the thermos bottle.

"They must be collecting leaves from all over the grounds," I said. "Should we go somewhere else? . . . Rude practicality has invaded our dream world."

Beth shook her head. "It's Saturday afternoon. They won't work much longer." We watched several of the piles grow to more than ten feet high. "What are you going to do with them?" Beth asked one of the gardeners.

"Too dry to burn them . . . We'll compost them next week," one of them replied, wiping his brow and looking longingly at the water. "Cripes, if I were a kid I'd strip bollicky and go swimming in this little puddle." He scooped up some water and splashed it across his face.

"Come on," the other gardener said. "It's twelve-thirty. We're knocking off. You kids go to Harrad?"

We nodded.

"What kind of monkeyshines are goin' on there? I heard a rumor you kids sleep together. Is that true?" he demanded.

"Does it sound likely?" Beth asked, her eyebrows raised.

"Hell's bells, with the younger generation anything is likely. I tell my son, I know you won't be good . . . but for godsake be careful."

They drove away chuckling, leaving us with the blippety sound of the water and the skeletons of the trees. I stretched out on the ground beside Beth and I looked up at the few remaining leaves wispy and brown against the clear blue sky. Beth read, in a deep throaty imitation of a Welsh voice, Thomas' *Fern Hill, Do not go gentle into that Good Night, Poem in October* and *In my Craft or Sullen Art* while I listened dreamily, charmed as much by her seriousness as the words of the poems.

We finished the wine, and for a long time, her back against a tree, her eyes closed, Beth said nothing. Then softly:

"Harry, I think sometimes I am a very erotic person."

"Why?" I asked.

"I get very sensuous ideas. Once in the middle of winter, I took off all my clothes and ran out in our back yard. It was snowing and blustery. Drifts four and five feet high swirled into small knife-edge mountains. The snow was soft and powdery. For a moment, though I knew I was half frozen, I felt that I wasn't me. I was snow itself, and I was whirling in a mad snow dance. Then you know what I did? I jumped and rolled in the biggest drift and rubbed the snow all over me."

"Did you catch cold?"

"My, you are practical, aren't you, Harry?"

"I would have liked to have been there," I said.

"Would you have jumped in the snow with me . . . or would you have watched?"

"I guess I am practical."

"Well, jiminy I could have used you, anyway . . . to snuggle against. Afterwards, I got into bed and shivered all night. Why did I do that, Harry?"

"I don't know. Maybe you were all tense, and it relaxed you. You seem to have a wonderful ability to just let go. Everybody has to find some form of release."

"No, I don't think so, Harry. I think it was a throwback."

"Throwback?"

"Did you ever see a dog or cat roll on the ground . . . right in the dirt?

"Or a pig or rhinoceros in the zoo just wallow in the mud?"

"Sure. My guess is that it is a sexual response of some kind."

"Maybe masochistic?"

"Ugh . . . no! Just plain sensual. After all, man is linked to the earth. One's body crying for the earth from which it came, and an ecstasy at being re-united."

"If you'd like to roll in the mud," I said laughing, "go ahead. I'll roll with you."

"Let's play in the leaves instead. Did you ever play in the leaves when you were a kid, Harry?"

"Sure. We had leaf houses and burrowed in them, and had leaf fights and itched for days afterwards. But they weren't our leaves. They belonged to the city. Maybe that's why I never got the urge to roll in the snow. We have no back yard, and when it snows the city cleans it off the streets within a day."

"Come on, Harry," Beth said. "Stop mourning your youth. Take off your clothes and follow me!" In seconds she stripped off her blouse, skirt, bra, and panties. Yelling with sheer joy, she plunged naked into huge piles of leaves. Tossing them about her in mad abandon, she sank deep into them and disappeared from view.

Naked myself, I followed, burrowed in after her, and grabbed her. Laughing hilariously, we tumbled and leaped and jumped, and worked our way deep into the pile, tossing leaves at each other, and in the air . . . and then we rolled together and Beth hugged me as we sank deep into the crackly pyramid. Sunlight filtered down through the leaves covering us. Beth kissed me fiercely.

"What is love?" she whispered.

"A girl, a boy, their hearts beating . . . happy with simple things like leaves and each other," I said.

"You look like Pan . . . or maybe like Bacchus. At least you're full of wine," she said. "Harry, you said a boy and girl. Not a man and woman? Love is youth? When you are fifty, and a staid old Doctor, you wouldn't roll in the leaves naked, would you? I guess not. Daddy and Mommy wouldn't . . . but I will, Harry, because I believe love is laughter, too."

I couldn't answer her. I could only see her through a film of tears that came in my eyes. Oh, Beth . . .

"Rub the leaves on my body, Harry," she sighed.

And she lay there, luxuriating, sensuous, while the leaves crumbled in my hands and turned her white breasts and shoulders and stomach dusty brown.

"We're going to need a bath," she chuckled, rubbing leaves over me until I was as dusty as she.

"Harry," she whispered, lying back in the leaves, her legs wide apart. "I am a very devious person. I practiced with that diaphragm this morning. It's kind of god-awful . . . but . . ."

"But what?"

"I left it in."

"I never did it before, Beth," I said.

"According to everything I have read in the books, you are ready enough." She grinned at me and carefully picked the leaves off my penis. "Please, Harry. We've waited long enough."

She shuddered and raked my back with her fingernails. "Harry . . . Harry . . . hold me . . . I'm afraid . . . I'm afraid . . ." she whimpered, and then with a banshee wail she clasped her legs around me, rocked me fiercely, kissing me and sobbing while I kissed her dusty face and breasts and held her so hard that her poor body must ache even now.

We lay together for a long time in our leafy womb, and I could feel the soft undulating movement of her vagina keeping me happily within her.

"Was that love, Harry?" she asked.

"Yes . . . and this whole day, and yesterday and tomorrow is love, too."

She gave me one million two hundred and thirty-nine thousand little kisses, and then, laughing and screaming at the cold chill of the brook water, we washed the dirt and powdered leaves off each other, and dried ourselves as best we could with my shorts and her panties.

And then last night she slept in her own bed; and today she has been very serious and subdued. When I said: "I love you, Beth," she smiled affectionately, but she didn't say: "I love you, too, Harry."

Oh, Beth . . . why am I afraid to just ask you what you are thinking?

A KIND MEMORY

Robert Anderson

The following excerpt is taken from a play which attempts to reveal some possible consequences of living in a social milieu which demands strict adherence to prescribed sex roles. The males of *Tea and Sympathy* must behave as males; to do otherwise is to risk social ostracism. Ironically, the play dramatizes that those males who flaunt their "masculinity" are sometimes the most vulnerable, while those who do not seek to prove their masculinity are truly the most complete, the most genuine of human beings. In this concluding scene from the drama, Laura, the wife of a man who has been given the task of "making a man" of young Tom, has just accused her husband, Bill, of that "weakness" which Tom is supposed to possess.

LAURA: (*Quietly*) I will be . . . (*Going towards him*) Oh, Bill, I'm sorry. I shouldn't have said that . . . it was cruel. (*She reaches for him as he goes out the door*) This was the weakness you cried out for me to save you from, wasn't it . . . And I have tried. (*He is gone*) I have tried. (*Slowly she turns back into the room and looks at it*) I did try. (*For a few minutes she stands stunned and tired from her outburst. Then she moves slowly to* TOM'S *raincoat, picks it up and turns and goes out of the room and to the stair-landing. She goes to the boy's study door and knocks*) Tom. (*She opens it and goes in out of sight. At* TOM'S *door, she calls again*) Tom. (TOM *turns his head slightly and listens.* LAURA *opens* TOM'S *door and comes in*) Oh, I'm sorry. May I come in? (*She sees she's not going to get an answer from him, so she goes*

From *TEA AND SYMPATHY*, by Robert Anderson. Copyright 1953 by Robert Anderson. Reprinted by permission of Random House, Inc.

in) I brought back your raincoat. You left it last night. (*She puts it on chair. She looks at him*) This is a nice room . . . I've never seen it before . . . As a matter of fact I've never been up here in this part of the house. (*Still getting no response, she goes on.* TOM *slowly turns and looks at her back, while she is examining something on the walls. She turns, speaking*) It's very cozy. It's really quite . . . (*She stops when she sees he has turned around looking at her*) Hello.

TOM: (*Barely audible*) Hello.

LAURA: Do you mind my being here?

TOM: You're not supposed to be.

LAURA: I know. But everyone's out, and will be for some time . . . I wanted to return your raincoat.

TOM: Thank you. (*After a pause he sits up on the bed, his back to her*) I didn't think you'd ever want to see me again.

LAURA: Why not?

TOM: After last night. I'm sorry about what happened downstairs.

LAURA: (*She looks at him a while, then*) I'm not.

TOM: (*Looks at her. Can't quite make it out*) You've heard everything, I suppose.

LAURA: Yes.

TOM: Everything?

LAURA: Everything.

TOM: I knew your husband would be anxious to give you the details.

LAURA: He did. (*She stands there quietly looking down at the boy.*)

TOM: So now you know too.

LAURA: What?

TOM: That everything they said about me is true.

LAURA: Tom!

TOM: Well, it is, isn't it?

LAURA: Tom?

TOM: I'm no man. Ellie knows it. Everybody knows it. It seems everybody knew it, except me. And now I know it.

LAURA: (*Moves towards him*) Tom . . . Tom . . . dear. (TOM *turns away from her*) You don't think that just because . . .

TOM: What else am I to think?

LAURA: (*Very gently*) Tom, that didn't work because you didn't believe in it . . . in such a test.

TOM: (*With the greatest difficulty*) I touched her, and there was nothing.

LAURA: You aren't in love with Ellie.

TOM: That's not supposed to matter.

LAURA: But it does.

TOM: I wish they'd let me kill myself.

LAURA: Tom, look at me. (TOM *shakes his head*) Tom, last night you kissed me.

TOM: Jesus!

LAURA: Why did you kiss me?

TOM: (*Turns suddenly*) And it made you sick, didn't it? Didn't it? (*Turns away from her again.*)

LAURA: How can you think such a thing?

TOM: You sent me away . . . you . . . Anyway, when you heard this morning it must have made you sick.

LAURA: (*Sits on edge of bed*) Tom, I'm going to tell you something. (TOM *won't turn*) Tom? (*He still won't turn*) It was the nicest kiss I've ever had . . . from anybody. (TOM *slowly turns and looks at her*) Tom, I came up to say good-bye. (TOM *shakes his head, looking at her*) I'm going away . . . I'll probably never see you again. I'm leaving Bill. (TOM *knits his brows questioning*) For a lot of reasons . . . one of them, what he's done to you. But before I left, I wanted you to know, for your own comfort, you're more of a man now than he ever was or will be. And one day you'll meet a girl, and it will be right. (TOM *turns away in disbelief*) Tom, believe me.

TOM: I wish I could. But a person knows . . . knows inside. Jesus, do you think after last night I'd ever . . . (*He stops. After a moment, he smiles at her*) But thanks . . . thanks a lot. (*He closes his eyes.* LAURA *looks at him a long time. Her face shows the great compassion and tenderness she feels for this miserable boy. After some time, she gets up and goes out the door. A moment later she appears in the hall door. She pauses for a moment, then reaches out and closes it, and stays inside.*

TOM, when he hears the door close, his eyes open. He sees she has left his bedroom. Then in complete misery, he lies down on the bed, like a wounded animal, his head at the foot of the bed.

LAURA in a few moments appears in the bedroom doorway. She stands there, and then comes in, always looking at the slender figure of the boy on the bed. She closes the bedroom door.

TOM hears the sound and looks around. When he sees she has come back, he turns around slowly, wonderingly, and lies on his back, watching her.

LAURA seeing a bolt on the door, slides it to. Then she stands looking at TOM, her hand at her neck. With a slight and delicate movement, she unbuttons the top button of her blouse, and moves towards TOM. When she gets alongside the bed, she reaches out her hand, still keeping one hand at her blouse. TOM makes no move. Just watches her.

LAURA makes a little move with the outstretched hand, asking for his hand. TOM slowly moves his hand to hers.)

LAURA: (*Stands there holding his hand and smiling gently at him. Then she sits and looks down at the boy, and after a moment, barely audible*) And now . . . nothing? (TOM's *other hand comes up and with both his hands he brings her hand to his lips.*)

LAURA: (*Smiles tenderly at this gesture, and after a moment*) Years from now . . . when you talk about this . . . and you will . . . be kind. (*Gently she brings the boy's hands toward her opened blouse, as the lights slowly dim out . . . and . . .*

THE CURTAIN FALLS

THE MAN LIVES

D. H. Lawrence

In the austere, self-denying, celibate existence which Christ observed to his "death," was there a sin of omission? This is the question which D. H. Lawrence seems to ponder in his novella, *The Man Who Died,* from which the following excerpt is taken. As the scene opens we find a man who, having been crucified and left for dead, has managed to recoup from his wounds and has journeyed on foot into Egypt, where he meets "the woman of Isis." Through his encounter with "the woman of Isis," Christ discovers a new dimension of his "humanness," something that causes him to look toward heaven and say: "Father! Why did you hide this from me?" Lawrence invites us to suspend temporarily any preconception we might have of the divine nature of Christ so that we might explore the psychic and physical sensation of a man who deprived himself of mundane experience, who "offered only kindness" but was given "unjust cruelty" in return.

He was absorbed and enmeshed in new sensations. The woman of Isis was lovely to him, not so much in form, as in the wonderful womanly glow of her. Suns beyond suns had dipped her in mysterious fire, the mysterious fire of a potent woman, and to touch her was like touching the sun. Best of all was her tender desire for him, like sunshine, so soft and still.

"She is like sunshine upon me," he said to himself, stretching his limbs. "I have never before stretched my limbs in such sunshine as her desire for me. The greatest of all gods granted me this."

At the same time he was haunted by the fear of the outer world. "If they can, they will kill us," he said to himself. "But there is a law of the sun which protects us."

And again he said to himself: "I have risen naked and branded. But if I am naked enough for this contact, I have not died in vain. Before I was clogged."

He rose and went out. The night was chill and starry, and of a great wintery splendour. "There are destinies of splendour," he said to the night, "after all our doom of littleness and meanness and pain."

So he went up silently to the temple, and waited in darkness against the inner wall, looking out on a gray darkness, stars, and rims of trees. And he said again to himself: "There are destinies of splendour, and there is a greater power."

So at last he saw the light of her silk lanthorn swinging, coming intermittent between the trees, yet coming swiftly. She was alone, and near, the light softly swishing on her mantle-hem. And he trembled with fear and with joy, saying to himself: "I am almost more afraid of this touch than I was of death. For I am more nakedly exposed to it."

"I am here, Lady of Isis," he said softly out of the dark.

"Ah!" she cried, in fear also, yet in rapture. For she was given to her dream.

She unlocked the door of the shrine, and he followed after her. Then she latched the door shut again. The air inside was warm and close and perfumed. The man who had died stood by the closed door, and watched the woman. She had come first to the goddess. And dim-lit, the goddess-statue stood surging forward, a little fearsome like a great woman-presence urging.

The priestess did not look at him. She took off her saffron mantle and laid it on a low couch. In the dim light she was bare armed, in her girdled white tunic. But she was still hiding herself away from him. He stood back in shadow, and watched her slowly fan the brazier and fling on incense. Faint clouds of sweet aroma arose on the air. She turned to the statue in the ritual of approach, softly swaying forward with a slight lurch, like a moored boat, tipping towards the goddess.

He watched the strange rapt woman, and he said to himself: "I must leave her alone in her rapture, her female mysteries." So she tipped in her strange forward-swaying rhythm before the goddess. Then she broke into a murmur of Greek, which he could not understand. And, as she murmured, her swaying softly subsided, like a boat on a sea that grows still. And as he watched her, he saw her soul in its aloneness, and its female difference. He said to himself: "How different she is from me, how strangely different! She is afraid of me, and my male difference. She is getting herself naked and clear of her fear. How sensitive and softly alive she is, with a life so different from mine! How beautiful with a soft strange courage, of life, so different from my courage of death! What a beautiful thing, like the heart of a rose, like the core of a flame. She is making herself completely penetrable. Ah! how terrible to fail her, or to trespass on her!"

She turned to him, her face glowing from the goddess.

"You are Osiris, aren't you?" she said naïvely.

"If you will," he said.

"Will you let Isis discover you? Will you not take off your things?"

He looked at the woman, and lost his breath. And his wounds, and especially the death-wound through his belly, began to cry again.

"It has hurt so much!" he said. "You must forgive me if I am still held back."

But he took off his cloak and his tunic, and went naked towards the idol, his breast panting with the sudden terror of overwhelming pain, memory of overwhelming pain, and grief too bitter.

"They did me to death!" he said in excuse of himself, turning his face to her for a moment.

And she saw the ghost of the death in him, as he stood there thin and stark before her, and suddenly she was terrified, and she felt robbed. She felt the shadow of the gray, grisly wing of death triumphant.

"Ah, Goddess," he said to the idol, in the vernacular. "I would be so glad to live, if you would give me my clue again."

For here again he felt desperate, faced by the demand of life, and burdened still by his death.

"Let me anoint you!" the woman said to him softly. "Let me anoint the scars! Show me, and let me anoint them!"

He forgot his nakedness in this re-evoked old pain. He sat on the edge of the couch, and she poured a little ointment into the palm of his hand. And as she chafed his hand, it all came back, the nails, the holes, the cruelty, the unjust cruelty against him who had offered only kindness. The agony of injustice and cruelty came over him again, as in his death-hour. But she chafed the palm, murmuring: "What was torn becomes a new flesh, what was a wound is full of fresh life; this scar is the eye of the violet."

And he could not help smiling at her, in her naïve priestess's absorption. This was her dream, and he was only a dream-object to her. She would never know or understand what he was. Especially she would never know the death that was gone before in him. But what did it matter? She was different. She was woman: her life and her death were different from his. Only she was good to him.

When she chafed his feet with oil and tender, tender healing, he could not refrain from saying to her:

"Once a woman washed my feet with tears, and wiped them with her hair, and poured on precious ointment."

The woman of Isis looked up at him from her earnest work, interrupted again.

"Were they hurt then?" she said. "Your feet?"

"No, no! It was while they were whole."

"And did you love her?"

"Love had passed in her. She only wanted to serve," he replied. "She had been a prostitute."

"And did you let her serve you?" she asked.

"Yea."

"Did you let her serve you with the corpse of her love?"

"Ay!"

Suddenly it dawned on him: "I asked them all to serve me with the corpse of their love. And in the end I offered them only the corpse of my love. This is my body—take and eat—my corpse—"

A vivid shame went through him. "After all," he thought, "I wanted them to love with dead bodies. If I had kissed Judas with live love, perhaps he would never have kissed me with death. Perhaps he loved me in the flesh, and I willed that he should love me body-lessly, with the corpse of love—"

There dawned on him the reality of the soft warm love which is in touch, and which is full of delight. "And I told them, blessed are they that mourn," he said to himself. "Alas, if I mourned even this woman here, now I am in death, I should have to remain dead, and I want so much to live. Life has brought me to this woman with warm hands. And her touch is more to me now than all my words. For I want to live—"

"Go then to the goddess!" she said softly, gently pushing him towards Isis. And as he stood there dazed and naked as an unborn thing, he heard the woman murmuring to the goddess, murmuring, murmuring with a plaintive appeal. She was stooping now, looking at the scar in the soft flesh of the socket of his side, a scar deep and like an eye sore with endless weeping, just in the soft socket above the hip. It was here that his blood had left him, and his essential seed. The woman was trembling softly and murmuring in Greek. And he

in the recurring dismay of having died, and in the anguished per-
plexity of having tried to force life, felt his wounds crying aloud, and
the deep places of the body howling again: "I have been murdered,
and I lent myself to murder. They murdered me, but I lent myself
to murder—"

The woman, silent now, but quivering, laid oil in her hand and
put her palm over the wound in his right side. He winced, and the
wound absorbed his life again, as thousands of times before. And in
the dark, wild pain and panic of his consciousness rang only one cry:
"Oh, how can she take this death out of me? How can she take from
me this death? She can never know! She can never understand! She
can never equal it! . . ."

In silence, she softly rhythmically chafed the scar with oil. Absorbed now in her priestess's task, softly, softly gathering power,
while the vitals of the man howled in panic. But as she gradually
gathered power, and passed in a girdle round him to the opposite
scar, gradually warmth began to take the place of the cold terror,
and he felt: "I am going to be warm again, and I am going to be
whole! I shall be warm like the morning. I shall be a man. It doesn't
need understanding. It needs newness. She brings me newness—"

And he listened to the faint, ceaseless wail of distress of his
wounds, sounding as if for ever under the horizons of his consciousness. But the wail was growing dim, more dim.

He thought of the woman toiling over him: "She does not know!
She does not realise the death in me. But she has another consciousness. She comes to me from the opposite end of the night."

Having chafed all his lower body with oil, having worked with
her slow intensity of a priestess, so that the sound of his wounds grew
dimmer and dimmer, suddenly she put her breast against the wound
in his left side, and her arms round him, folding over the wound in
his right side, and she pressed him to her, in a power of living
warmth, like the folds of a river. And the wailing died out altogether,
and there was a stillness, and darkness in his soul, unbroken dark
stillness, wholeness.

Then slowly, slowly, in the perfect darkness of his inner man,
he felt the stir of something coming. A dawn, a new sun. A new sun
was coming up in him, in the perfect inner darkness of himself. He
waited for it breathless, quivering with a fearful hope . . . "Now I am
not myself. I am something new . . ."

And as it rose, he felt, with a cold breath of disappointment, the
girdle of the living woman slip down from him, the warmth and the

glow slipped from him, leaving him stark. She crouched, spent, at the feet of the goddess, hiding her face.

Stooping, he laid his hand softly on her warm, bright shoulder, and the shock of desire went through him, shock after shock, so that he wondered if it were another sort of death: but full of magnificence.

Now all his consciousness was there in the crouching, hidden woman. He stooped beside her and caressed her softly, blindly, murmuring inarticulate things. And his death and his passion of sacrifice were all as nothing to him now, he knew only the crouching fulness of the woman there, the soft white rock of life. . . . "On this rock I built my life." The deep-folded, penetrable rock of the living woman! The woman, hiding her face. Himself bending over, powerful and new like dawn.

He crouched to her, and he felt the blaze of his manhood and his power rise up in his loins, magnificent.

"I am risen!"

Magnificent, blazing indomitable in the depths of his loins, his own sun dawned, and sent its fire running along his limbs, so that his face shone unconsciously.

He untied the string on the linen tunic, and slipped the garment down, till he saw the white glow of her whitegold breasts. And he touched them, and he felt his life go molten. "Father!" he said, "why did you hide this from me?" And he touched her with the poignancy of wonder, and the marvellous piercing transcendence of desire. "Lo!" he said, "this is beyond prayer." It was the deep, interfolded warmth, warmth living and penetrable, the woman, the heart of the rose! "My mansion is the intricate warm rose, my joy is this blossom!"

She looked up at him suddenly, her face like a lifted light, wistful, tender, her eyes like many wet flowers. And he drew her to his breast with a passion of tenderness and consuming desire, and the last thought: "My hour is upon me, I am taken unawares—"

So he knew her, and was one with her.

Afterwards, with a dim wonder, she touched the great scars in his sides with her finger-tips, and said:

"But they no longer hurt?"

"They are suns!" he said. "They shine from your touch. They are my atonement with you."

And when they left the temple, it was the coldness before dawn. As he closed the door, he looked again at the goddess, and he said: "Lo, Isis is a kindly goddess; and full of tenderness. Great gods are warm-hearted, and have tender goddesses."

The woman wrapped herself in her mantle and went home in silence, sightless, brooding like the lotus softly shutting again, with its gold core full of fresh life. She saw nothing, for her own petals were a sheath to her. Only she thought: "I am full of Osiris. I am full of the risen Osiris! . . ."

But the man looked at the vivid stars before dawn, as they rained down to the sea, and the dog-star green towards the sea's rim. And he thought: "How plastic it is, how full of curves and folds like an invisible rose of dark-petalled openness that shows where the dew touches its darkness! How full it is, and great beyond all gods. How it leans around me, and I am part of it, the great rose of Space. I am like a grain of its perfume, and the woman is a grain of its beauty. Now the world is one flower of many petalled darknesses, and I am in its perfume as in a touch."

So, in the absolute stillness and fulness of touch, he slept in his cave while the dawn came. And after the dawn, the wind rose and brought a storm, with cold rain. So he stayed in his cave in the peace and the delight of being in touch, delighting to hear the sea, and the rain on the earth, and to see one white-and-gold narcissus bowing wet, and still wet. And he said: "This is the great atonement, the being in touch. The gray sea and the rain, the wet narcissus and the woman I wait for, the invisible Isis and the unseen sun are all in touch, and at one."

He waited at the temple for the woman, and she came in the rain. But she said to him:

"Let me sit awhile with Isis. And come to me, will you come to me, in the second hour of night?"

So he went back to the cave and lay in stillness and in the joy of being in touch, waiting for the woman who would come with the night, and consummate again the contact. Then when night came the woman came, and came gladly, for her great yearning too was upon her, to be in touch, to be in touch with him, nearer.

So the days came, and the nights came, and days came again, and the contact was perfected and fulfilled. And he said: "I will ask her nothing, not even her name, for a name would set her apart."

And she said to herself: "He is Osiris. I wish to know no more."

Plum-blossom blew from the trees, the time of the narcissus was past, anemones lit up the ground and were gone, the perfume of bean-field was in the air. All changed, the blossom of the universe changed its petals and swung round to look another way. The spring was fulfilled, a contact was established, the man and the woman were fulfilled of one another, and departure was in the air.

One day he met her under the trees, when the morning sun was hot, and the pines smelled sweet, and on the hills the last pear-bloom was scattering. She came slowly towards him, and in her gentle lingering, her tender hanging back from him, he knew a change in her.

"Hast thou conceived?" he asked her.

"Why?" she said.

"Thou art like a tree whose green leaves follow the blossom, full of sap. And there is a withdrawing about thee."

"It is so," she said. "I am with young by thee. Is it good?"

"Yea!" he said. "How should it not be good? So the nightingale calls no more from the valley-bed. But where wilt thou bear the child, for I am naked of all but life."

"We will stay here," she said.

"But the lady, your mother?"

A shadow crossed her brow. She did not answer.

"What when she knows?" he said.

"She begins to know."

"And would she hurt you?"

"Ah, not me! What I have is all my own. And I shall be big with Osiris. . . . But thou, do you watch her slaves."

She looked at him, and the peace of her maternity was troubled by anxiety.

"Let not your heart be troubled!" he said. "I have died the death once."

So he knew the time was come again for him to depart. He would go alone, with his destiny. Yet not alone, for the touch would be upon him, even as he left his touch on her. And invisible suns would go with him.

LISE

Hermann Hesse

Hesse's *Narcissus and Goldmund*, from which the following excerpt is taken, is a delicate work, filled with a myriad of conflicts—both visible and invisible. Some have argued that the characters of Narcissus and Goldmund are two sides of a hopelessly divided personality. Such critical insights notwithstanding, "Lise" represents a sexual initiation for Goldmund. The soft, dream-like quality of its description is typical of Hesse's art; and it is included here as a specimen of an impressionistic version of what has been treated with stark severity in other portions of this collection. The tone of this selection makes it possible to add layers of meaning to the ideas of love that are difficult, if not impossible, to deal with in a more literal and realistic narrative.

From the distant forest someone came walking, a young woman in a faded blue skirt, with a red kerchief tied around black hair, and a tanned summer face. The woman came closer; she was carrying a bundle; a fire-red gillyflower shone between her lips. She noticed the sitting man, watched him from afar for a long while, curious and distrustful, saw that he was asleep, tiptoed closer on naked brown feet, stood in front of Goldmund and looked at him. Her suspicions vanished; this fine young sleeper did not look dangerous; he pleased her greatly—what had brought him out here to these fallow fields? With a smile she saw that he had been picking flowers; they were already wilted.

Goldmund opened his eyes, returning from a forest of dreams. His head was bedded softly; it was lying in a woman's lap. Strangely close, two warm brown eyes were looking into his, which were sleepy and astonished. He felt no fear; no danger shone in those warm brown stars; they looked friendly. The woman smiled at his astonishment, a very friendly smile, and slowly he, too, began to smile. Her mouth came down on his smiling lips; they greeted each other with a gentle kiss, and Goldmund remembered the evening in the village and the little girl with the braids. But the kiss was not over yet. The woman's mouth lingered, began to play, teased and tempted, and finally seized his lips with greed and violence, set fire to his blood, made it throb in his veins; in slow, patient play the brown woman gave herself to the boy, teaching him gently, letting him seek and find, setting him afire and stilling the flames. The exalted, brief joy of love vaulted above him, burned with a golden glow, sank down and died. He lay with eyes closed, his face against the woman's breast. Not a word had been said. The woman didn't move, softly she stroked his hair, gave him time to come to himself. Finally he opened his eyes.

"You!" he said. "You! But who are you?"

"I'm Lise," she said.

"Lise," he repeated after her, tasting her name. "Lise, you are sweet."

She brought her mouth close to his ear and whispered into it: "Tell me, was this the first time? Did you never love anyone before me?"

He shook his head. Abruptly he sat up and looked across the fields and up into the sky.

"Oh!" he cried, "the sun is almost down. I must get back."

"Where to?"

"To the cloister, to Father Anselm."

"To Mariabronn? Is that where you belong? Don't you want to stay with me a little longer?"

"I'd like to."

"Well, stay then!"

"No, that would not be right. And I must pick more of these herbs."

"Do you live in the cloister?"

"Yes, I'm a student. But I'll not stay there. May I come to you, Lise? Where do you live, where is your home?"

"I live nowhere, dear heart. But won't you tell me your name?—
Ah, Goldmund is what they call you. Give me another kiss, little
Goldmouth, then you may go."

"You live nowhere? But where do you sleep?"

"If you like, in the forest with you, or in the hay. Will you come
tonight?"

"Oh, yes. But where? Where will I find you?"

"Can you screech like a barn owl?"

"I've never tried."

"Try."

He tried. She laughed, satisfied.

"All right, come out of the cloister tonight and screech like a
barn owl. I'll be close by. Do you like me, little Goldmouth, my
darling?"

"Oh, Lise, I do like you. I'll come. Now go with God, I must
hurry."

It was twilight when Goldmund returned to the cloister on his
steaming horse, and he was glad to find Father Anselm occupied. A
brother had been wading barefoot in the brook and cut himself on
a shard of crockery.

Now it was important to find Narcissus. He asked one of the lay
brothers who waited at table in the refectory. No, he was told, Narcissus would not be down for supper; this was his fasting day; he'd
probably be asleep now since he held vigils during the night. Goldmund hurried off. During the long exercises, his friend slept in one
of the penitents' cells in the inner cloister. Goldmund ran there
without thinking. He listened at the door; there wasn't a sound. He
entered softly. That it was strictly forbidden made no difference
now.

Narcissus was lying on the narrow cot. In the half light he looked
like a corpse, rigid on his back, with pale, pointed face, his hands
crossed on his chest. His eyes were open; he was not asleep. He
looked at Goldmund without speaking, without reproach, but without stirring, so obviously elsewhere, absorbed in a different time and
world, that he had difficulty recognizing his friend and understanding his words.

"Narcissus! Forgive me, dear friend, forgive me for disturbing
you. I'm not doing it lightly. I realize that you ought not to speak
to me, but do speak to me, I beg you with all my heart."

Narcissus reflected, his eyes blinked violently for a moment as
though he were struggling to come awake.

"Is it necessary?" he asked in a spent voice.

"Yes, it is necessary. I've come to say farewell."

"Then it is necessary. You shall not have come in vain. Here, sit with me. I have fifteen minutes before the first vigil."

Haggard, he sat on the bare sleeping plank. Goldmund sat down beside him.

"Please forgive me!" he said guiltily. The cell, the bare cot, Narcissus's strained face, drawn with lack of sleep, his half-absent eyes—all this showed plainly how much he disturbed his friend.

"There is nothing to forgive. Don't worry about me; there's nothing amiss with me. You've come to take leave, you say? You're going away then?"

"I'm going this very day. Oh, I don't know how to tell you! Suddenly everything has been decided."

"Has your father come, or a message from him?"

"No, nothing. Life itself has come to me. I'm leaving, without father, without permission. I'm bringing shame upon you, you know; I'm running away."

Narcissus looked down at his long white fingers. Thin and ghost-like, they protruded from the wide sleeves of the habit. There was no smile in his severe, exhausted face, but it could be felt in his voice as he said: "We have very little time, dear friend. Tell me only the essentials, tell me clearly and briefly. Or must I tell you what has happened to you?"

"You tell me," Goldmund begged.

"You've fallen in love, little boy, you've met a woman."

"How do you always know these things?"

"You're making it easy for me. Your condition, *amicus meus*, shows all the signs of that drunkenness called being in love. But speak now, please."

Timidly Goldmund touched his friend's shoulder.

"You have just said it. Although this time you didn't say it well, Narcissus, not accurately. It is altogether different. I was out in the fields, and I fell asleep in the heat, and when I woke up, my head was resting on the knees of a beautiful woman and I immediately felt that my mother had come to take me home. I did not think that this woman was my mother. Her eyes were brown and her hair was black; my mother had blond hair like mine. This woman didn't look in the least like her. And yet it was my mother, my mother's call, a message from her. It was as though an unknown beautiful woman had suddenly come out of the dreams of my own heart and was holding my head in her lap, smiling at me like a flower and being sweet to me. At her first kiss I felt something melt inside me that hurt in an exquisite way. All my longings, all my dreams and sweet anguish, all the secrets that slept within me, came awake, everything was transformed and enchanted, everything made sense. She taught me what a woman is and what secrets she has. In half an hour she aged me by many years. I know many things now. I also suddenly knew that I could no longer remain in this house, not for another day. I'm going as soon as night falls."

Narcissus listened and nodded.

"It happened suddenly," he said, "but it is more or less what I expected. I shall think of you often. I'll miss you, *amicus.* Is there anything I can do for you?"

"Yes, if you can, please say a word to our Abbot, so that he does not condemn me completely. He is the only person in this house, besides you, whose thoughts about me are not indifferent to me. His and yours."

"I know. Is there anything else?"

"Yes, one thing, please. Later, when you think of me, will you pray for me from time to time? And—thank you."

"For what, Goldmund?"

"For your friendship, your patience, for everything. Also for listening to me today, when it was hard for you. And also for not trying to hold me back."

"How could I want to hold you back? You know how I feel about it.—But where will you go, Goldmund? Have you a goal? Are you going to that woman?"

"Yes, I'm going with her. I have no goal. She is a stranger— homeless, it seems; perhaps a gypsy."

"Well, all right. But do you know, my dear Goldmund, that your road with her will be extremely short? I don't think you should count on her too much. Perhaps she has relatives, a husband perhaps; who knows what kind of reception awaits you there."

Goldmund leaned against his friend.

"I know," he said, "although I had not thought of it yet. As I told you, I have no goal. This woman who was so very sweet to me is not my goal. I'm going to her, but I'm not going because of her. I'm going because I must, because I have heard the call."

He sighed and was silent. They sat shoulder to shoulder, sad and yet happy in the feeling of their indestructible friendship. Then Goldmund continued: "Do not think that I'm completely blind and naïve. No. I'm happy to go, because I feel that it has to be, and because something so marvelous happened to me today. But I'm not imagining that I'll meet with nothing but joy and mirth. I think the road will be hard. But it will also be beautiful, I hope. It is extremely beautiful to belong to a woman, to give yourself. Don't laugh if I sound foolish. But to love a woman, you see, to abandon yourself to her, to absorb her completely and feel absorbed by her, that is not what you call 'being in love,' which you mock a little. For me it is the road to life, the way toward the meaning of life. Oh, Narcissus, I must leave you! I love you, Narcissus, and thank you for sacrificing a moment of sleep to me today. I find it hard to leave you. You won't forget me?"

"Don't make us both sad! I'll never forget you. You will come back, I ask it of you, I expect it. If you are in need some day, come to me, or call to me. Farewell, Goldmund, go with God!"

He had risen. Goldmund embraced him. Knowing his friend's aversion of caresses, he did not kiss him; he only stroked his hands.

Night was falling. Narcissus closed the cell behind him and walked over to the church, his sandals slapping the flagstones. Goldmund followed the bony figure with loving eyes, until it vanished like a shadow at the end of the corridor, swallowed by the darkness of the church door, claimed by exercises, duties, and virtues. How extraordinary, how infinitely puzzling and confusing everything was! This, too—how strange and frightening: to have come to his friend with his heart overflowing, drunk with blossoming love, at the very moment his friend was in meditation, devoured by fasting and vigils, crucifying his youth, his heart, his senses—all offered up in sacrifice; at the very moment his friend was subjecting himself to the most rigorous obedience, pledging to serve only the mind, to become nothing but a minister *verbi divini!* There he had lain, tired unto death, extenuated, with his pale face and bony hands, corpselike, and yet he had listened to his friend, lucid and sympathetic, had lent his ear to this love-drunken man with the smell of a woman still on him, had sacrificed his few moments of rest between penances. It was strange and divinely beautiful that there was also this kind of love, this selfless, completely spiritualized kind. How different it was from today's love in the sunny field, the reckless, intoxicated play of the senses. And yet both were love. Oh, and now Narcissus had gone from him, after showing him once again, clearly, at the last moment, how utterly different and dissimilar they were from one another.

BALTHAZAR B

J. P. Donleavy

For those readers who may have read J. P. Donleavy's *The Ginger Man*, the irreverence and gentle sensuality of the precocious Balthazar B should be immediately recognizable. Balthazar is as much a sexual outlaw as Sebastian Dangerfield—has all his sensual proclivities—only at a younger, more delicate age. The following chapter is about Balthazar's falling in love with his beautiful governess, Miss Hortense, and their precarious sexual experiences together; the rest of the novel entails his loss of her, and learning to live out his adolescent years in loneliness, to be finally swept away to the high and low life of Dublin. The tension from this passage arises when Miss Hortense realizes that the tenderness she has felt for Balthazar has turned suddenly to intimate longings, which she rejects for fear of community censure. Her sense of duty and convential morality clashes with her actual feelings of love and sexual desire.

Balthazar's mother moved from the big house off Avenue Foch to a sprawling apartment overlooking the gardens of the Palais Royal. Miss Hortense with her tall flowing gay willing way came each Christmas, Easter and summer holiday. Taking Balthazar back and forth to Paris by taxi ship and train. While his mother went hither and thither to Baden Baden, Liechtenstein and Biarritz, to one for a cure, to the next for taxes and to the last to swim.

And this summer now hot and dry. A white dust rising to whiten leaves in the Tuilleries. Balthazar's mother asleep till late afternoons. At nights to dinners and balls and weekends away from Gare St.

Lazare to the country. A Czechoslovakian woman came to cook and a Russian to clean. They had their lunch in the big kitchen with the high walls hung with pots and pans.

Mornings Miss Hortense would sit doing the English paper cross-word puzzle and play dominoes between the plates with Balthazar. And in the warm cool at night, hand in hand they sat on the balcony above the garden. The shadowy stone urns with upturned seventeen spears, and four fish hook prongs to keep out intruders. And one year ago Miss Hortense said I think it's time you called me Bella.

Each day to laugh down the steps and out across the gardens. To sit a while where the solemn little children played under the thick chestnut trees. Or watch the marionettes in the Tuilleries. And the favourite hours to quietly read away an afternoon on the sentinel pale green chairs. Miss Hortense to be seated with her pillow, her elegant long legs crossed in the hot sunshine. By a bed of pink roses while the sparrows pecked and scratched and bathed.

The mornings at dawn Balthazar heard the keeper open the gates. And sometimes alone and dressed, Bella asleep, to go down and skip along the brown and black tiles of the arcade and pirouette on each four leaved shamrock. Bella said it was good for Irish luck. Then pause to read the garden rules which said no writing on the walls, no sound instruments and no games which can bring trouble to the tranquillity of the pedestrian.

And on this soft summer Saturday night. As Balthazar and Bella walked hand in hand past the black fence bars topped with golden spears. By the stamp shop and where the old strange watches stood in the window with coloured pictures on their faces. And near to me was Bella. The close up of her grey eyes was green. And her breath as sweet as roses. When she told her secrets in wide eyed words. And whispered dreams. And laughed when she lost at chess.

"Balthazar."

"Yes my Bella."

"You know something."

"What."

"I am going away."

"Where. What do you mean."

"I am going away from you."

"Why."

"It is too complicated to explain."

"Has my mother told you to."

"No not yet."

"Then why. Don't you enjoy coming to Paris anymore."

"Yes."

"Then why."

"Because this is all very foolish."

"What is foolish."

"You are growing up. You're getting tall. A full inch above my shoulder last year. And now, see. You come right to the top of my ear. When first we met you were only up to here. Soon you will be thirteen. You don't need me anymore."

"That's rather an unfortunate thing for you to say Bella. I don't understand why you've chosen to discuss this at all."

"Because it is ruining my life coming here three times a year."

Passing the windows of the red carpeted theatre. And into the peristyle courtyard. Crossing between the stone pillars, they stood near the restaurant with the golden walls and carved and painted ceilings and the mirror you could look up at from the courtyard and see down from the restaurant ceiling on to tables where customers where leisurely lavishly eating. To see now this moment a gentleman's hand with gold rings, his fingers opening and closing upon a glass stem which he raised to swirl a wine beneath his nose. On the restaurant window it said Sherry, Goblers and Lemon Squash. Miss Hortense took a deep breath and raised her eyebrows and bent forward as she walked.

"Bella, I did not know I was ruining your life."

"It was unfair of me to say."

"You told me it was nice these holidays like this. And you could give all the gentlemen about Kensington a merry dance. And you had your nice little change of situations."

"O God what a mess. Don't you see I love you. And you are far too old to be loved like that."

A strange shiver comes upon the back of the head and goes down the spine and lingers between the legs. The sound of our slow feet passing over the waves worn in the tiles. The lace shop. Rooms alight behind curved shiny windows above under the roof of the arcade. And through all the black muddy months there loomed her middle parted brown long hair. And how she bent each thumb backwards on her wrist and could spin her skirt high up over her knees and always forgot to castle her king.

To come now through to the empty street and back to the little bell and great dark green enamel door. Yesterday so bright and sunny. Shopping at Corcellet, where Miss Hortense smiled to rub her shoe on the brass letters of the entrance floor under the iron bunch of grapes. And she laughed and laughed as she sewed on her bedroom chaise longue. Of the story about Uncle Edouard. When a month ago he dined at a terrace on the Champs Elysèes. When a gust of wind exploded upon the cafe, tore off the awning, and carried away the umbrellas over the tables. Le Baron the balloonist extraordinaire remained calm, giving instructions to the waiters to stand back from the cyclone. And as he held to his own table umbrella it rose with a bang. Uncle Edouard clinging tightly as it pulled him off his feet and down the boulevard. Shouting, I am in control, I am in control.

Now climbing up these dark stairs. And the big brown doors. The incense smelling vestibule.

"Bella I am fond of you too."

"Don't you see that is the trouble."

Feeling a tender trembling and shaking. Her summer tanned back and the cool brown across her shoulders. The white skin under the straps of her light blue summer frock. My breath seems pushing up against the back of my eyes. And the first time off the train at Paris when I gave the address and opened the door for her into the taxi she smiled and took my hand and said your manners make you such a little gentleman and if only you were bigger I would have you for my man.

Miss Hortense swept into the salon and went quickly from table to table to turn on all the blazing lights.

"Why have you done that, Bella."

"I don't know. I think it's as well. Your mother is away. There's no one here the whole weekend. I've turned on the lights that's all."

"You're awfully upset."

"The fact of the matter is I'm twenty-four and should be married."

"But every man will have you."

"That does not mean I want one of them. There's little to choose between a cunning solicitor and a rich dunce, except my choice would be neither of them."

"If you marry the cunning solicitor he's sure to be very rich one day."

"And his heart and soul completely poor."

"But Bella you said yourself that only money matters, and for a woman it's better even to have her own."

"Yes. I said that and it's true. I'll be cured next week when I buy a new hat."

"Shall we play chess."

"I don't feel like it tonight."

"It is not too late to go to the theatre."

"No."

"Do you want me to go away and leave you alone."

"For heaven's sake no."

"I am awfully sorry that I have made you so unhappy."

Miss Hortense against the edge of the high grey marble table where she put back her arms and pressed the heels of her hands. And her fingers whitening as they tightened around the cold hard stone.

"O God it's crazy. It's crazy. In fact it's far too funny. Here I am, good Lord, in love with a twelve year old boy."

Miss Hortense turned from where she leaned and slowly rolled herself over the arm rest and fell deep into the green brocaded sofa of eiderdown. This still night the end of June. Faint horns honking along Rue St. Honoré and the memory of an afternoon three years ago when I went down into the Métro of the Palais Royal, past the blue smocked woman at a desk with her plateful of centimes and stood to wee wee elbow high to a nearby man. Upon whose gleaming patent leather shoe I peed. And he reared backwards stamping his foot, his own pee crazily sprinkling his trousers and tiled floor. I quickly buttoned up and ran. Out past the phalanx of dark brown cubicles and up into the street into Miss Hortense's arms. And when she asked what did you do I said I peed on a man and there he is now with his black briefcase shaking his umbrella. And Miss Hortense turned and smiled and made him a fluttering curtsy.

"Bella why do you say this when I have told you that I love you too."

"Balthazar it's not your fault. I can't expect you to understand. What could you ever know about women."

"I want to learn. I have read some most unseemly books."

"God you're so sweet. And I mustn't say I could kiss you."

The tinkling eight thirty chime of the gold mantel clock. Miss Hortense's brown long legs shooting akimbo on the gleaming parquet. Her big toes upturned from her sandals. A great heaving sigh whispering out her lips. And back now these years. For all the hushed little nights when Beefy said across bedsides. Of what girls were for, and what you could do to them. More than botty bashing. More than pulling or playing put it in the ring. That his granny's maid said she had a hole like a penny slot and one day he would have hair there too. And out of his horn a white hot syrup could come. And Beefy would whisper as each urgent piece of news arrived about girls. That they had their own little knob upon which you could play. That nipples could get big and hard but he was not positively sure of this yet. And girls were of two types. One to whom you did the vile and odious thing and whom you would not love. She would be a servant, a waitress or a maid or be in a back alley of the town. But girls you loved were cousins at the race meetings or partners at dancing school or at aunts' and uncles' houses in their pretty dresses. You married them and always and always they had their own bed and dressing room and you would not go in there unless it was desperately necessary. Beefy never said what he knew about nannies for each one he had departed after a few days.

"I don't like you staring at me like that Balthazar. Do you think you should go and find something to do."
"Why."
"Because I think it would be proper."
"Why."
"Don't ask me why."
"Then I will not go and find something to do."
"Don't."
"I won't."
"I don't care if you don't."
"And I don't care that you don't care that I don't."
"Then don't."
"I'm not."
"Then I am going to go and sew."
Miss Hortense standing. Her sandals making a flapping noise on the floor. Passing by Balthazar as he stood near the door. His blue jacket closed and his flannel trousers long and white. Miss Hortense went by the fruit basket on the dining table and snatched out a pear. The strong muscles in the backs of her legs. And the thin tapering ankle and tendon down into her heels. Her bedroom door closing. I tremble and my heart thumps. Tight and hot in my head above the eyes. When I made a squeaking noise on a leaf between my palms, Bella laughed and said I can do that. I said beware my spit, I'll find a new leaf. O no I like your spit. On a bench near the Trocadero after I showed Bella my father's tomb. And I said I would not want a germ to harm you. She laughed and suddenly threw her arms about my shoulders and squeezed me tight and said I could eat you all up.

Balthazar turned off the lights of the salon, save one by the window and bookcase where he knelt and pulled volumes from the shelves. A faded green spine which faintly read The Neighbourhood of Dublin. His father's large scrawled signature inside the cover. Tales Uncle Edouard told. Of the noble and splendid blood of the Celt flowing through our veins. After the battle of the Boyne our ancestor fled in the Flight of the Wild Geese from Ireland to France. They were brave men of unquenchable principle. And he was one brilliant fellow, a Royal Astronomer of Ireland. He knew much of ether and even electricity. And from this great house he watched by telescope out into the solar system. It was only because of the clouds that he did not get much chance to see the stars. Remember always you are of Irish kings as well as of France, and all Irishmen are kings but not all kings are Irishmen.

With four tomes under arm and Paris bells tolling eleven o'clock Balthazar passed along the dark hallway to his room. The dry creaking of the boards beneath the feet. Miss Hortense's door with a bright dot of keyhole. To pause to knock. And no. She may never like me anymore. And tomorrow we were going to go to Sevres. To see the porcelain in the museum. All our splendid days we wandered here and there. Along the banks and book stalls of the Seine. In and out the alley darkened streets, Huchette, Suger, St. André des Arts, passing under grey peeling walls, buildings like full old bellies, buttons bursting and washerwomen's eyes staring sullenly down. Often they stopped at St. Germain des Près for citron pressé and all the young gentlemen giggled at Miss Hortense's horsey elegant beauty, twitching their shoulders as they went by and laughing in their little groups to catch Bella's cool grey green eye. She would rise up tall between the cafe tables. Her white beaded summer bag tucked neatly beneath a breast. And with the other cool hand to throw her hair back upon her shoulder and putting aloft her head, the tiniest smile across her lips, she stepped out on the boulevard, her hips gently shifting to and fro. A grin on her face as a cry went up from the cafe table, long live mademoiselle so magnificently callipyge.

Balthazar bent an eye to the keyhole. A yellow light and golden drapes at the end of the room. To be shut out from all her warmth and love. Across the polished floor and persian carpet hangs her light blue dressing gown from a chair. And a night three summers ago I awoke to rumbling thunder to stumble afeared out into the corridor. To say outside this door. Nannie, o dear I am most frightened. But not loud enough for her to hear. Too shy to knock and too shy to show my fear. And suddenly her door opened and lightning whitened her window and flashed behind her. Her body so long and slender and outlined against the light through her sleeping gown. She held me there and then said come, get into bed with me, put your head on my pillow and I will tell you why there is no need to be afraid. Because they are playing skittles in the sky and when they want to throw a ball, it's only that God puts on the lightning so that they can see. And then there's the big boom and the rain comes down to wash away all the mess. And in sleep I snuggled and clutched to her and dreamt I flew on a white horse up steps right into the sky and jumped over clouds and put my fingers into soft crushed berries and cream. And at morn to wake and see her brown long hair streaming across the pillow. As the triangle of sunlight rose up the green wall. And the clutch of deep dark small freckles on her back and I put a finger there to rub one away and she rolled over and smiled, her eyes so gaily alight and sparkling and she slowly withdrew one of her long long arms from under the covers and reached out and pushed me on the nose and said hey you, you must get out of here now.

"Balthazar. Is that you out there."

"Yes."

"What are you doing there."

"Looking through your keyhole."

"What can you see."

"Nothing."

"Come in then."

Balthazar turning down the handle on the door. Opening it into the soft light and blinking his eyes. Miss Hortense in her bed. The blue linen counterpane drawn to the bottom and up into the soft peach blanket stuck her knees and toes. The pillows piled high, a book clipped open by her elbow and shiny needle in her hand.

"Goodness Balthazar what are you doing with that awful pile of books."

"Reading."

"Sit down. Reading what."

"This one is about tunnels and railways. And this, it's a book about Dublin. Have you ever been there."

"No. My father has, he was born in Belfast."

"What is that."

"That's a city in the north of Ireland. Where they march and beat great drums and say they are up to their knees in catholic blood and up to their necks in slaughter."

"That's not awfully nice."

"No. It's not."

"Did he ever talk of Dublin."

"Yes he liked it there. And the pints of stout and chunks of cheese that he had in the mornings in a pub. He read Divinity at Trinity College. He said it was the happiest time of his life. And he always said, that there in Dublin, the sun shone in on our lives."

"Bella, you're not cross at me are you."

"No. Of course not, why should I be."

"I don't know. I feel awfully badly when I think you're cross with me. And now I feel much worse that perhaps you might be going to go away."

"You're such a silly boy."

"You know I'm not silly."

"Yes I know you're not silly. I'm silly I suppose. And really you're old enough to know. That I am going to have to go. Aren't you. But it's not that I want to. It is nice to be with you. And we do like so many things together. And so you know don't you that it's not that I want to. And that it has been the happiest time of my whole life. That I've ever had. Don't hang your face down like that."

"I'm not."

"You are. Come sit over here on the bed."

Balthazar put his tomes on the floor. And crossed to Miss Hortense's bed. Where the light shone down on the white folded sheet and her slender arms sat in cushioned little white cloth valleys. She lifted up an embroidery frame. Its streaming blue and green and yellow threads.

"Do you think this is nice."

"It looks such a bore to do."

"After all my work that's what you say. Anyway this is what I want to tell you. That this is not good for either of us. Soon you will want to be with girls your own age. And God knows I ought to be putting a rope around some gentleman and tying his ankle to my stove. You see Balthazar when I'm not with you. Well I don't know what I'm going to say. Many men have asked me to marry. It may be me or my little money. They all seem to get to know rather too quickly for my liking that I have a small income. But each time something always goes wrong and either I hate them or they hate me."

"I want to marry you."

"Balthazar."

"You mustn't laugh. You are only twelve years older."

"But your whole life, what you are going to do, where you are going to go."

"I think I am going to go to Dublin."

"Ah, that is something nice."

Miss Hortense's arm fell slowly and her hand touched Balthazar's blue serge sleeve. As she always did when she was pleased, reach out and touch me gently. With a closed mouth smile.

"And you know Bella how awfully rich I am. And when I am of age I can go where I want and you can come too."

"Yes."

"To go on big ships. To Africa and America. Will you wait for me to grow up. Will you please, Bella."

"That is the most wonderful proposal I have ever had."

"Will you then. Will you please. When I finish school before I go to college we could be married."

"You're so serious aren't you. And I will then be over thirty."

"I would not care."

"Yes you would. Your eye would be seeking out the young ladies."

"I would never want anyone else."

"Heavens, heavens. And what am I to do then from now till you become of age."

"Three times a year you would be here with me in Paris. We could go to Bucharest and from there to St. Petersburgh. We could go to Dublin. And have cheese like your father did and the sun would shine in on us."

"You rascal. You are. You have more daring than on a trapeze. God how girls are going to waste their tears on you."

Balthazar slowly stood up from the bed. Miss Hortense laid her embroidery away at her side. Her dressing table with her ivory brush and mirror and comb. The crimson lining of her open pigskin writing case with envelopes blue and pink. A lone bottle of scent and toilet water. Where his mother's bath was shelved high with colognes and sweet essences of faint colours and perfumes in all their tall fat crystal bottles. To bend now to pick up these tomes.

"O please don't go away like that."

"I will. Because at least I have told you of what is in my heart."

"Don't go away like this Balthazar."

"I am. Why should I not."

"No. Don't. Come back here."

Balthazar turned and laid the books on the chair. He walked back to the bed. And as his knees touched the edge, Bella's hand reached out and switched off the table light. And her hand felt and took his hand and she pulled him gently down. Her fingers up through the short hairs on the back of my head, and cool they touch in behind my ear. Tumbling down into her arms she whispers out o God come to me. Her kisses over my mouth. On the cheeks and eyes. Her tongue along the side of my neck and deep into my ringing ear. All the bells of Paris. And stormy choirs sing when it is not yet mass or Sunday but her silky long slender arms, smooth wrists, and soft slim hands. She breathed her breath catching in her lungs. And I can hardly breathe at all. Her hard teeth as she bites into my mouth. Her hand at my throat to undo my tie. Pulling herself up out of the sheets. Hair strings of shadow hanging round her head. I watched in the gardens once her fingernails as she sat and scratched her thigh and they made big long white marks on her sunny skin. Distant fingers unbuttoning my shirt one by one. And close by lips kissing me upon the breasts. Bella tell me what to do. Nothing nothing. Just take off your clothes. And so strange to wonder. Of all these years of dreams. To reach one day in the laundry room to secretly touch her drying underthings more close to her than I ever hoped to be. And now lay side by side all along her body and feel it pressed to mine, like two bodies all of your own. One here and one you reach around. Bella is what we're doing love. Yes yes. Hurry tell me how. You'll see you'll see. And I see. Bella on top of my mind chewing a cashew nut. Bella what do I do. Nothing nothing now. Like that flush of jealous courage two days ago. Waiting for a seat on the back of the bus to Place du Pont Neuf. When the conductor pinched her on the bottom and Miss Hortense widened her eyes, squared her shoulders, raised her brows and parasol and said in English keep your hands to yourself you miserable little man and the conductor laughed and as they returned once more to alight, he reached to pinch again and her parasol came slashing down across his wrist. It was an unfriendly time. To reach and gouge out his grinning eyes. Or wait one day till I was big enough to slap his cheek and shake his molars. For now I touch. All of this most precious prize. Here from the top of her head to the tip of her big toes. Can I touch and put my hand running over you you're so smooth. Yes you can you can and come on top of me. Bella Bella it's coming out of me. It won't stop. All over you. O darling you mustn't mind, sweetest and dearest, let it come out over me, you must not mind. Bella tell me what did I do. It's all right now. It should have been inside you. Yes but it's all right, you mustn't mind. I know it means you'll never marry me. And I hope I haven't been vile. Balthazar it's really all right, really it is. I feel all ashamed and all awful inside. You must tell me, Balthazar, tell me if you do. All around in me it's going very strange indeed, you're not a servant or a town girl in the street but if I've done this I can't be in love. O God what are you talking about, love is for everybody wherever it may be no matter what you are. You're so young you see, full of all those tall tales of all those little boys. It's not vile, it's not that at all, but what I'm doing to you is so wrong. Why do you say it's wrong.

Because it's my duty to take care of you. But isn't this the best care there could be then. Balthazar you're asking such damn questions and knowing answers too damn fast, but nothing can be answered here, just lie now with your silly sad little face, and maybe a devil too, you know don't you that we should never do this again. If anyone found us I would be in an awful mess.

"But there's no one here but us. And if we never do it again you'll never teach me."

"You know enough already you little rabbit."

"What have you done with men Bella."

"And what have you done with girls Balthazar."

"Please Bella, what have you done."

"You mustn't ask me questions like that."

"I must know."

"Why must you know."

"Because if you did I may never speak to you again."

"O dear. Turn around your head. Come on. Turn around. You're quite spoiled you know. Look at me. Are you jealous. A little aren't you."

"I'm not discussing it. Do you do this. Without your clothes and be in bed with other men."

"And I'm not discussing it."

"If you've been like this with other men I will kill myself. With arsenic."

"O Lord."

"I will."

"Snuggle up close and comfy to me. Don't let me hear you say that again. Or I will be off to Bristol or something like that and go on a ship. To the south seas."

"Bella I love you so much. So awfully awfully much."

"There you mustn't cry. You really mustn't."

"And I never want you to go away for ever and ever."

"I'm here now. You crazy little rabbit. I'm here."

"If you don't stay with me I don't want to grow up at all."

"But you little rabbit you can't stop growing up. You'll know all sorts of girls. Through a whole bunch of years. Innocent and smiling ones who would make you think butter would not melt in their mouths."

"I don't care, if there isn't you I don't want anybody. No one could ever take your place."

"O God."

"Are you cross."

"No no I'm not cross. Just crosseyed. How are you to understand. I just feel I'm somehow sitting on my backside. In the middle of some very grand ball. And I can't get up off the floor. For months and months. I've wanted to just seize and hug you and hold you to me. And I knew, I knew this would happen. That we never should have been left alone. That all it needed was bumping into you at night in the hall or just the nosey moments in the evening when you get long faced when I tell you not to read my letters. And each time you sulked I had to do everything I could to stop myself hugging and kissing you. Don't you see how it's been for me. O but don't you get cross now."

"I'm not cross."

"You are."

"I'm not."

"O Balthazar. Don't you see. To you the world is just as you find it. Just as each day it's time to get up, to dress, to eat, to sleep. The trip to school. And to Paris. And here we kind of live in a little estate all of our own. Larking about in each other's hair. But the world is not like that. Like we are now. And if we were ever found. Really like we are now. God if we ever were. Did I lock the door."

"Yes. And you hung up the keys under the telephone."

"O God. I don't even know that I may be doing something criminal. I don't know but I might be."

"I am a criminal then too and we are still together."

"Yes. Till they cart us off to prison. And sling us into cells."

"Uncle Edouard would see that we were freed."

"Uncle Edouard, I wonder. Don't depend upon him."

"Why do you say that."

"I just do. He's nice. But don't depend upon anybody Balthazar."

"Did he attempt to entice you."

"O nothing. Three years ago."

"What did he do."

"Jealous jealous."

"I'm not. What did he try."

"Nothing. He invited me to the Bois. And so you came too. That's all. And once to Biarritz. And I said I went nowhere without my boyfriend. And he laughed and was quite nice. And probably he did want to take me to bed. You see how difficult you have made me for other men. And then one day you'll see a creature without whom you think you cannot live. And she'll throw her arms up and spin about and raise her skirt on her legs. And you'll like what you see. And she'll look beautiful and flutter her eyes. Put rouge on her cheeks. And tell you nice little lies. And squeal when you feel her breast. And as she shrinks away she'll say come hither come thither and do not dither dear blond beautiful Balthazar. O God she'll get her bloody hands into your hair. And you'll marry her. And she will be up to her elbows rummaging in your fortune when she isn't skipping down the Faubourg St. Honoré. For soap and saddles and suits and rose bouquets."

"I would never a marry a girl like that. And who would put rouge on her cheeks."

"I hope when all the years have gone by. And I'm retired in my little country cottage somewhere in Devon. With all, I hope, my many emoluments. That you'll come and see me. And put your hat on a hook and a cane against the wall. You may even be tall and straight and grey. And bow as I sit in black and lace near my fire. With probably the same old embroidery frame. And you'll take up and kiss my hand. O God let me kiss you, kiss you. While you're still here here here."

The night hushed and still. Faint breeze out on the garden tree leaves. Paris cools in darkness. The slow slow sounds that transport over the city. A shout. And listen, a strange answer. Some night time philosopher advising himself. To avoid hunger perhaps and a tread-mill day. Like the shadowy men standing inside the cathedral doors in all their silent poverty. Where do they go at night. And Bella said there they are on the benches and in winter they will lie on the Métro grating. To curl up in wait for another day. And the day Bella said let's, when I said why don't we go on a train. As we stood outside the building of the Légion d'Honneur as the sun shone down the Rue de Bellechasse. She made big eyes on the street and made me laugh. And said maybe we should take a picnic and never come back again. We two. Go in search of the holy grail. And we go. Don't we go. Into the great Gare d'Orsay. And I looked up at her flowing hair as all the eyes watched her trotting by. Searching wide eyed between the wondering citizens. Under the darkened glass roof and monstrous tiled walls. First stop St. Michel and through Gare d'Austerlitz. And when we got off the train at a town, any town. Bretigny. There were kids with a flag marching through the street. Blowing bugles and workmen putting up coloured lights for a fete. When it started to rain. Houses shuttered up. And curtains elsewhere twitching. As we walked hand in hand down the street. And Bella said no holy grail I'm sure will be found, we are Balthazar in a most uninviting town. Would we ever live here. Yes with you. With you I would too. And back on the train in a carriage with three. Of gentlemen. Who stood and turned and sat and sniffed as Bella crossed her legs. And they said ah we are well fixed, I have just come out of the hospital and I am very well placed, to live just far enough outside Paris where it is country and close enough too. Each of them their eyes dropping on Bella's knees and looking when they could at her face. And when they left the carriage and in the corridor, one said my God if I were a young man what I wouldn't give to do what I could do to that one, and I Monsieur would not need to be young to do what I would do to that one. And we came back through the station and the urine smell. A man passed and said to Bella ah up there the unmarried employees live. And she said why tell me. Ah Mademoiselle because to have such beauty passing so close by I feel somehow that it is justice you should know. And we went to a restaurant up through the streets. Where she sat and I thought and thought of the men on the train what did they mean what they would do to that one. What would they do. And Bella let me have a full glass of wine. What would they do to you those men. O it's just talk, men never grow tired of flattering themselves. We raced and ran all the way back up the stairs and into her room. And Bella is this what they do. When I put my hand here and feel your breast the way it swells up from the rest of you. And I don't know yet what you've got down there in your secret hair. Yes dearest it's what they would do. They would kiss me only I'm kissing you. They would grab me tight only I'm grabbing you. And they would do what I'm telling you. Come Balthazar on top of me. On top. Like that. And never would I want you to be them. You're sweet and sweet. And my own loveliest little man of mine. Get in between my legs. There. God it's so hard. I'll guide you in. Don't worry don't worry. O God there you are, there you are. O God Balthazar. You have it up in me. And all the thoughts you never knew you'd know. Of some strange miracle happening to it there. In that part of her. Was it her. Like her face and teeth and hair. These speaking lips so close. Just step out of my brain and into hers. And hello where's the holy grail. Like rolling down in grass in all the wet sweet smell of hay and stop and stare up into a sky of chestnut blossoms. White white planets everywhere. Bella. Have I done it right. Yes yes. O Bella o Bella please it's coming out of me, it's coming out of me, hold me please. Yes yes my dearest let it come. Bella don't let me die. O please. And bleed away all my blood. O Balthazar I won't let you die or bleed away all your blood and God I'm dying too. In all the nooks and crannies and shadows of the sheets. Torn back from bodies one wild one pale. Her hand bumping and counting on my spine. And put my fingers on the hard bone behind her tiny ear. Your face Bella has your eyes closed. And you smile all around your mouth. Everything now so still. Save another long cry from the street philosopher. In search of the holy grail. And you went back up on your shoulders and groaned and groaned. Bella it wasn't unhappy was it. No no not unhappy, you silly boy. I worried you were in pain, you went all so stiff and shook. Sweet that's the way it is when it happens, with happiness, happiness. Why then do you have tears in your eyes. I don't know why. Tell me why. Bella. You must. Tell me why you're crying and you are. And her elbows pointed out into the dark as she held up hands. Tips of fingers across her brows, palms flat on her cheeks showing just her lips and nose. I know I'm crying. And try to lift her fingers. O please what's the matter Bella, please tell me what's the matter. O Bella what has happened to you, what have I done. I love you so, I do I love you so dearly so and now I've done something, please speak and don't cry. Please speak. I can't I can't. The mattress trembling. Her stuttering sobs. Bella you're frightening me, please what's the matter. I won't be frightened if you tell me. O Balthazar I wish I were dead. I wish so desperately I were dead. O Bella you must not wish you were dead. You must be alive with me. Let me see under your hand. Bella. I always know what's in your eyes. Please let me see under your hand. No. Please and then I can make you better again and dry up your tears. Come you snuggle in Bella now, I'll take care of you and hold your head and make you nice again. Maybe you have a little stomach ache. Little men with hammers who jump around in your belly tinkering and banging on your pipes that's what you used to say to me when I had a tummy pain. You see Bella I make a cozy corral of arms for you to be in with me. Don't you feel safe. No harm will ever get you now. Balthazar I desperately wish it were so. I like you holding me and I know that everything you say is real and is true and what you believe, you must know that I do. But it just cannot be.

"Bella I love you and have told you everything in my heart."

"I know you have, I know you have."

"I will love you through all of my life."

"You can't Balthazar, you can't."

"I can I can."

"I've got to give my notice to your mother. I'm twenty four, twenty four."

"You'll not give it."

"I have to. We're sure to get caught at this."

"We won't we will go to hotels."

"O Christ."

"And I will go to my lawyers for the money. I like doing this to you."

"O Lord. But for God's sake Balthazar you must never never breathe a word of this. Never never no matter what happens."

"Why not if we're in love."

"Now listen to me, people just won't understand. You would never be that foolish would you."

"Yes."

"O God please now Balthazar I'm very serious. This is no joke. You would not want to see me ruined and that's what would happen if ever a word of this were breathed. To anyone."

"Promise then you'll stay."

"I can't."

"Yes you can."

"But what can we do together now. I mean you see it's all different now."

"You can teach me more about antiques."

"You know more than I do."

"Well then I'll teach you. Bella I won't tell anyone. But you must not go. I want everything to stay just like today."

"I know sweet but dearest, things change. Everything will be different in just a very few years. And you'll not care at all that I'm gone. Now hush. Listen. Balthazar, nothing stays the same. I won't and you won't. Even a day can come when I really will be dead. Yes. I will."

"If that day ever comes, all I will do as long as I live is remember you. I would build you a big monument too. In the Passy cemetery. I would have it have a big high roof. And it would be the grandest there was. With tall bronze doors. And inside I would have pictures of you and all your favourite flowers every day. I would come and sweep it out myself and polish the way all those old ladies do."

"Hey, you little devil. I'm not dead yet."

"Only if you were."

"I should hope so. Now maybe it's a good idea if you get out of here."

"It's only just rung half past twelve. I heard it."

"Gather up all your things now. Come on."

"No."

"Come on Balthazar."

"No."

"Now Balthazar you must. You can't stay here all night. There. Here's your tie. Heavens everything's everywhere. Out."

"No."

"Out."

"No."

"Out please."

"No."

"O come on Balthazar, don't be like that. Don't make me upset please. What if someone came."

"I should then depart in what is commonly called a jiffy."

"You mischief."

"Bella Bella I'm a mischief, that's what I am. A mischief."

"Push you out then."

"Push, push."

"Stop stop get your hands away. Stop it Balthazar. O stop. O you've got to stop. O you really really must stop. You must. But o not yet. O God Balthazar. Not yet not yet."

Miss Hortense with her hard little knuckled fists dug into Balthazar's sides. Opened out her hands. And reached his head to pull it smothering down upon her breasts. Cushion his silky blond face back and forth in all the milky softness. Her arms so tight around. And I press my sallow body to hers. To snake my own arms under and put them round her back. And I hold her now. More than she holds me. Why did God give her so much beauty and make her born before me. To give her years to flash teeth with love and laughter. And make me race and chase after her and feel before she should go, her warm soft tongue in my mouth and whisper of rabbit rabbit in my ear. I want to catch up. Ask you wait for me. The most nicest people are always taken away. And Bella I feel I have climbed up on a dark and strange tree. Flowering dewy wet and new. Beefy said there are more things in the world than jelly beans and lemon delights. Like your bottom Bella turns up as you roll over on top of me. Down there on your big spacious mounds I can put my fingers pressing softly. Where the conductor tried to pinch. On that white bright sunny day under all the trees' full greenery. And the hot silence against the stone walls along the Seine. Where we crossed the Pont Neuf and went down the dark stone steps to the Vert Galant and walked along the cobbles and sandy path. The barges throbbing by on the green grey river like your eyes. And we came to the point of this little island

land. Dark figures grouped together by the park wall. I said look Bella. A man and woman clutching a greasy gathering of belongings, lay next each other in rags. The sun burned down on their dirt and dust encrusted faces dried and cracking. Toothless heads, lips drawn in over gums, strange purple swollen lips and mucous covered eyes. And before I could ask why. Were they so poor and why were they there. Bella said come along Balthazar we mustn't stay here. And I stood. Bella waiting. Three ragged men each with a bottle clutched in their blackened fists, came to stand over the sleeping couple. They began to kick them in the sides and head and bottom of their feet. And they awoke from sleep shielding their heads with raised tattered arms. And the kicks rained upon them and shouts, get out of our place. The man slowly struggled under the blows to his knees, his eyes blinking up into the sunshine. A foot smashed against his face and he fell forward as blood poured from both his eyes. The woman clawed screaming at the striking feet. The dark legs closed in on her. They struck sending dust from her ragged covered bosoms and she crumbled groaning to the ground. And as I stood there watching, the man and woman clutching at the sandy stony ground slowly began to crawl away. More blows raining on their backs and heads as they howled. Bella said you must not watch and pulled me by the arm. A day that grew grey and dark over Paris. And cast shadows through the museums, on the boats, and along the boulevards. In the passing Paris eyes were cunning monsters brooding. To lift aside some shallow gaiety and see all the writhing sewer fears. To wish to be back in England. Upon a green unworried day. The crack of a cricket bat, the choir voices of evensong. Prayerful hands and glowing altars. Lay my head as it is now between Bella's soft neck and shoulder. Gone is my fever. I felt all these long days. And listen. Another shout out on the streets. He looks for his mother. On a golden most narrow day. To fit lips upon her breast. To lie quietly now on top of one another. She's mine. No one will ever take her from me.

The summer light comes up all over the sky. Bella it's morning. Yes dearest the sun came racing across the Ukraine over the Danube and valleys of the Rhone and Rhine. And it's coming in your window now. Yes. Up south over the Seine. And Bella northwards to Metz and Reims. And now across your naked golden legs. Do you hear the birds. I stayed with you the whole night. I'm glad you did. Hear the garden keeper singing. Yes I do. Bella promise me you'll never forget this night. Of course I won't, go away now and brush your teeth. And I'll bring you breakfast. Bella I want to shout and sing and go dancing down the street. Yes I know, now really you must must go. But it's nice, you were a boy when you came in last night. And I am happy for you.

> For
> Now
> Out walks
> A man.

THE GRANGE

Radclyffe Hall

Radclyffe Hall's *The Well of Loneliness* is a sensitive, psychological study of the shaping influences of Stephen Gordon's lesbian love, and of its adulthood consequences. Rejected as a child by a jealous mother, and raised by an overly-attentive father, Stephen finds in the passages that follow the first strength of spirit and peace of mind she has known. Having had her passions aroused for the first time by Angela Crossby, Stephen comes to understand her earlier instinctive rejection of a male friend who had pressed his affections upon her, and experiences all the turbulent emotions of first love. Stephen encounters Angela at the end of adolescence, just at the moment her father's death has left her feeling particularly lonely and rejected; hence her meeting with Angela and consequent sexual awakening has all the earmarks of a spiritual rebirth. Thoughts of Angela leave her exultant—very much alive and full of purpose—and she likens herself to "some queer flower that had grown up in darkness, like some rare, pale flower, without blemish or stain."

It was only five days till Sunday, yet for Stephen those five days seemed like as many years. Every evening now she rang up The Grange to inquire about Angela's hand and Tony, so that she grew quite familiar with the butler, with his quality of voice, with his habit of coughing, with the way he hung up the receiver.

She did not stop to analyse her feelings, she only knew that she felt exultant—for no reason at all she was feeling exultant, very much alive too and full of purpose, and she walked for miles alone on the hills, unable to stay really quiet for a moment. She found herself becoming acutely observant, and now she discovered all manner of wonders; the network of veins on the leaves, for instance, and the delicate hearts of the wild dog-roses, the uncertain shimmering flight of the larks as they fluttered up singing, close to her feet. But above all she rediscovered the cuckoo—it was June, so the cuckoo had changed his rhythm—she must often stand breathlessly still to listen: 'Cuckoo-kook, cuckoo-kook,' all over the hills; and at evening the songs of blackbirds and thrushes.

Her wanderings would sometimes lead her to the places that she and Martin had visited together, only now she could think of him with affection, with toleration, with tenderness even. In a curious way she now understood him as never before, and in consequence condoned. It had just been some rather ghastly mistake, his mistake, yet she understood what he must have felt; and thinking of Martin she might grow rather frightened—what if she should ever make such a mistake? But the fear would be driven into the background by her sense of well-being, her fine exultation. The very earth that she trod seemed exalted, and the green, growing things that sprang out of the earth, and the birds, 'Cuckoo-kook,' all over the hills—and at evening the songs of blackbirds and thrushes.

She became much more anxious about her appearance; for five mornings she studied her face in the glass as she dressed—after all she was not so bad looking. Her hair spoilt her a little, it was too thick and long, but she noticed with pleasure that at least it was wavy— then she suddenly admired the colour of her hair. Opening cupboard after cupboard she went through her clothes. They were old, for the most part distinctly shabby. She would go into Malvern that very afternoon and order a new flannel suit at her tailor's. The suit should be grey with a little white pin stripe, and the jacket, she decided, must have a breast pocket. She would wear a black tie—no, better a grey one to match the new suit with the little white pin stripe. She ordered not one new suit but three, and she also ordered a pair of brown shoes; indeed she spent most of the afternoon in ordering things for her personal adornment. She heard herself being ridiculously fussy about details, disputing with her tailor over buttons; disputing with her bootmaker over the shoes, their thickness of sole, their amount of broguing; disputing regarding the match of her ties with the young man who sold her handkerchiefs and neckties—for such trifles had assumed an enormous importance; she had, in fact, grown quite longwinded about them.

That evening she showed her smart neckties to Puddle, whose manner was most unsatisfactory—she grunted.

And now some one seemed to be always near Stephen, some one for whom these things were accomplished—the purchase of the three new suits, the brown shoes, the six carefully chosen, expensive neckties. Her long walks on the hills were a part of this person, as were also the hearts of the wild dog-roses, the delicate network of veins on the leaves and the queer June break in the cuckoo's rhythm. The night with its large summer stars and its silence, was pregnant with a new and mysterious purpose, so that lying at the mercy of that age-old purpose, Stephen would feel little shivers of pleasure creeping out of the night and into her body. She would get up and stand by the open window, thinking always of Angela Crossby.

Sunday came and with it church in the morning; then two interminable hours after lunch, during which Stephen changed her necktie three times, and brushed back her thick chestnut hair with water, and examined her shoes for imaginary dust, and finally gave a hard rub to her nails with a nail pad snatched brusquely away from Puddle.

When the moment for departure arrived at last, she said rather tentatively to Anna: 'Aren't you going to call on the Crossbys, Mother?'

Anna shook her head: 'No, I can't do that, Stephen—I go nowhere these days; you know that, my dear.'

But her voice was quite gentle, so Stephen said quickly: 'Well then, may I invite Mrs. Crossby to Morton?'

Anna hesitated a moment, then she nodded: 'I suppose so—that is if you really wish to.'

The drive only took about twenty minutes, for now Stephen was so nervous that she positively flew. She who had been puffed up with elation and self-satisfaction was crumbling completely—in spite of her careful new necktie she was crumbling at the mere thought of Angela Crossby. Arrived at The Grange she felt over life-size; her hands seemed enormous, all out of proportion, and she thought that the butler stared at her hands.

'Miss Gordon?' he inquired.

'Yes,' she mumbled, 'Miss Gordon.' Then he coughed as he did on the telephone, and quite suddenly Stephen felt foolish.

She was shown into a small oak-panelled parlour whose long, open casements looked on to the herb-garden. A fire of apple wood burnt on the hearth, in spite of the fact that the weather was warm, for Angela was always inclined to feel chilly—the result, so she said, of the English climate. The fire gave off rather a sweet, pungent odour—the odour of slightly damp logs and dry ashes. By way of a really propitious beginning, Tony barked until he nearly burst his stitches, so that Angela, who was lying on the lounge, had perforce to get up in order to soothe him. An extremely round bullfinch in an ornate brass cage, was piping a tune with his wings half extended. The tune sounded something like 'Pop goes the weasel.' At all events it was an impudent tune, and Stephen felt that she hated that bullfinch. It took all of five minutes to calm down Tony, during which Stephen stood apologetic but tongue-tied. She hardly knew whether to laugh or to cry at this very ridiculous anti-climax.

Then Angela decided the matter by laughing: 'I'm so sorry, Miss Gordon, he's feeling peevish. It's quite natural, poor lamb, he had a bad night, he just hates being all sewn up like a bolster.'

Stephen went over and offered him her hand, which Tony now licked, so that trouble was ended; but in getting up Angela had torn her dress, and this seemed to distress her—she kept fingering the tear.

'Can I help?' inquired Stephen, hoping she'd say no—which she did, quite firmly, after one look at Stephen.

At last Angela settled down again on the lounge. 'Come and sit over here,' she suggested, smiling. Then Stephen sat down on the edge of a chair as though she were sitting in the Prickly Cradle.

She forgot to inquire about Angela's dog-bite, though the bandaged hand was placed on a cushion; and she also forgot to adjust her new necktie, which in her emotion had slipped slightly crooked. A thousand times in the last few days had she carefully rehearsed this scene of their meeting, making up long and elaborate speeches; assuming in her mind, many dignified poses; and yet there she sat on the edge of a chair as though it were the Prickly Cradle.

And now Angela was speaking in her soft, Southern drawl: 'So you've found your way here at last,' she was saying. And then, after a pause: 'I'm so glad, Miss Gordon, do you know that your coming has given me real pleasure?'

Stephen said: 'Yes—oh, yes—' Then fell silent again, apparently intent on the carpet.

'Have I dropped my cigarette ash or something?' inquired her hostess, whose mouth twitched a little.

'I don't think so,' murmured Stephen, pretending to look, then glancing up sideways at the impudent bullfinch.

The bullfinch was now being sentimental; he piped very low and with great expression. 'O, Tannebaum, O, Tannebaum, wie grün sind

Deine Blätter' he piped, hopping rather heavily from perch to perch, with one beady black orb fixed on Stephen.

Then Angela said: 'It's a curious thing, but I feel as though I've known you for ages. I don't want to behave as though we were strangers—do you think that's very American of me? Ought I to be formal and stand-offish and British? I will if you say so, but I don't feel British.' And her voice, although quite steady and grave, was somehow distinctly suggestive of laughter.

Stephen lifted troubled eyes to her face: 'I want very much to be your friend if you'll have me,' she said; and then she flushed deeply.

Angela held out her undamaged hand which Stephen took, but in great trepidation. Barely had it lain in her own for a moment, when she clumsily gave it back to its owner. Then Angela looked at her hand.

Stephen thought: 'Have I done something rude or awkward?' And her heart thumped thickly against her side. She wanted to retrieve the lost hand and stroke it, but unfortunately it was now stroking Tony. She sighed, and Angela, hearing that sigh, glanced up, as though in inquiry.

The butler arrived bringing in the tea.

'Sugar?' asked Angela.

'No, thanks,' said Stephen; then she suddenly changed her mind, 'three lumps, please,' she has always detested tea without sugar.

The tea was too hot; it burnt her mouth badly. She grew scarlet and her eyes began to water. To cover her confusion she swallowed more tea, while Angela looked tactfully out of the window. But when she considered it safe to turn round, her expression, although still faintly amused, had something about it that was tender.

And now she exerted all her subtlety and skill to make this queer guest of hers talk more freely, and Angela's subtlety was no mean thing, neither was her skill if she chose to exert it. Very gradually the girl became more at her ease; it was up-hill work but Angela triumphed, so that in the end Stephen talked about Morton, and a very little about herself also. And somehow, although Stephen appeared to be talking, she found that she was learning many things about her hostess; for instance, she learnt that Angela was lonely and very badly in need of her friendship. Most of Angela's troubles seemed to centre round Ralph, who was not always kind and seldom agreeable. Remembering Ralph she could well believe this, and she said:

'I don't think your husband liked me.'

Angela sighed: 'Very probably not. Ralph never likes the people I do; he objects to my friends on principle I think.'

Then Angela talked more openly of Ralph. Just now he was staying away with his mother, but next week he would be returning to The Grange, and then he was certain to be disagreeable: 'Whenever he's been with his mother he's that way—she puts him against me, I never know why—unless, of course, it's because I'm not English. I'm the stranger within the gates, it may be that.' And when Stephen protested, 'Oh, yes indeed, I'm quite often made to feel like a stranger. Take the people round here, do you think they like me?'

Then Stephen, who had not yet learnt to dissemble, stared hard at her shoes, in embarrassed silence.

Just outside the door a clock boomed seven. Stephen started; she had been there nearly three hours. 'I must go,' she said, getting abruptly to her feet, 'you look tired, I've been making a visitation.'

Her hostess made no effort to retain her: 'Well,' she smiled, 'come again, please come very often—that is if you won't find it dull, Miss Gordon; we're terribly quiet here at The Grange.'

Stephen drove home slowly, for now that it was over she felt like a machine that had suddenly run down. Her nerves were relaxed, she was thoroughly tired, yet she rather enjoyed this unusual sensation. The hot June evening was heavy with thunder. From somewhere in the distance came the bleating of sheep, and the melancholy sound seemed to blend and mingle with her mood, which was now very gently depressed. A gentle but persistent sense of depression enveloped her whole being like a soft, grey cloak; and she did not wish to shake off this cloak, but rather to fold it more closely around her.

At Morton she stopped the car by the lakes and sat staring through the trees at the glint of water. For a long while she sat there without knowing why, unless it was that she wished to remember. But she found that she could not even be certain of the kind of dress that Angela had worn—it had been of some soft stuff, that much she remembered, so soft that it had easily torn, for the rest her memories of it were vague—though she very much wanted to remember that dress.

A faint rumble of thunder came out of the west, where the clouds were banking up ominously purple. Some uncertain and rather hysterical swallows flew high and then low at the sound of the thunder. Her sense of depression was now much less gentle, it increased every moment, turning to sadness. She was sad in spirit and mind and body—her body felt dejected, she was sad all over. And now some one was whistling down by the stables, old Williams, she suspected, for the whistle was tuneless. The loss of his teeth had disgruntled his whistle; yes, she was sure that that must be Williams. A horse whinnied as one bucket clanked against another—sounds came clearly this evening; they were watering the horses. Anna's young carriage horses would be pawing their straw, impatient because there were feeling thirsty.

Then a gate slammed. That would be the gate of the meadow where the heifers were pastured—it was yellow with king-cups. One of the men from the home farm was going his rounds, securing all gates before sunset. Something dropped on the bonnet of the car with a ping. Looking up she met the eyes of a squirrel; he was leaning well forward on his tiny front paws, peering crossly; he had dropped his nut on the bonnet. She got out of the car and retrieved his supper, throwing it under his tree while he waited. Like a flash he was down and then back on his tree, devouring the nut with his legs well straddled.

All around were the homely activities of evening, the watering of horses, the care of cattle—pleasant, peaceable things that preceded the peace and repose of the coming nightfall. And suddenly Stephen longed to share them, an immense need to share them leapt up within her, so that she ached with this urgent longing that was somehow a part of her bodily dejection.

She drove on and left the car at the stables, then walked round to the house, and when she got there she opened the door of the study and went in, feeling terribly lonely without her father. Sitting down in the old arm-chair that had survived him, she let her head rest where his head had rested; and her hands she laid on the arms of the chair where his hands, as she knew, had lain times without number. Closing her eyes, she tried to visualize his face, his kind face that had sometimes looked anxious; but the picture came slowly and faded at once, for the dead must often give place to the living. It was Angela Crossby's face that persisted as Stephen sat in her father's old chair.

In the small panelled room that gave on to the herb-garden, Angela yawned as she stared through the window; then she suddenly laughed out loud at her thoughts; then she suddenly frowned and spoke crossly to Tony.

She could not get Stephen out of her mind, and this irritated while it amused her. Stephen was so large to be tongue-tied and frightened—a curious creature, not devoid of attraction. In a way—her own way—she was almost handsome; no, quite handsome; she had fine eyes and beautiful hair. And her body was supple like that of an athlete, narrow-hipped and wide shouldered, she should fence very well. Angela was anxious to see her fence; she must certainly try to arrange it somehow.

Mrs. Antrim had conveyed a number of things, while actually saying extremely little; but Angela had no need of her hints, not now that she had come to know Stephen Gordon. And because she was idle, discontented and bored, and certainly not overburdened with virtue, she must let her thoughts dwell unduly on this girl, while her curiosity kept pace with her thoughts.

Tony stretched and whimpered, so Angela kissed him, then she sat down and wrote quite a short little letter: 'Do come over to lunch the day after to-morrow and advise me about the garden,' ran the letter. And it ended—after one or two casual remarks about gardens—with: 'Tony says *please* come, Stephen!'

On a beautiful evening three weeks later, Stephen took Angela over Morton. They had had tea with Anna and Puddle, and Anna had been coldly polite to this friend of her daughter's, but Puddle's manner had been rather resentful—she deeply mistrusted Angela Crossby. But now Stephen was free to show Angela Morton, and this she did gravely, as though something sacred were involved in this first introduction to her home, as though Morton itself must feel that the coming of this small, fair-haired woman was in some way momentous. Very gravely, then, they went over the house—even into Sir Philip's old study.

From the house they made their way to the stables, and still grave, Stephen told her friend about Raftery. Angela listened, assuming an interest she was very far from feeling—she was timid of horses, but she liked to hear the girl's rather gruff voice, such an earnest young voice, it intrigued her. She was thoroughly frightened when Raftery sniffed her and then blew through his nostrils as though disapproving, and she started back with a sharp exclamation, so that Stephen slapped him on his glossy grey shoulder: 'Stop it, Raftery, come up!' And Raftery, disgusted, went and blew on his oats to express his hurt feelings.

They left him and wandered away through the gardens, and quite soon poor Raftery was almost forgotten, for the gardens smelt softly of night-scented stock and of other pale flowers that smell sweetest at evening, and Stephen was thinking that Angela Crossby resembled such flowers—very fragrant and pale she was, so Stephen said to her gently:

'You seem to belong to Morton.'

Angela smiled a slow, questioning smile: 'You think so, Stephen?'

And Stephen answered: 'I do, because Morton and I are one,' and she scarcely understood the portent of her words, but Angela, understanding, spoke quickly:

'Oh, I belong nowhere—you forget I'm the stranger.'

'I know that you're you,' said Stephen.

They walked on in silence while the light changed and deepened, growing always more golden and yet more elusive. And the birds, who loved that strange light, sang singly and then all together: 'We're happy, Stephen!'

And turning to Angela, Stephen answered the birds: 'Your being here makes me so happy.'

'If that's true, then why are you so shy of my name?'

'Angela—" mumbled Stephen.

Then Angela said: 'It's just over three weeks since we met—how quickly our friendship's happened. I suppose it was meant, I believe in Kismet. You were awfully scared that first day at The Grange; why were you so scared?'

Stephen answered slowly: 'I'm frightened now—I'm frightened of you.'

'Yet you're stronger than I am—'

'Yes, that's why I'm so frightened, you make me feel strong—do you want to do that?'

'Well—perhaps—you're so very unusual, Stephen.'

'Am I?'

'Of course, don't you know that you are? Why, you're altogether different from other people.'

Stephen trembled a little: 'Do you mind?' she faltered.

'I know that you're you,' teased Angela, smiling again, but she reached out and took Stephen's hand.

Something in the queer, vital strength of that hand stirred her deeply, so that she tightened her fingers: 'What in the Lord's name are you?' she murmured.

'I don't know. Go on holding like that to my hand—hold it tighter—I like the feel of your fingers.'

'Stephen, don't be absurd!'

'Go on holding my hand, I like the feel of your fingers.'

'Stephen, you're hurting, you're crushing my rings!'

And now they were under the trees by the lakes, their feet falling softly on the luminous carpet. Hand in hand they entered that place of deep stillness, and only their breathing disturbed the stillness for a moment, then it folded back over their breathing.

'Look,' said Stephen, and she pointed to the swan called Peter, who had come drifting past on his own white reflection. 'Look,' she said, 'this is Morton, all beauty and peace—it drifts like that swan does, on calm, deep water. And all this beauty and peace is for you, because now you're a part of Morton.'

Angela said: 'I've never known peace, it's not in me—I don't think I'd find it here, Stephen.' And as she spoke she released her hand, moving a little away from the girl.

But Stephen continued to talk on gently; her voice sounded almost like that of a dreamer: 'Lovely, oh, lovely it is, our Morton. On evenings in winter these lakes are quite frozen, and the ice looks like slabs of gold in the sunset, when you and I come and stand here in the winter. And as we walk back we can smell the log fires long before we can see them, and we love that good smell because it means home, and our home is Morton—and we're happy, happy— we're utterly contented and at peace, we're filled with the peace of this place—'

'Stephen—don't!'

'We're both filled with the old peace of Morton, because we love each other so deeply—and because we're perfect, a perfect thing, you and I—not two separate people but one. And our love has lit a great, comforting beacon, so that we need never be afraid of the dark any more—we can warm ourselves at our love, we can lie down together, and my arms will be round you—'

She broke off abruptly, and they stared at each other.

'Do you know what you're saying?' Angela whispered.

And Stephen answered: 'I know that I love you, and that nothing else matters in the world.'

Then, perhaps because of that glamorous evening, with its spirit of queer, unearthly adventure, with its urge to strange, unendurable sweetness, Angela moved a step nearer to Stephen, then another, until their hands were touching. And all that she was, and all that she had been and would be again, perhaps even to-morrow, was fused at that moment into one mighty impulse, one imperative need, and that need was Stephen. Stephen's need was now hers, by sheer force of its blind and uncomprehending will to appeasement.

Then Stephen took Angela into her arms, and she kissed her full on the lips, as a lover.

MAURICE

E. M. Forster

The seduction that occurs in chapters nine and ten of E. M. Forster's *Maurice* manifests itself only in caresses and kisses. But because it involves an illicit love affair of two male school chums that has been six years in the brewing, it results in such an overwhelming emotional crisis for the protagonist that he thinks of suicide as a way of ending his guilt and shame. The tentative stirrings of his homosexual nature first awakens Maurice's sense of sin, and terrifies him as "the worst crime in the books." But eventually his painful *rite de passage* puts him beyond the world's judgments and leads him to the recognition that his power to love, whatever its form, is the key to personal strength and a full life in a harmonious universe. Flinging down all barriers, he pours all the dignity and richness of his being into his relationship.

During the previous term he had reached an unusual level mentally, but the vac pulled him back towards public-schoolishness. He was less alert, he again behaved as he supposed he was supposed to behave—a perilous feat for one who is not dowered with imagination. His mind, not obscured totally, was often crossed by clouds, and though Miss Olcott had passed, the insincerity that led him to her remained. His family were the main cause of this. He had yet to realize that they were stronger than he and influenced him incalculably. Three weeks in their company left him untidy, sloppy, victorious in every item, yet defeated on the whole. He came back thinking, and even speaking, like his mother or Ada.

Till Durham arrived he had not noticed the deterioration. Durham had not been well, and came up a few days late. When his face, paler than usual, peered round the door, Maurice had a spasm of despair, and tried to recollect where they stood last term, and to gather up the threads of the campaign. He felt himself slack, and afraid of action. The worst part of him rose to the surface, and urged him to prefer comfort to joy.

"Hullo, old man," he said awkwardly.

Durham slipped in without speaking.

"What's wrong?"

"Nothing"; and Maurice knew that he had lost touch. Last term he would have understood this silent entrance.

"Anyhow, take a pew."

Durham sat upon the floor beyond his reach. It was late afternoon. The sounds of the May term, the scents of the Cambridge year in flower, floated in through the window and said to Maurice, "You are unworthy of us." He knew that he was three parts dead, an alien, a yokel in Athens. He had no business here, nor with such a friend.

"I say, Durham—"

Durham came nearer. Maurice stretched out a hand and felt the head nestle against it. He forgot what he was going to say. The sounds and scents whispered, "You are we, we are youth." Very gently he stroked the hair and ran his fingers down into it as if to caress the brain.

"I say, Durham, have you been all right?"

"Have you?"

"No."

"You wrote you were."

"I wasn't."

The truth in his own voice made him tremble. "A rotten vac and I never knew it," and wondered how long he should know it. The mist would lower again, he felt sure, and with an unhappy sigh he pulled Durham's head against his knee, as though it was a talisman for clear living. It lay there, and he had accomplished a new tenderness—stroked it steadily from temple to throat. Then, removing both hands, he dropped them on either side of him and sat sighing.

"Hall."

Maurice looked.

"Is there some trouble?"

He caressed and again withdrew. It seemed as certain that he hadn't as that he had a friend.

"Anything to do with that girl?"

"No."

"You wrote you liked her."

"I didn't—don't."

Deeper sighs broke from him. They rattled in his throat, turning to groans. His head fell back, and he forgot the pressure of Durham on his knee, forgot that Durham was watching his turbid agony. He stared at the ceiling with wrinkled mouth and eyes, understanding nothing except that man has been created to feel pain and loneliness without help from heaven.

Now Durham stretched up to him, stroked his hair. They clasped one another. They were lying breast against breast soon, head was on shoulder, but just as their cheeks met someone called "Hall" from the court, and he answered: he always had answered when people called. Both started violently, and Durham sprang to the mantelpiece where he leant his head on his arm. Absurd people came thundering up the stairs. They wanted tea. Maurice pointed to it, then was drawn into their conversation, and scarcely noticed his friend's departure. It had been an ordinary talk, he told himself, but too sentimental, and cultivated a breeziness against their next meeting.

This took place soon enough. With half a dozen others he was starting for the theatre after hall when Durham called him.

"I knew you read the *Symposium* in the vac," he said in a low voice.

Maurice felt uneasy.

"Then you understand—without me saying more—"

"How do you mean?"

Durham could not wait. People were all around them, but with eyes that had gone intensely blue he whispered, "I love you."

Maurice was scandalized, horrified. He was shocked to the bottom of his suburban soul, and exclaimed, "Oh, rot!" The words, the manner, were out of him before he could recall them. "Durham, you're an Englishman. I'm another. Don't talk nonsense. I'm not offended, because I know you don't mean it, but it's the only subject absolutely beyond the limit as you know, it's the worst crime in the calendar, and you must never mention it again. Durham! a rotten notion really—"

But his friend was gone, gone without a word, flying across the court, the bang of his door heard through the sounds of spring.

A slow nature such as Maurice's appears insensitive, for it needs time even to feel. Its instinct is to assume that nothing either for good or evil has happened, and to resist the invader. Once gripped, it feels acutely, and its sensations in love are particularly profound. Given time, it can know and impart ecstasy; given time, it can sink to the heart of Hell. Thus it was that his agony began as a slight regret; sleepless nights and lonely days must intensify it into a frenzy that consumed him. It worked inwards, till it touched the root whence body and soul both spring, the "I" that he had been trained to obscure, and, realized at last, doubled its power and grew superhuman. For it might have been joy. New worlds broke loose in him at this, and he saw from the vastness of the ruin what ecstasy he had lost, what a communion.

They did not speak again for two days. Durham would have made it longer, but most of their friends were now in common, and they were bound to meet. Realizing this, he wrote Maurice an icy note suggesting that it would be a public convenience if they behaved as if nothing had happened. He added, "I shall be obliged if you will not mention my criminal morbidity to anyone. I am sure you will do this from the sensible way in which you took the news." Maurice did not reply, but first put the note with the letters he had received during the vac and afterwards burnt them all.

He supposed the climax of agony had come. But he was fresh to real suffering as to reality of any kind. They had yet to meet. On the second afternoon they found themselves in the same four at tennis and the pain grew excruciating. He could scarcely stand or see; if he returned Durham's service the ball sent a throb up his arm. Then they were made to be partners; once they jostled, Durham winced, but managed to laugh in the old fashion.

Moreover, it proved convenient that he should come back to college in Maurice's side-car. He got in without demur. Maurice, who had not been to bed for two nights, went light-headed, turned the machine into a by-lane, and travelled top speed. There was a wagon in front, full of women. He drove straight at them, but when they screamed stuck on his brakes, and just avoided disaster. Durham made no comment. As he indicated in his note, he only spoke when others were present. All other intercourse was to end.

That evening Maurice went to bed as usual. But as he laid his head on the pillows a flood of tears oozed from it. He was horrified. A man crying! Fetherstonhaugh might hear him. He wept stifled in the sheets, he sprang about kicking, then struck his head against the wall and smashed the crockery. Someone did come up the stairs. He grew quiet at once and did not recommence when the footsteps died away. Lighting a candle, he looked with surprise at his torn pyjamas and trembling limbs. He continued to cry, for he could not stop, but the suicidal point had been passed, and, remaking the bed, he lay down. His gyp was clearing away the ruins when he opened his eyes. It seemed queer to Maurice that a gyp should have been dragged in. He wondered whether the man suspected anything, then slept again. On waking the second time he found letters on the floor—one from old Mr. Grace, his grandfather, about the party that was to be given when he came of age, another from a don's wife asking him to lunch ("Mr. Durham is coming too, so you won't be shy"), another from Ada with mention of Gladys Olcott. Yet again he fell asleep.

Madness is not for everyone, but Maurice's proved the thunderbolt that dispels the clouds. The storm had been working up not for three days as he supposed, but for six years. It had brewed in the obscurities of being where no eye pierces, his surroundings had thickened it. It had burst and he had not died. The brilliancy of day was around him, he stood upon the mountain range that overshadows youth, he saw.

Most of the day he sat with open eyes, as if looking into the Valley he had left. It was all so plain now. He had lied. He phrased it "been fed upon lies," but lies are the natural food of boyhood, and he had eaten greedily. His first resolve was to be more careful in the future. He would live straight, not because it mattered to anyone now, but for the sake of the game. He would not deceive himself so much. He would not—and this was the test—pretend to care about women when the only sex that attracted him was his own. He loved men and always had loved them. He longed to embrace them and mingle his being with theirs. Now that the man who returned his love had been lost, he admitted this.

THREE
Frustration

Love is a sickness full of woes,
    All remedies refusing;
A plant that with most cutting grows,
    Most barren with best using.
       Why so?
    More we enjoy it, more it dies;
If not enjoyed it sighing cries,
       Hey ho.
Love is a torment of the mind,
    A tempest everlasting;
And Jove hath made it of a kind
    Not well, nor full, nor fasting.
       Why so?
    More we enjoy it, more it dies;
If not enjoyed it sighing cries,
       Hey ho.

from HYMEN'S TRIUMPH
Michael Drayton

THE TEST OF MIRIAM

D. H. Lawrence

Probably no other writer has written with greater power or conviction about the ability of a satisfactory sex life to render our lives beautiful or ugly, vital or sterile, than D. H. Lawrence. Lawrence believed that sexual relations should be a deeply emotional and religious experience, but that man must not protest against his physical nature or think it inferior. The act of love, he said, involves the nourishing, sacred flow of life between man and woman, a communion of the blood which brings renewed vitality and the resurrection of the spirit. To this end, Lawrence recounts in *Sons and Lovers* the disastrous effects on his psychological and spiritual growth of his possessive, overly-attentive mother, and of the totally spiritual girl, Miriam—both of whom try to dominate his affection. In the following passage, Paul Morel's problem is in convincing Miriam that the physical side of love is not cheap or vulgar, and that while people live by love, they may die or cause death if they love too much.

With the spring came again the old madness and battle. Now he knew he would have to go to Miriam. But what was his reluctance? He told himself it was only a sort of overstrong virginity in her and him which neither could break through. He might have married her; but his circumstances at home made it difficult, and, moreover, he did not want to marry. Marriage was for life, and because they had become close companions, he and she, he did not see that it should inevitably follow they should be man and wife. He did not feel that he wanted marriage with Miriam. He wished he did. He would have given his head to have felt a joyous desire to marry her and to have her. Then why couldn't he bring it off? There was some obstacle; and what was the obstacle? It lay in the physical bondage. He shrank from the physical contact. But why? With her he felt bound up inside himself. He could not go out to her. Something struggled in him, but he could not get to her. Why? She loved him. Clara said she even wanted him; then why couldn't he go to her, make love to her, kiss her? Why, when she put her arm in his, timidly, as they walked, did he feel he would burst forth in brutality and recoil? He owed himself to her; he wanted to belong to her. Perhaps the recoil and the shrinking from her was love in its first fierce modesty. He had no aversion for her. No, it was the opposite; it was a strong desire battling with a still stronger shyness and virginity. It seemed as if virginity were a positive force, which fought and won in both of them. And with her he felt it so hard to overcome; yet he was nearest to her, and with her alone could he deliberately break through. And he owed himself to her. Then, if they could get things right, they could marry; but he would not marry unless he could feel strong in the joy of it— never. He could not have faced his mother. It seemed to him that to sacrifice himself in a marriage he did not want would be degrading, and would undo all his life, make it a nullity. He would try what he *could* do.

And he had a great tenderness for Miriam. Always, she was sad, dreaming her religion; and he was nearly a religion to her. He could not bear to fail her. It would all come right if they tried.

He looked round. A good many of the nicest men he knew were like himself, bound in by their own virginity, which they could not break out of. They were so sensitive to their women that they would go without them for ever rather than do them a hurt, an injustice. Being the sons of mothers whose husbands had blundered rather brutally through their feminine sanctities, they were themselves too diffident and shy. They could easier deny themselves than incur any reproach from a woman; for a woman was like their mother, and they were full of the sense of their mother. They preferred themselves to suffer the misery of celibacy, rather than risk the other person.

He went back to her. Something in her, when he looked at her, brought the tears almost to his eyes. One day he stood behind her as she sang. Annie was playing a song on the piano. As Miriam sang her mouth seemed hopeless. She sang like a nun singing to heaven. It reminded him so much of the mouth and eyes of one who sings beside a Botticelli Madonna, so spiritual. Again, hot as steel, came up the pain in him. Why must he ask her for the other thing? Why was there his blood battling with her? If only he could have been always gentle, tender with her, breathing with her the atmosphere of reverie and religious dreams, he would give his right hand. It was not fair to hurt her. There seemed an eternal maidenhood about her; and when he thought of her mother, he saw the great brown eyes of a maiden who was nearly scared and shocked out of her virgin maidenhood, but not quite, in spite of her seven children. They had been born almost leaving her out of count, not of her, but upon her. So she could never let them go, because she never had possessed them.

Mrs. Morel saw him going again frequently to Miriam, and was astonished. He said nothing to his mother. He did not explain nor excuse himself. If he came home late, and she reproached him, he frowned and turned on her in an overbearing way:

"I shall come home when I like," he said; "I am old enough."

"Must she keep you till this time?"

"It is I who stay," he answered.

"And she lets you? But very well," she said.

And she went to bed, leaving the door unlocked for him; but she lay listening until he came, often long after. It was a great bitterness to her that he had gone back to Miriam. She recognised, however, the uselessness of any further interference. He went to Willey Farm as a man now, not as a youth. She had no right over him. There was a coldness between him and her. He hardly told her anything. Discarded, she waited on him, cooked for him still, and loved to slave for him; but her face closed again like a mask. There was nothing for her to do now but the housework; for all the rest he had gone to Miriam. She could not forgive him. Miriam killed the joy and the warmth in him. He had been such a jolly lad, and full of the warmest affection; now he grew colder, and more and more irritable and gloomy. It reminded her of William; but Paul was worse. He did things with more intensity, and more realisation of what he was about. His mother knew how he was suffering for want of a woman, and she saw him going to Miriam. If he had made up his mind, nothing on earth would alter him. Mrs. Morel was tired. She began to give up at last; she had finished. She was in the way.

He went on determinedly. He realised more or less what his mother felt. It only hardened his soul. He made himself callous towards her; but it was like being callous to his own health. It undermined him quickly; yet he persisted.

He lay back in the rocking-chair at Willey Farm one evening.
He had been talking to Miriam for some weeks, but had not come
to the point. Now he said suddenly:

"I am twenty-four, almost."

She had been brooding. She looked up at him suddenly in surprise.

"Yes. What makes you say it?"

There was something in the charged atmosphere that she dreaded.

"Sir Thomas More says one can marry at twenty-four."

She laughed quaintly, saying:

"Does it need Sir Thomas More's sanction?"

"No; but one ought to marry about then."

"Ay," she answered broodingly; and she waited.

"I can't marry you," he continued slowly, "not now, because
we've no money, and they depend on me at home."

She sat half-guessing what was coming.

"But I want to marry now—"

"You want to marry?" she repeated.

"A woman—you know what I mean."

She was silent.

"Now at last, I must," he said.

"Ay," she answered.

"And you love me?"

She laughed bitterly.

"Why are you ashamed of it," he answered. "You wouldn't be
ashamed before your God, why are you before people?"

"Nay," she answered deeply, "I am not ashamed."

"You are," he replied bitterly; "and it's my fault. But you know
I can't help being—as I am—don't you?"

"I know you can't help it," she replied.

"I love you an awful lot—then there is something short."

"Where?" she answered, looking at him.

"Oh, in me! It is I who ought to be ashamed—like a spiritual
cripple. And I am ashamed. It is misery. Why is it?"

"I don't know," replied Miriam.

"And I don't know," he repeated. "Don't you think we have
been too fierce in what they call purity? Don't you think that to be
so much afraid and averse is a sort of dirtiness?"

She looked at him with startled dark eyes.

"You recoiled away from anything of the sort, and I took the
motion from you, and recoiled also, perhaps worse."

There was silence in the room for some time.

"Yes," she said, "it is so."

"There is between us," he said, "all these years of intimacy. I feel naked enough before you. Do you understand?"

"I think so," she answered.

"And you love me?"

She laughed.

"Don't be bitter," he pleaded.

She looked at him and was sorry for him; his eyes were dark with torture. She was sorry for him; it was worse for him to have this deflated love than for herself, who could never be properly mated. He was restless, for ever urging forward and trying to find a way out. He might do as he liked, and have what he liked of her.

"Nay," she said softly, "I am not bitter."

She felt she could bear anything for him; she would suffer for him. She put her hand on his knee as he leaned forward in his chair. He took it and kissed it; but it hurt to do so. He felt he was putting himself aside. He sat there sacrificed to her purity, which felt more like nullity. How could he kiss her hand passionately, when it would drive her away, and leave nothing but pain? Yet slowly he drew her to him and kissed her.

They knew each other too well to pretend anything. As she kissed him, she watched his eyes; they were staring across the room, with a peculiar dark blaze in them that fascinated her. He was perfectly still. She could feel his heart throbbing heavily in his breast.

"What are you thinking about?" she asked.

The blaze in his eyes shuddered, became uncertain.

"I was thinking, all the while, I love you. I have been obstinate."

She sank her head on his breast.

"Yes," she answered.

"That's all," he said, and his voice seemed sure, and his mouth was kissing her throat.

Then she raised her head and looked into his eyes with her full gaze of love. The blaze struggled, seemed to try to get away from her, and then was quenched. He turned his head quickly aside. It was a moment of anguish.

"Kiss me," she whispered.

He shut his eyes, and kissed her, and his arms folded her closer and closer.

When she walked home with him over the fields, he said:

"I am glad I came back to you. I feel so simple with you—as if there was nothing to hide. We will be happy?"

"Yes," she murmured, and the tears came to her eyes.

"Some sort of perversity in our souls," he said, "makes us not want, get away from, the very thing we want. We have to fight against that."

"Yes," she said, and she felt stunned.

As she stood under the drooping-thorn tree, in the darkness by the roadside, he kissed her, and his fingers wandered over her face. In the darkness, where he could not see her but only feel her, his passion flooded him. He clasped her very close.

"Sometime you will have me?" he murmured, hiding his face on her shoulder. It was so difficult.

"Not now," she said.

His hopes and his heart sunk. A dreariness came over him.

"No," he said.

His clasp of her slackened.

"I love to feel your arm *there!*" she said, pressing his arm against her back, where it went round her waist. "It rests me so."

He tightened the pressure of his arm upon the small of her back to rest her.

"We belong to each other," he said.

"Yes."

"Then why shouldn't we belong to each other altogether?"

"But——" she faltered.

"I know it's a lot to ask," he said; "but there's not much risk for you really—not in the Gretchen way. You can trust me there?"

"Oh, I can trust you." The answer came quick and strong. "It's not that—it's not that at all—but——"

"What?"

She hid her face in his neck with a little cry of misery.

"I don't know!" she cried.

She seemed slightly hysterical, but with a sort of horror. His heart died in him.

"You don't think it ugly?" he asked.

"No, not now. You have *taught* me it isn't."

"You are afraid?"

She calmed herself hastily.

"Yes, I am only afraid," she said.

He kissed her tenderly.

"Never mind," he said. "You should please yourself."

Suddenly she gripped his arms round her, and clenched her body stiff.

"You *shall* have me," she said, through her shut teeth.

His heart beat up again like fire. He folded her close, and his mouth was on her throat. She could not bear it. She drew away. He disengaged her.

"Won't you be late?" she asked gently.

He sighed, scarcely hearing what she said. She waited, wishing he would go. At last he kissed her quickly and climbed the fence. Looking round he saw the pale blotch of her face down in the darkness under the hanging tree. There was no more of her but this pale blotch.

"Good-bye!" she called softly. She had no body, only a voice and a dim face. He turned away and ran down the road, his fists clenched; and when he came to the wall over the lake he leaned there, almost stunned, looking up the black water.

Miriam plunged home over the meadows. She was not afraid of people, what they might say; but she dreaded the issue with him. Yes, she would let him have her if he insisted; and then, when she thought of it afterwards, her heart went down. He would be disappointed, he would find no satisfaction, and then he would go away. Yet he was so insistent; and over this, which did not seem so all-important to her, was their love to break down. After all, he was only like other men, seeking his satisfaction. Oh, but there was something more in him, something deeper! She could trust to it, in spite of all desires. He said that possession was a great moment in life. All strong emotions concentrated there. Perhaps it was so. There was something divine in it; then she would submit, religiously, to the sacrifice. He should have her. And at the thought her whole body clenched itself involuntarily, hard, as if against something; but Life forced her through this gate of suffering, too, and she would submit. At any rate, it would give him what he wanted, which was her deepest wish. She brooded and brooded and brooded herself towards accepting him.

He courted her now like a lover. Often, when he grew hot, she put his face from her, held it between her hands, and looked in his eyes. He could not meet her gaze. Her dark eyes, full of love, earnest and searching, made him turn away. Not for an instant would she let him forget. Back again he had to torture himself into a sense of his responsibility and hers. Never any relaxing, never any leaving himself to the great hunger and impersonality of passion; he must be brought back to a deliberate, reflective creature. As if from a swoon of passion she called him back to the littleness, the personal relationship. He could not bear it. "Leave me alone—leave me alone!" he wanted to cry; but she wanted him to look at her with eyes full of love. His eyes, full of the dark, impersonal fire of desire, did not belong to her.

There was a great crop of cherries at the farm. The trees at the back of the house, very large and tall, hung thick with scarlet and crimson drops, under the dark leaves. Paul and Edgar were gathering the fruit one evening. It had been a hot day, and now the clouds were rolling in the sky, dark and warm. Paul climbed high in the tree, above the scarlet roofs of the buildings. The wind, moaning steadily, made the whole tree rock with a subtle, thrilling motion that stirred the blood. The young man, perched insecurely in the slender branches, rocked till he felt slightly drunk, reached down the boughs, where the scarlet beady cherries hung thick underneath, and tore off handful after handful of the sleek, cool-fleshed fruit. Cherries touched his ears and his neck as he stretched forward, their chill finger-tips sending a flash down his blood. All shades of red, from a golden vermilion to a rich crimson, glowed and met his eyes under a darkness of leaves.

The sun, going down, suddenly caught the broken clouds. Immense piles of gold flared out in the south-east, heaped in soft, glowing yellow right up the sky. The world, till now dusk and grey, reflected the gold glow, astonished. Everywhere the trees, and the grass, and the far-off water, seemed roused from the twilight and shining.

Miriam came out wondering.

"Oh!" Paul heard her mellow voice call, "isn't it wonderful?"

He looked down. There was a faint gold glimmer on her face, that looked very soft, turned up to him.

"How high you are!" she said.

Beside her, on the rhubarb leaves, were four dead birds, thieves that had been shot. Paul saw some cherry stones hanging quite bleached, like skeletons, picked clear of flesh. He looked down again to Miriam.

"Clouds are on fire," he said.

"Beautiful!" she cried.

She seemed so small, so soft, so tender, down there. He threw a handful of cherries at her. She was startled and frightened. He laughed with a low, chuckling sound, and pelted her. She ran for shelter, picking up some cherries. Two fine red pairs she hung over her ears; then she looked up again.

"Haven't you got enough?" she asked

"Nearly. It is like being on a ship up here."

"And how long will you stay?"

"While the sunset lasts."

She went to the fence and sat there, watching the gold clouds fall to pieces, and go in immense, rose-coloured ruin towards the darkness. Gold flamed to scarlet, like pain in its intense brightness. Then the scarlet sank to rose, and rose to crimson, and quickly the passion went out of the sky. All the world was dark grey. Paul scrambled quickly down with his basket, tearing his shirt-sleeve as he did so.

"They are lovely," said Miriam, fingering the cherries.

"I've torn my sleeve," he answered.

She took the three-cornered rip, saying:

"I shall have to mend it." It was near the shoulder. She put her fingers through the tear. "How warm!" she said.

He laughed. There was a new, strange note in his voice, one that made her pant.

"Shall we stay out?" he said.

"Won't it rain?" she asked.

"No, let us walk a little way."

They went down the fields and into the thick plantation of fir-trees and pines.

"Shall we go in among the trees?" he asked.

"Do you want to?"

"Yes."

It was very dark among the firs, and the sharp spines pricked her face. She was afraid. Paul was silent and strange.

"I like the darkness," he said. "I wish it were thicker—good, thick darkness."

He seemed to be almost unaware of her as a person: she was only to him then a woman. She was afraid.

He stood against a pine-tree trunk and took her in his arms. She relinquished herself to him, but it was a sacrifice in which she felt something of horror. This thick-voiced oblivious man was a stranger to her.

Later it began to rain. The pine-trees smelled very strong. Paul lay with his head on the ground, on the dead pine needles, listening to the sharp hiss of the rain—a steady, keen noise. His heart was down, very heavy. Now he realised that she had not been with him all the time, that her soul had stood apart, in a sort of horror. He was physically at rest, but no more. Very dreary at heart, very sad, and very tender, his fingers wandered over her face pitifully. Now again she loved him deeply. He was tender and beautiful.

"The rain!" he said.

"Yes—is it coming on you?"

She put her hands over him, on his hair, on his shoulders, to feel if the raindrops fell on him. She loved him dearly. He, as he lay with his face on the dead pine-leaves, felt extraordinarily quiet. He did not mind if the raindrops came on him: he would have lain and got wet through: he felt as if nothing mattered, as if his living were smeared away into the beyond, near and quite lovable. This strange, gentle reaching-out to death was new to him.

"We must go," said Miriam.

"Yes," he answered, but did not move.

To him now, life seemed a shadow, day a white shadow; night, and death, and stillness, and inaction, this seemed like *being*. To be alive, to be urgent and insistent—that was *not-to-be*. The highest of all was to melt out into the darkness and sway there, identified with the great Being.

"The rain is coming in on us," said Miriam.

He rose, and assisted her.

"It is a pity," he said.

"What?"

"To have to go. I feel so still."

"Still!" she repeated.

"Stiller than I have ever been in my life."

He was walking with his hand in hers. She pressed his fingers, feeling a slight fear. Now he seemed beyond her; she had a fear lest she should lose him.

"The fir-trees are like presences on the darkness: each one only a presence."

She was afraid, and said nothing.

"A sort of hush: the whole night wondering and asleep: I suppose that's what we do in death—sleep in wonder."

She had been afraid before of the brute in him: now of the mystic. She trod beside him in silence. The rain fell with a heavy "Hush!" on the trees. At last they gained the cart-shed.

"Let us stay here awhile," he said.

There was a sound of rain everywhere, smothering everything.

"I feel so strange and still," he said; "along with everything."

"Ay," she answered patiently.

He seemed again unaware of her, though he held her hand close.

"To be rid of our individuality, which is our will, which is our effort—to live effortless, a kind of curious sleep—that is very beautiful, I think; that is our after-life—our immortality."

"Yes?"

"Yes—and very beautiful to have."

"You don't usually say that."

"No."

In a while they went indoors. Everybody looked at them curiously. He still kept the quiet, heavy look in his eyes, the stillness in his voice. Instinctively, they all left him alone.

About this time Miriam's grandmother, who lived in a tiny cottage in Woodlinton, fell ill, and the girl was sent to keep house. It was a beautiful little place. The cottage had a big garden in front, with red brick walls, against which the plum trees were nailed. At the back another garden was separated from the fields by a tall old hedge. It was very pretty. Miriam had not much to do, so she found time for her beloved reading, and for writing little introspective pieces which interested her.

At the holiday-time her grandmother, being better, was driven to Derby to stay with her daughter for a day or two. She was a crotchety old lady, and might return the second day or the third; so Miriam stayed alone in the cottage, which also pleased her.

Paul used often to cycle over, and they had as a rule peaceful and happy times. He did not embarrass her much; but then on the Monday of the holiday he was to spend a whole day with her.

It was perfect weather. He left his mother, telling her where he was going. She would be alone all the day. It cast a shadow over him; but he had three days that were all his own, when he was going to do as he liked. It was sweet to rush through the morning lanes on his bicycle.

He got to the cottage at about eleven o'clock. Miriam was busy preparing dinner. She looked so perfectly in keeping with the little kitchen, ruddy and busy. He kissed her and sat down to watch. The room was small and cosy. The sofa was covered all over with a sort of linen in squares of red and pale blue, old, much washed, but pretty. There was a stuffed owl in a case over a corner cupboard. The sunlight came through the leaves of the scented geraniums in the window. She was cooking a chicken in his honour. It was their cottage for the day, and they were man and wife. He beat the eggs for her and peeled the potatoes. He thought she gave a feeling of home almost like his mother; and no one could look more beautiful, with her tumbled curls, when she was flushed from the fire.

The dinner was a great success. Like a young husband, he carved. They talked all the time with unflagging zest. Then he wiped the dishes she had washed, and they went out down the fields. There was a bright little brook that ran into a bog at the foot of a very steep bank. Here they wandered, picking still a few marsh-marigolds and many big blue forget-me-nots. Then she sat on the bank with her hands full of flowers, mostly golden water-blobs. As she put her face down into the marigolds, it was all overcast with a yellow shine.

"Your face is bright," he said, "like a transfiguration."

She looked at him, questioning. He laughed pleadingly to her, laying his hands on hers. Then he kissed her fingers, then her face.

The world was all steeped in sunshine, and quite still, yet not asleep, but quivering with a kind of expectancy.

"I have never seen anything more beautiful than this," he said. He held her hand fast all the time.

"And the water singing to itself as it runs—do you love it?" She looked at him full of love. His eyes were very dark, very bright.

"Don't you think it's a great day?" he asked.

She murmured her assent. She *was* happy, and he saw it.

"And our day—just between us," he said.

They lingered a little while. Then they stood up upon the sweet thyme, and he looked down at her simply.

"Will you come?" he asked.

They went back to the house, hand in hand, in silence. The chickens came scampering down the path to her. He locked the door, and they had the little house to themselves.

He never forgot seeing her as she lay on the bed, when he was unfastening his collar. First he saw only her beauty, and was blind with it. She had the most beautiful body he had ever imagined. He stood unable to move or speak, looking at her, his face half-smiling with wonder. And then he wanted her, but as he went forward to her, her hands lifted in a little pleading movement, and he looked at her face, and stopped. Her big brown eyes were watching him, still and resigned and loving; she lay as if she had given herself up to sacrifice: there was her body for him; but the look at the back of her eyes, like a creature awaiting immolation, arrested him, and all his blood fell back.

"You are sure you want me?" he asked, as if a cold shadow had come over him.

"Yes, quite sure."

She was very quiet, very calm. She only realised that she was doing something for him. He could hardly bear it. She lay to be sacrificed for him because she loved him so much. And he had to sacrifice her. For a second, he wished he were sexless or dead. Then he shut his eyes again to her, and his blood beat back again.

And afterwards he loved her—loved her to the last fibre of his being. He loved her. But he wanted, somehow, to cry. There was something he could not bear for her sake. He stayed with her till quite late at night. As he rode home he felt that he was finally initiated. He was a youth no longer. But why had he the dull pain in his soul? Why did the thought of death, the after-life, seem so sweet and consoling?

He spent the week with Miriam and wore her out with his passion before it was gone. He had always, almost wilfully, to put her out of count, and act from the brute strength of his own feelings. And he could not do it often, and there remained afterwards always the sense of failure and of death. If he were really with her, he had to put aside himself and his desire. If he would have her, he had to put her aside.

"When I come to you," he asked her, his eyes dark with pain and shame, "you don't really want me, do you?"

"Ah, yes!" she replied quickly.

He looked at her.

"Nay," he said.

She began to tremble.

"You see," she said, taking his face and shutting it out against her shoulder—"you see—as we are—how can I get used to you? It would come all right if we were married."

He lifted her head, and looked at her.

"You mean, now, it is always too much shock?"

"Yes—and——"

"You are always clenched against me."

She was trembling with agitation.

"You see," she said, "I'm not used to the thought——"

"You are lately," he said.

"But all my life. Mother said to me: 'There is one thing in marriage that is always dreadful, but you have to bear it.' And I believed it."

"And still believe it," he said.

"No!" she cried hastily. "I believe, as you do, that loving, even in *that* way, is the high-water mark of living."

"That doesn't alter the fact that you never *want* it."

"No," she said, taking his head in her arms and rocking in despair. "Don't say so! You don't understand." She rocked with pain. "Don't I want your children?"

"But not me."

"How can you say so? But we must be married to have children——"

"Shall we be married, then? *I* want you to have my children."

He kissed her hand reverently. She pondered sadly, watching him.

"We are too young," she said at length.

"Twenty-four and twenty-three——"

"Not yet," she pleaded, as she rocked herself in distress.

"When you will," he said.

She bowed her head gravely. The tone of hopelessness in which he said these things grieved her deeply. It had always been a failure between them. Tacitly, she acquiesced in what he felt.

And after a week of love he said to his mother suddenly one Sunday night, just as they were going to bed:

"I shan't go so much to Miriam's, mother."

She was surprised, but she would not ask him anything.

"You please yourself," she said.

So he went to bed. But there was a new quietness about him which she had wondered at. She almost guessed. She would leave him alone, however. Precipitation might spoil things. She watched him in his loneliness, wondering where he would end. He was sick, and much too quiet for him. There was a perpetual little knitting of his brows, such as she had seen when he was a small baby, and which had been gone for many years. Now it was the same again. And she could do nothing for him. He had to go on alone, make his own way.

He continued faithful to Miriam. For one day he had loved her utterly. But it never came again. The sense of failure grew stronger. At first it was only a sadness. Then he began to feel he could not go on. He wanted to run, to go abroad, anything. Gradually he ceased to ask her to have him. Instead of drawing them together, it put them apart. And then he realised, consciously, that it was no good. It was useless trying: it would never be a success between them.

For some months he had seen very little of Clara. They had occasionally walked out for half an hour at dinner-time. But he always reserved himself for Miriam. With Clara, however, his brow cleared, and he was gay again. She treated him indulgently, as if he were a child. He thought he did not mind. But deep below the surface it piqued him.

Sometimes Miriam said:

"What about Clara? I hear nothing of her lately."

"I walked with her about twenty minutes yesterday," he replied.

"And what did she talk about?"

"I don't know. I suppose I did all the jawing—I usually do. I think I was telling her about the strike, and how the women took it."

"Yes."

So he gave the account of himself.

But insidiously, without his knowing it, the warmth he felt for Clara drew him away from Miriam, for whom he felt responsible, and to whom he felt he belonged. He thought he was being quite faithful to her. It was not easy to estimate exactly the strength and warmth of one's feelings for a woman till they have run away with one.

He began to give more time to his men friends. There was Jessop, at the art school; Swain, who was chemistry demonstrator at the university; Newton, who was a teacher; besides Edgar and Miriam's younger brothers. Pleading work, he sketched and studied with Jessop. He called in the University for Swain, and the two went "down town" together. Having come home in the train with Newton, he called and had a game of billiards with him in the Moon and Stars. If he gave to Miriam the excuse of his men friends, he felt quite justified. His mother began to be relieved. He always told her where he had been.

During the summer Clara wore sometimes a dress of soft cotton stuff with loose sleeves. When she lifted her hands, her sleeves fell back, and her beautiful strong arms shone out.

"Half a minute," he cried. "Hold your arm still."

He made sketches of her hand and arm, and the drawings contained some of the fascination the real thing had for him. Miriam, who always went scrupulously through his books and papers, saw the drawings.

"I think Clara has such beautiful arms," he said.

"Yes! When did you draw them?"

"On Tuesday, in the work-room. You know, I've got a corner where I can work. Often I can do every single thing they need in the department, before dinner. Then I work for myself in the afternoon, and just see to things at night."

"Yes," she said, turning the leaves of his sketch-book.

Frequently he hated Miriam. He hated her as she bent forward and pored over his things. He hated her way of patiently casting him up, as if he were an endless psychological account. When he was with her, he hated her for having got him, and yet not got him, and he tortured her. She took all and gave nothing, he said. At least, she gave no living warmth. She was never alive, and giving off life. Looking for her was like looking for something which did not exist. She was only his conscience, not his mate. He hated her violently, and was more cruel to her. They dragged on till the next summer. He saw more and more of Clara.

At last he spoke. He had been sitting working at home one evening. There was between him and his mother a peculiar condition of people frankly finding fault with each other. Mrs. Morel was strong on her feet again. He was not going to stick to Miriam. Very well; then she would stand aloof till he said something. It had been coming a long time, this bursting of the storm in him, when he would come back to her. This evening there was between them a peculiar condition of suspense. He worked feverishly and mechanically, so that he could escape from himself. It grew late. Through the open door, stealthily, came the scent of madonna lilies, almost as if it were prowling abroad. Suddenly he got up and went out of doors.

The beauty of the night made him want to shout. A half-moon, dusky gold, was sinking behind the black sycamore at the end of the garden, making the sky dull purple with its glow. Nearer, a dim white fence of lilies went across the garden, and the air all round seemed to stir with scent, as if it were alive. He went across the bed of pinks, whose keen perfume came sharply across the rocking, heavy scent of the lilies, and stood alongside the white barrier of flowers. They flagged all loose, as if they were panting. The scent made him drunk. He went down to the field to watch the moon sink under.

A corncrake in the hay-close called insistently. The moon slid quite quickly downwards, growing more flushed. Behind him the great flowers leaned as if they were calling. And then, like a shock, he caught another perfume, something raw and coarse. Hunting round, he found the purple iris, touched their fleshy throats and their dark, grasping hands. At any rate, he had found something. They stood stiff in the darkness. Their scent was brutal. The moon was melting down upon the crest of the hill. It was gone; all was dark. The corncrake called still.

Breaking off a pink, he suddenly went indoors.

"Come, my boy," said his mother. "I'm sure it's time you went to bed."

He stood with the pink against his lips.

"I shall break off with Miriam, mother," he answered calmly.

She looked up at him over her spectacles. He was staring back at her, unswerving. She met his eyes for a moment, then took off her glasses. He was white. The male was up in him, dominant. She did not want to see him too clearly.

"But I thought——" she began.

"Well," he answered, "I don't love her. I don't want to marry her—so I shall have done."

"But," exclaimed his mother, amazed, "I thought lately you had made up your mind to have her, and so I said nothing."

"I had—I wanted to—but now I don't want. It's no good. I shall break off on Sunday. I ought to, oughtn't I?"

"You know best. You know I said so long ago."

"I can't help that now. I shall break off on Sunday."

"Well," said his mother, "I think it will be best. But lately I decided you had made up your mind to have her, so I said nothing, and should have said nothing. But I say as I have always said, I *don't* think she is suited to you."

"On Sunday I break off," he said, smelling the pink. He put the flower in his mouth. Unthinking, he bared his teeth, closed them on the blossom slowly, and had a mouthful of petals. These he spat into the fire, kissed his mother, and went to bed.

On Sunday he went up to the farm in the early afternoon. He had written Miriam that they would walk over the fields to Hucknall. His mother was very tender with him. He said nothing. But she saw the effort it was costing. The peculiar set look on his face stilled her.

"Never mind, my son," she said. "You will be so much better when it is all over."

Paul glanced swiftly at his mother in surprise and resentment. He did not want sympathy.

Miriam met him at the lane-end. She was wearing a new dress of figured muslin that had short sleeves. Those short sleeves, and Miriam's brown-skinned arms beneath them—such pitiful, resigned arms—gave him so much pain that they helped to make him cruel. She had made herself look so beautiful and fresh for him. She seemed to blossom for him alone. Every time he looked at her—a mature young woman now, and beautiful in her new dress—it hurt so much that his heart seemed almost to be bursting with the restraint he put on it. But he had decided, and it was irrevocable.

On the hills they sat down, and he lay with his head in her lap, whilst she fingered his hair. She knew that "he was not there," as she put it. Often, when she had him with her, she looked for him, and could not find him. But this afternoon she was not prepared.

It was nearly five o'clock when he told her. They were sitting on the bank of a stream, where the lip of turf hung over a hollow bank of yellow earth, and he was hacking away with a stick, as he did when he was perturbed and cruel.

"I have been thinking," he said, "we ought to break off."

"Why?" she cried in surprise.

"Because it's no good going on."

"Why is it no good?"

"It isn't. I don't want to marry. I don't want ever to marry. And if we're not going to marry, it's no good going on."

"But why do you say this now?"

"Because I've made up my mind."

"And what about these last months, and the things you told me then?"

"I can't help it! I don't want to go on."

"You don't want any more of me?"

"I want us to break off—you be free of me, I free of you."

"And what about these last months?"

"I don't know. I've not told you anything but what I thought was true."

"Then why are you different now?"

"I'm not—I'm the same—only I know it's no good going on."

"You haven't told me why it's no good."

"Because I don't want to go on—and I don't want to marry."

"How many times have you offered to marry me, and I wouldn't?"

"I know; but I want us to break off."

There was silence for a moment or two, while he dug viciously at the earth. She bent her head, pondering. He was an unreasonable child. He was like an infant which, when it has drunk its fill, throws away and smashes the cup. She looked at him, feeling she could get hold of him and *wring* some consistency out of him. But she was helpless. Then she cried:

"I have said you were only fourteen—you are only *four*!"

He still dug at the earth viciously. He heard.

"You are a child of four," she repeated in her anger.

He did not answer, but said in his heart: "All right; if I'm a child of four, what do you want me for? *I* don't want another mother." But he said nothing to her, and there was silence.

"And have you told your people?" she asked.

"I have told my mother."

There was another long interval of silence.

"Then what do you *want*?" she asked.

"Why, I want us to separate. We have lived on each other all these years; now let us stop. I will go my own way without you, and you will go your way without me. You will have an independent life of your own then."

There was in it some truth that, in spite of her bitterness, she could not help registering. She knew she felt in a sort of bondage to him, which she hated because she could not control it. She hated her love for him from the moment it grew too strong for her. And, deep down, she had hated him because she loved him and he dominated her. She has resisted his domination. She had fought to keep herself free of him in the last issue. And she *was* free of him, even more than he of her.

"And," he continued, "we shall always be more or less each other's work. You have done a lot for me, I for you. Now let us start and live by ourselves."

"What do you want to do?" she asked.

"Nothing—only to be free," he answered.

She, however, knew in her heart that Clara's influence was over him to liberate him. But she said nothing.

"And what have I to tell my mother?" she asked.

"I told my mother," he answered, "that I was breaking off—clean and altogether."

"I shall not tell them at home," she said.

Frowning, "You please yourself," he said.

He knew he had landed her in a nasty hole, and was leaving her in the lurch. It angered him.

"Tell them you wouldn't and won't marry me, and have broken off," he said. "It's true enough."

She bit her finger moodily. She thought over their whole affair. She had known it would come to this; she had seen it all along. It chimed with her bitter expectation.

"Always—it has always been so!" she cried. "It has been one long battle between us—you fighting away from me."

It came from her unawares like a flash of lightning. The man's heart stood still. Was this how she saw it?

"But we've had *some* perfect hours, *some* perfect times, when we were together!" he pleaded.

"Never!" she cried; "never! It has always been you fighting me off."

"Not always—not at first!" he pleaded.

"Always, from the very beginning—always the same!"

She had finished, but she had done enough. He sat aghast. He had wanted to say: "It has been good, but it is at an end." And she—she whose love he had believed in when he had despised himself—denied that their love had ever been love. "He had always fought away from her?" Then it had been monstrous. There had never been anything really between them; all the time he had been imagining something where there was nothing. And she had known. She had known so much, and had told him so little. She had known all the time. All the time this was at the bottom of her!

He sat silent in bitterness. At last the whole affair appeared in a cynical aspect to him. She had really played with him, not he with her. She had hidden all her condemnation from him, had flattered him, and despised him. She despised him now. He grew intellectual and cruel.

"You ought to marry a man who worships you," he said;"then you could do as you liked with him. Plenty of men will worship you, if you get on the private side of their natures. You ought to marry one such. They would never fight you off."

"Thank you!" she said. "But don't advise me to marry someone else any more. You've done it before."

"Very well," he said; "I will say no more."

He sat still, feeling as if he had had a blow, instead of giving one. Their eight years of friendship and love, *the* eight years of his life, were nullified.

"When did you think of this?" she asked.

"I thought definitely on Thursday night."

"I knew it was coming," she said.

That pleased him bitterly. "Oh, very well! If she knew, then it doesn't come as a surprise to her," he thought.

"And have you said anything to Clara?" she asked.

"No; but I shall tell her now."

There was a silence.

"Do you remember the things you said this time last year, in my grandmother's house—nay last month even?"

"Yes," he said; "I do! And I meant them! I can't help that it's failed."

"It has failed because you want something else."

"It would have failed whether or not. *You* never believed in me."

She laughed strangely.

He sat in silence. He was full of a feeling that she had deceived him. She had despised him when he thought she worshipped him. She had let him say wrong things, and had not contradicted him. She had let him fight alone. But it stuck in his throat that she had despised him whilst he thought she had worshipped him. She should have told him when she found fault with him. She had not played fair. He hated her. All these years she had treated him as if he were a hero, and thought of him secretly as an infant, a foolish child. Then why had she left the foolish child to his folly? His heart was hard against her.

She sat full of bitterness. She had known—oh, well she had known! All the time he was away from her she had summed him up, seen his littleness, his meanness, and his folly. Even she had guarded her soul against him. She was not overthrown, not prostrated, not even much hurt. She had known. Only why, as he sat there, had he still this strange dominance over her? His very movements fascinated her as if she were hypnotised by him. Yet he was despicable, false, inconsistent, and mean. Why this bondage for her? Why was it the movement of his arm stirred her as nothing else in the world could? Why was she fastened to him? Why, even now if he looked at her and commanded her, would she have to obey? She would obey him, in his trifling commands. But once he was obeyed, then she had him in her power, she knew, to lead him where she would. She was sure of herself. Only, this new influence! Ah, he was not a man! He was a baby that cries for the newest toy. And all the attachment of his soul would not keep him. Very well, he would have to go. But he would come back when he had tired of his new sensation.

He hacked at the earth till she was fretted to death. She rose. He sat flinging lumps of earth in the stream.

"We will go and have tea here?" he asked.

"Yes," she answered.

They chattered over irrelevant subjects during tea. He held forth on the love of ornament—the cottage parlour moved him thereto—and its connection with aesthetics. She was cold and quiet. As they walked home, she asked:

"And we shall not see each other?"

"No—or rarely," he answered.

"Nor write?" she asked, almost sarcastically.

"As you will," he answered. "We're not strangers—never should be, whatever happened. I will write to you now and again. You please yourself."

"I see!" she answered cuttingly.

But he was at that stage at which nothing else hurts. He had made a great cleavage in his life. He had had a great shock when she had told him their love had been always a conflict. Nothing more mattered. If it never had been much, there was no need to make a fuss that it was ended.

He left her at the lane-end. As she went home, solitary, in her new frock, having her people to face at the other end, he stood still with shame and pain in the highroad, thinking of the suffering he caused her.

In the reaction towards restoring his self-esteem, he went into the Willow Tree for a drink. There were four girls who had been out for the day, drinking a modest glass of port. They had some chocolates on the table. Paul sat near with his whisky. He noticed the girls whispering and nudging. Presently one, a bonny dark hussy, leaned to him and said:

"Have a chocolate?"

The others laughed loudly at her impudence.

"All right," said Paul. "Give me a hard one—nut. I don't like creams."

"Here you are, then," said the girl; "here's an almond for you."

She held the sweet between her fingers. He opened his mouth. She popped it in, and blushed.

"You *are* nice!" he said.

"Well," she answered, "we thought you looked overcast, and they dared me offer you a chocolate."

"I don't mind if I have another—another sort," he said.

And presently they were all laughing together.

It was nine o'clock when he got home, falling dark. He entered the house in silence. His mother, who had been waiting, rose anxiously.

"I told her," he said.

"I'm glad," replied the mother, with great relief.

He hung up his cap wearily.

"I said we'd have done altogether," he said.

"That's right, my son," said the mother. "It's hard for her now, but best in the long run. I know. You weren't suited for her."

He laughed shakily as he sat down.

"I've had such a lark with some girls in a pub," he said.

His mother looked at him. He had forgotten Miriam now. He told her about the girls in the Willow Tree. Mrs. Morel looked at him. It seemed unreal, his gaiety. At the back of it was too much horror and misery.

"Now have some supper," she said very gently.

Afterwards he said wistfully:

"She never thought she'd have me, mother, not from the first, and so she's not disappointed."

"I'm afraid," said his mother, "she doesn't give up hopes of you yet."

"No," he said, "perhaps not."

"You'll find it's better to have done," she said.

"I don't know," he said desperately.

"Well, leave her alone," replied his mother.

So he left her, and she was alone. Very few people cared for her, and she for very few people. She remained alone with herself, waiting.

THE ECLIPSE
OF THE MOON

Herman Wouk

The time is the mid and late 1930s, and the place is New York City. The romance of Marjorie Morningstar and Noel Airman has been lengthy, more dream-like than real, and—until the evening of the eclipse of the moon—totally platonic. As the daughter of very conservative, middle-class Jewish parents, Marjorie is the victim of a tradition of cultural propriety—a tradition that has caused her to think and act in accordance with an explicit and implicit set of religious and social assumptions. When she finally decides, because of increasing social pressure, to compromise this tradition—to give herself sexually for the first time to a man she thinks she loves—the result, for Marjorie, is extremely painful: physically and psychologically. What Wouk is dealing with here is the price we must pay when we make decisions entirely on the basis of social conventions and the expectations of others, rather than on the basis of gratifying deeply felt emotional needs.

He slid his fingers along the keyboard, came to her; he put his arm around her shoulders. They looked out at the moonlight together. He stared at the sky, craning his neck, and then pointed at the moon. "Yes, of course, I clean forgot. I think it's starting. There's an eclipse of the moon tonight, the paper said. Look at the left side of that moon, will you? Isn't it getting sort of dark red and queer?"

"I thought the moon blacked out in an eclipse," Marjorie said, peering in awe at the discolored moon. "I've never seen an eclipse of the moon."

Noel smiled. "It can't black out. The earth's air diffuses the sunlight. You just get a dull red color."

"Walking encyclopedia," Marjorie said. "Well, this is the opportunity of a lifetime, isn't it? Perfect view, perfect night. Let's watch the eclipse, by all means."

"It takes a couple of hours, dear."

Marjorie laughed. "How long before it's total, d'you suppose?"

"I don't know. Quarter, half hour, maybe."

"Well, why don't you just go and rewrite your duet? I'll watch till it's total, maybe. If I get bored I'll go home."

Noel returned to the piano. For about ten minutes he played fragments of the melody and scrawled on the pad. Marjorie sat on the arm of a chair, looking out at the eclipse. The coppery color crawled very slowly across the face of the moon. Now and then she glanced at Noel. Sometimes she found his eyes on her. She finished her drink and put down the glass. He stood. "I'll get you another."

"Positively not. Eclipse is getting there, all right. I'll have a cigarette, and then I'll go home. And you're not taking me home, either. I'll leave you to wrestle with the muse."

He brought her a cigarette, lit it, and embraced her waist with one arm. She leaned against him. They looked at the dulling moon, his cheek against her hair. After a while he said in a troubled voice, "Pretty slow kind of show, at that, an eclipse of the moon."

"It does lack something in the way of entertainment," Marjorie said, her voice shaking too.

He turned her around by the shoulders. It was a terrific release to kiss Noel. She broke away from him long enough to murmur, "It's been a very very long time, hasn't it?" They kissed again, with more passion.

Without a word he went to the hallway, and came back with her coat. "No doubt I'm being an imbecile, I'm throwing you out. Here's your coat. I love you. Good night. See you soon."

Marjorie slowly smiled, and shrugged. She started to put one arm into a sleeve. Then the coat was on the floor, and Noel was straining her to him until only her toes touched the floor. After kissing her furiously on the mouth, the eyes, the ears, the forehead, he said, "You don't exactly want me to work, do you?"

She said something, she didn't know what. He was leading her by the hand to the sofa, and she was following.

At one point, as they necked—she was quite defenseless against him, and quite without desire to defend herself—she murmured, "What about the redheaded chorus girl? Isn't she all you want?"

He said, "If you mean a kid named Carol, I took her once to dinner with Marsha and Lou. She's not quite you, unfortunately. That's always the trouble."

Soon they sat up, straightening their disarranged clothes. He took her face in his hands, kissed her on the mouth, and said huskily, "Well, now, Marjorie, my dear sweet love, this isn't what grown people do, is it? You've grown up, haven't you, at long last? I wonder. I think you have. Have you grown up?"

They stared at each other for a very long time. Marjorie's gesture at last was not even a nod; it was a slight, a very slight, ashamed dip of the head. It didn't seem to her she willed the movement; it happened. Then she tossed her head and laughed. "If you really think it's such a good idea."

He said, his face flushed and eager, "God knows I've always thought so."

"You devil. You've always known I would, too."

He stood and pulled her up by a hand. When he took a step toward the bedroom she held back; then she followed him.

Something happened at the bedroom door when he snapped on the light. It might have been the sight of the bed piled with papers; or of the open bathroom door, with the toilet beyond; it might have been that the overhead bedroom lights glared after the indirect glow in the living room, and shocked her eyes. The mood broke. She stood leaning in the doorway, while he agitatedly cleared away the books, scripts, and papers on the bed. He seemed comical to her in his excitement, as other men usually did, even though he was Noel; comical and boyish.

He tumbled the collected stuff in a heap in a chair, and turned to her. His arms dropped to his sides. "What's so funny, my love?"

She said, "You, my love."

He smiled. "The snorting pawing male, eh? Yes, indeed. Well, come on."

The smile faded from her face. She saw now something she had not noticed for a year and a half. She saw that his left arm hung crookedly. He held out his arms and came toward her. She said hurriedly, "Do you have a robe? Let me have it."

He gave her a yellow-and-red silk robe. She went into the bathroom, and as she closed the door she heard him kick off his shoes.

She looked at herself in the full-length mirror on the back of the door, in the white glare of the bathroom, and wondered in a vague way whether this girl she saw before her, Marjorie Morgenstern, this girl in the familiar blue dress with the gray trim, was really about to take off that dress in a man's apartment and lose her virginity. She wondered whether it would hurt. She felt detached, cold, and amused. Her teeth kept baring in a smile. She took off her shoes and then pulled off the dress over her head, in the same way she always took it off before going to sleep. Habit was so strong that she wanted to remove her smeared makeup—what was left of it, after the necking. But this seemed too cool and methodical a thing to do; no doubt hotel chambermaids were used to cosmetic smears on bed linen. She wondered how much of her clothing it was proper to take off. She was quite sure she couldn't go back naked to Noel. The question was, what was decently indecent for a girl of twenty-one, doing this for the first time? She took off her stockings and some of her underclothing. She kept on her slip, and hugged the robe around her as she combed her hair with his big black comb. Regretting that she hadn't brought her purse in with her, she considered dashing out and getting it, because she really needed powder and a touch of lipstick. But she was sure Noel would be offended at her appearing and disappearing again. Obviously she was to emerge, throw herself into his eager arms, and abandon all to love.

The trouble was that she hadn't the faintest desire to do it. She was, she supposed, scared; how scared, she wasn't sure. Mainly she was out of the mood for sex. She couldn't have been less in the mood had she been in the middle of baking a cake. She thought of taking a shower, pleading sudden fatigue, and going home. But in plain fact she was too embarrassed at the idea of backing out. All her reasonable objections to sleeping with Noel were gone. If she could have thought of a good argument against it, she might have come out of the bathroom and argued with him, even at this point, and argued herself inviolate back into her clothes and out of his apartment. She couldn't think of a reason. An appeal to morality was nonsense. She couldn't say she didn't love him; not after her performance on the sofa. Nor could she demand a guarantee of marriage, having started up with him again of her own accord, knowing full well how he felt, and what he was.

She knew she shouldn't have come to the dress rehearsal. She shouldn't have come to the hotel suite. She shouldn't have lingered— this was fatal—after the others had left. She shouldn't have responded so readily to the first kiss in a year. She shouldn't have used the coy excuse of staying to watch the eclipse. She shouldn't have gone to the sofa with him. But she had done these things.

She pictured herself putting her clothes back on, emerging from the bathroom, and announcing, "Sorry, I've changed my mind, dear. I'm going home. Please forgive me."

It was a temptation. It was much more of a temptation, actually, than getting into a bed with Noel Airman. She could have forgone that treat with the greatest ease. But the thought of announcing a change of mind made her feel like a damned fool. She could do it; but she feared she might actually forfeit Noel forever. He wouldn't be likely to forgive such childish inconsistency and whimsy, at this point. He had been all too patient with her, too long. It might well be the end. She didn't want an end with Noel. She wanted him for her husband. The estrangement of a year seemed never to have existed. Reality was only being with him, with Noel Airman, and life was most real and most sweet and most true when this lean blond clever man was holding her and kissing her. That was as certain as the night outside the windows. She had no other certainty to cling to. All other certainties had faded or eroded away in growing up; or she had been talked out of them; or she had read books that had disintegrated them. The certainty that there was anything praise-worthy in virginity had long since been ridiculed out of her. There was nothing to believe in, except that she loved Noel and wanted him. If her only chance of getting him was to sleep with him—and Marsha was right to that extent, things were at that stand between them, and had been for a year—so be it! She would pass through this tunnel somehow and look for daylight on the other side. Fighting it off longer was pointless.

She put her hand on the doorknob and saw herself in the mirror, barefoot, her hair combed loosely to her shoulders, in the ludicrously big man's robe through which the pink of her slip peeked. She wrapped the robe close around her and tied the cord. She stood and stared for a few seconds at the mirror.

She had a race of last thoughts. What had plunged her over the line so suddenly and so finally? Marsha's tirade? The theremin, which had given him an excuse to hold her and hug her, and then to kidnap her from the wedding? The enchantment of *Princess Jones*, the knowledge that it probably would make him rich and well known?

It wasn't one thing. She had been working toward this moment for two years. She had been moving toward her first sex act, in this bedroom, in this hotel, with this man, like an asteroid moving to collide with a comet.

What of her mother, her father? What of Seth? How would it feel after this to go home, to sleep in a bed in a room in her family's apartment?

She snapped off the light and opened the door.

At first she could see nothing but a glowing cigarette in the gloom. It made a red arc in the darkness and went out, and Noel's voice said, "Hi, darling. I was beginning to think you'd found a fire escape."

She went to the bed and sat on the edge. She could see him dimly now in the faint light from the window. It startled her to see that he wore pajamas. She untied the robe, threw it off, and got into the bed beside him. It was all very clumsy. Her movements were hurried, his were uncertain. They poked each other with elbows and knees. They kissed awkwardly and unsatisfactorily. Then somehow they settled down.

"You love me?" she said.

"Yes."

"Do you suppose we'll ever be married?"

"I don't know, Marjorie. I just don't know. If it has to happen, it will."

"You love me more than you know. You're going to marry me. You'll be a wonderful wretch of a husband, and we'll be the two happiest people in the world."

"You think so?"

"I know it."

"Okay, darling. Maybe you can read fate. I've never loved anyone the way I love you. That, I know."

She wanted to kiss him then. For a while it was tender and sweet. There was something peculiarly pleasant in the comfort and nearness of being undressed. It was not so much exciting, as cosy and intimate.

Then all changed. It became rough and strange. She was powerless to stop it. She tried to seem pleasant and loving, but she was very uncomfortable and unhappy. It became rougher and more awkward. It became horrible. There were shocks, ugly uncoverings, pain, incredible humiliation, shock, shock, and it was over.

So it was that Marjorie qualified at last to portray true emotion on the stage. Her age was twenty-one years, four months, and seven days.

Noel said, "All right, darling?"

"Just fine," she answered, trying not to sound sick.

"The cigarettes are there on the night table. Toss me one, honey."

She groped on the table. There was a clinking and a crash. Instinctively she reached for the lamp cord and pulled it. Blinking in the blaze of light, holding the blanket to her bosom, she saw that she had knocked over a drinking glass. The pieces lay glittering on the marble top of the table. "Well, that's fine," she said. "We're supposed to break a glass, aren't we? Only you should have done it with your heel, I guess. Good luck, darling."

His lipstick-smeared face, white and tired, with the hair falling over his forehead, took on a pained alarmed look. She said hurriedly, "Good Lord, sweetheart, that was a joke. Smile, for heaven's sake."

He smiled. "Let's have the cigarettes."

She passed the pack to him. With her first puff she leaned back and sighed. Her glance went to the window. The moon hung in the sky over the buildings, a solid disk of reddish bronze, without a trace of white. "Well, bless me," she said, pointing. "Look, the eclipse is total. I got to see one, after all. Makes it easy to date this night, doesn't it, darling?"

"Marjorie," Noel said, in a strained tone, "I would appreciate it just as much if you weren't quite so brave and pathetic about all this. You're a big girl. It could have been more fun, and it will be, I promise you. I love you."

She looked at him, smiling, while tears came from nowhere and ran down her face in streams. "Why, darling, I wasn't being pathetic. I'm very glad. I love you too."

She put her face in the pillow. The tears were pouring; she could not possibly stop them, and she was ashamed of herself because she was crying.

A MEMOIR OF
THE FIRST TIME

Alix Kates Shulman

The only thing Sasha Davis and Marjorie Morningstar have in common is physical beauty. Whereas Marjorie is subject to a rigid set of rules of propriety, Sasha (a teenager of mid-America in the 1950s) is not. In fact, she seems to enjoy breaking the rules. She's been told by her girl friends that she cannot do anything she pleases just because she is beautiful. Such admonitions, however, don't deter Sasha from what she wants. Confident that her "transformation" into royalty (she was chosen queen of the hop) has freed her from the final set of rules governing the sexual behavior of her group, Sasha submits to Joe—the high school basketball star—after the coronation ball. It is important to note that the Sasha Davis narrating this graphic, sometimes journalistic, fatally stereotypic, account of a first sexual experience is not the Sasha Davis who, freeing herself of the image to which men have selfishly made her conform, emerges in **Alix Kates Shulman's** novel as one of the newly emancipated women of our time.

Music was spilling out of the cafeteria into the corridors of Baybury High. "Stardust," the S.L.T. theme song, announced that the annual S.L.T. Bunny Hop, celebrating spring and the big basketball game, was now under way.

I loved dances. But even before we arrived at the dance, I was already giddy from the evening. In a series of brilliant maneuvers

From *MEMOIRS OF AN EX-PROM QUEEN*, by Alix Kates Shulman. Copyright 1969, 1971, 1972 by Alix Kates Shulman. Reprinted by permission of Alfred A. Knopf, Inc.

beyond the hopes of anyone in Baybury Heights, my own Joey Ross had demolished snotty Shaker Heights and led Baybury to victory by scoring one spectacular basket after another. Of the eighty-one points scored by Baybury High against Shaker High's bleak thirty-four, Joey, still a sophomore, had made forty himself. After such a dazzling performance, he would surely be made captain of the team.

I floated out of the gym on Joey's arm, madly in love. "Great game, Joey," called Rooney Rogoff on his way to the locker room, snapping his towel at us.

"You too, stud," said Joey.

Hand in hand we mounted the stairs to the cafeteria. On the landing Joey shot one hand to the wall to trap me; then pressing his sinewy body flat against mine, he kissed me hard. When his tongue glided into the corners of my mouth I went limp like warm butter; I could have melted right down the stairs. "Don't," I managed to say. "They'll be judging us soon."

"So what?" said Joey, "you're gorgeous." But he lowered his arm obligingly and in we went.

The darkened cafeteria was undulating with mute couples grinding to a very slow instrumental. A canopy of paper streamers hung overhead. "Great game, Joey," someone said as we walked through the door.

"How ya doin'?" Joey answered modestly.

"Great game," said my friend Eloise the ticket taker. It was useless trying to hide my rapture.

At the opposite end of the large room Freddy and Fink (*More sound than you think/With Freddy and Fink*) had set up their amplifiers and turntables and were playing records on request. Behind them the girls on the Dance Committee were putting last-minute decorations on the table that would serve as a platform for the coronation. Tonight a new Queen would be chosen. My stomach sank when once again I remembered the contest, but Joey grabbed me around the waist and pulled me onto the dance floor and made everything all right again. Pressing thighs, eyes closed, we melted together and swayed as one. Nearing the open window where the April breeze was puffing out the cafeteria curtains like parachutes, we floated slowly down to a standstill and kissed again. Oh Joey.

The music stopped. "Great game!" said Nat Karlan, one of Joey's Keystone brothers. They twined their arms over each other's shoulders and moved away. But not before I overheard Nat whisper to Joey, with an intimacy I never achieved, "If you don't get in tonight, friend, you never will!"

I was stung by the thought. Of course: those forty points overwhelmingly weighted the scales. Tonight Joey would have a powerful advantage. But even if I managed to resist again tonight, who would believe me?

In the five months I had been going with Joey he'd come closer to "getting in" than anyone else, but I had always managed to resist. What happened to the girls who gave in, and even to those only suspected of giving in, was an unthinkable nightmare. I had myself sat through the now-famous S.L.T. meeting in which Renee Thomas had been expelled for allegedly going all the way. Only a year had passed and already Renee's name was legend. Girls sneered at her, boys abused her, her name appeared in all the graffiti, freshmen gaped at her in disbelief. She would never marry in Baybury. She'd have been better off dead. If only she had heeded the warnings that one thing inevitably leads to another.

Between me and Joey already one thing had led to another—kissing had led to French kissing, French kissing to necking, necking to petting, petting to bare-titting, bare-titting to dry humping—but somehow, thank God, I had always managed to stop at that penultimate step. When the Sunday morning telephone wires buzzed with intimate questions ("What did he try?" "How far did he get?") I bluffed my way through them with respectable answers, always a few steps behind the truth. But how long, I wondered, could I be believed? And how long could I go on holding out?

I knew there was some Renee in me, as there probably was in each of us. Renee, too, it was said, had started out by falling madly in love. So precariously did I totter between yes and no—from the first delicious kiss that made my knees go limp, to the very brink—that this new possibility appalled me. *If you don't get in tonight, friend, you never will.*

Actually, I had grown to dread necking with Joey, it had come to be such a struggle. Whatever I did, he wanted more. It wasn't even safe to neck in my house any more, where my parents trusted me. Gone were those long, voluptuous hours of kissing on my livingroom sofa or in the car at Shaker Lakes when I could abandon myself to Joey's sweet mouth, love his sinuous arms with my fingertips, and tickle my palms on his crew cut. The kissing and French kissing and petting I had so enjoyed had been reduced to a five-minute warm-up before the struggle, and I had been forced to trade abandon for vigilance.

"Please let me, Sasha."

"I can't, Joey."

"Please."

"No."

Now, after five kisses or ten, he'd slip his hand under my sweater or skirt and begin to tinker with me mechanically, then pin me under him on the back seat of his father's car and proceed to please himself. He was much too strong for me. In the beginning he used to lie on top of me so I could hardly move or breathe and rub his stiff clothed body against mine for a few minutes until a series of jerks let me know he was done and I could breathe again. I was bewildered by the shame and thrill of it. Later he stopped short of the jerks, turned suddenly away, opened his pants, and came into his handkerchief. Once he secretly unzipped and rubbed his bare penis on my thigh without my knowing until, suddenly aware, I managed to push him off and make him finish by himself.

Though he never again forced me to touch it, he started taking it out and begging me to feel it with my hand or let him rub it on my leg, and he would whine when I refused. "Come on, Sasha, you're torturing me," he would say. But it was really he who was torturing me, squeezing me between two guilts. I cowered whenever a car approached. I felt that if anyone ever discovered what Joey did with me in that car, I would have to run away. Poor Mother. Poor Daddy. Poor, poor Sasha.

It disgusted me to see Joey close his eyes and groan in ecstasy, his handkerchief over his crotch. When I had melted from his kisses it had been for love of him. But he certainly couldn't be groaning for love of me, it was all for himself. It was a tossup which was worse: to be appreciated as a mechanical ejaculator with all the attendant risks, or to be despised as a prude.

I had become so anxious over our sex that though we were going together and were therefore permitted to neck, I tried my best to avoid it. Passionate as I was, I looked for excuses to go straight home from a date. When Joey invariably parked the car anyway, I kept my coat buttoned all the way up as an act of protest. But of course, my protests went unheeded. I didn't dare get Joey really angry for fear he'd spread things about me. The girls' axiom about the boys was true: *they always go as far as they can, and never backwards.* By fifteen I knew love was a dangerous emotion. It was dynamite. I knew it was safer to be a sex reject than a sex object, but it was already too late for me to choose.

Freddy and Fink put on a fast record. Joey stepped back with his arm around his buddy Nat, while a Deltan twirled me off into the crowd. Athlete Joey, like all Keystones, danced only slow; the articulate Deltans danced as fast and as smoothly as they talked. As girls were divided by their looks and permissiveness, boys were divided by their accomplishments. I would have been a Deltan if I'd been a boy; maybe that was why I fell in love with a Keystone.

Whirling and bobbing and double-stepping, I danced with one Deltan after another. Couple after couple dropped off the floor while I danced on. Around us the circle of spectators swelled until it seemed the whole school was there. Breathless, pulse throbbing, I kept on going, to record after record, until Fink stopped the music and Freddy announced a break. I felt my face flush burgundy. Everyone exploded in applause. An intoxicating evening.

Freddy and Fink moved the coronation platform and mike into the center of the floor. "One-two-three-testing, one-two-three-testing." Time for the contest.

While the judges arranged their chairs in front of the platform, I ran to the girls' room with the three other finalists to primp and calm ourselves. My God, I thought, looking down the long mirror at those beautiful older girls, I haven't a chance. They seemed so poised, while I was falling apart. Long eyelashes, a tiny nose, and glowing skin simply couldn't be enough. The one power I had developed to perfection, the power of my glance, I didn't dare use on the judges. There was not a single way to improve my chances: I could only stand up and be judged.

As soon as we walked back into the cafeteria, Fink played a few bars of "Stardust" through the amplifier to set the ceremonial mood. Freddy caressed the mike and announced the contestants' names and fraternal sponsors. When he called my name I stepped up on a chair, then out onto the platform. Somehow I managed a smile for the eight judges below, two from each fraternity. *Please let me be chosen,* I prayed, climbing down again and taking my place beside the other contestants before the judges. I felt helpless, like a passenger riding in a "chicken" race.

Fink put on a slow ballad and a few couples danced in the corners. The judges consulted with Freddy, then whispered gravely among themselves. Feeling foolish, we whispered together too, not daring to look out, plucking at our sweaters nervously, waiting. "Who wants to be Queen anyway?" we said, hating each other. I needed to go to the bathroom again.

Freddy ran up to us. "Would you mind walking back and forth across the cafeteria once, girls, so these guys can get a better look at you?" he said.

"Oh, no!" we squealed. Didn't they see us every day? But of course, one at a time, we paraded before the judges. I remember making a little deferential curtsy at the end to camouflage my trembling knees—and I remember to my shame hearing someone laugh.

An eternity passed before Freddy ran back up to the front and tenderly took the mike in his hand. Fink stopped the music. "Okay, folks," said Freddy, "your attention please." He frowned and tapped the microphone until it hummed. Then he began again, laying on the famous Deltan smooth.

"There's such a stack of pulchritude up for Queen tonight that our judges have had a hard time making up their minds between these four gorgeous glamour girls." Everyone moved in a little closer. "But I'm happy to announce that they've finally reached a verdict."

He nodded to Fink, who started "Stardust" over again from the beginning, a little louder this time. Everyone fell silent. All suckers for ceremony.

My hands began shaking so hard that I clasped them behind my back. I wondered about my blushing skin. I had to go to the bathroom desperately. I thought about how it would feel to be Chinese or to live on the West Side, and then snapped back to Baybury Heights. Though I knew the decision was already settled, so there was no longer any possibility of influencing it, abandoning all prudence, I offered up one last wish to the Blue Fairy: *Make me Queen and I'll never ask for anything more.*

"I have the pleasure," said Freddy like a professional, "to present to you the new Queen of the S.L.T. Bunny Hop—I might even say the Basketball Queen of Baybury Heights."

Not me, throbbed my temples. *Never me.*

"—that beautiful miss from Sigma Lambda Tau, the Keystone's choice, the sweetest profile in Ohio, the Queen of the Bunny Hop, Sasha Davis!"

The music blared. Me! I couldn't believe it!

"That's you, Sasha," said Freddy, hugging me tightly and bending over to plant a loud kiss on my cheek. He pushed me up onto the platform. "Get up there now, honey, it's all yours!" I didn't dare take my eyes off him. "You're the Queen, Sasha," he yells up from below. "Smile!"

The others have disappeared. I'm all alone on the platform. The silver S.L.T. crown is on my head, and my arms enfold a huge bouquet of daffodils, tied with a blue satin ribbon on which are stitched in gold the letters S-L-T. In a circle below me everyone is singing out our song to the tune of "Stardust" and watching me. I smile till my gums show. I feel tears stream down my cheeks. Cameras are flashing. I feel so foolish and so happy. I am the Queen.

I confess, my coronation was such an undiluted triumph that I took it down in one long, sweet gulp that went straight to my head. Rashly I forgot that in the fall there would be another queen and the following spring another. Barely fifteen, that April night I reached such heady heights that the triumphs of the rest of my life were bound to seem anti-climactic.

Directly after my coronation I risked everything, celebrating with an act that wiped out months of restraint. Parked in our regular spot at Shaker Lakes, at last Joey got in. By allowing him to lie on me with his fly open, accepting his kisses with the delicious abandon of former days, I signaled that the struggle was over. It wasn't the forty points, or even Nat Karlan's prediction. It was simply that, being Queen, I dared to believe I could get away with it. There was something regal about going all the way.

I didn't get to remove my underpants, so eager was Joey to cross my threshold. He stretched the elastic of one leg and slipped his organ in; then with a little moan of joy he began humping me the same as always, plus in and out like an animal, wrinkling my skirt with his belly.

This is it! I said to myself. *This is love! Enjoy it!* I knew my daffodils were being crushed; nevertheless I tried to enjoy it, at least to attend to this celebrated moment in the most touted of acts.

It wasn't unpleasant with Joey inside me, but it wasn't particularly pleasant either. It didn't even hurt. I was surprised not to be feeling much, for Joey had pushed his entire appendage, so much larger than a finger, inside my opening. I couldn't imagine how it all fit in. Watching him move up and down on me in the darkness, I wondered: *is this all there is to it?* I had loved Joey to the melting point, but now I resented him. I received each thrust of his body like a doubt. Really all? When it was over a few moments later and Joey came groaning into his handkerchief as always, it struck me as hardly different from our usual sex. The only thing to recommend it was that it was ultimate. But, really, kissing felt much nicer.

Joey sat up. "I love you, Sasha. You'll never be sorry, I promise you."

He sounded so pious. I eyed him suspiciously. I wondered if I had done it all correctly, and if so, if it might not show or smell. Suppose some of the sperm had gotten in? Suppose Joey wouldn't keep his mouth shut? As I saw him wiping away the last traces of sperm, looking proud and lavishing on his withered organ more care than it deserved, I suddenly felt the enormity of my breach. I was utterly vulnerable.

I pulled down my skirt, hoping to become again inviolable. But there was clearly no going back.

If I get away with this, I consoled myself, I can probably get away with anything.

An hour later when Joey kissed me goodnight on my doorstep, I dutifully said "I love you," knowing Joey's new power to injure me. But for the first time, my knees did not go limp when he kissed me.

I was no longer simply "Joey's girl." I was a Queen myself with a life of my own.

NOBILITY

Robert Penn Warren

Jack Burden is twenty-one and in college, while Anne Stanton, the Governor's daughter, is only seventeen and on her way to a girl's finishing school as this excerpt from Robert Penn Warren's Pulitzer Prize novel begins. It's near the end of summer—one of those summers filled with romance, excitement, anticipation. One evening, in an empty house during a driving rainstorm, the two young people face each other and sense that "this was the moment the great current of summer had been steadily moving toward all the time." In a scene punctuated by panic, the seemingly fated union remains unconsummated. The curious aspect of the incident lies in the peculiar emotional responses of Jack and Anne as they prepare for this first sexual experience. Or is it just Jack whose response is peculiar? For he is the one who finds his mind straying from the anticipation of the moment and taking "wild leaps and centrifugal plunges like an animal with one foot in a trap or a June bug on a string."

Two nights before she was supposed to leave we went in to the Landing to a movie. It was raining when we came out of the movie. We had intended to go for a swim after the show, but we didn't. We had taken lots of swims in the rain, that summer and the summers before when Adam had been with us. We would no doubt have gone that night too, if the rain had been a different kind of rain, if it had been a light sweet rain, falling out of a high sky, the kind that barely whispers with a silky sound on the surface of the water you are swimming in, or if it had been a driven, needle-pointed, cold, cathartic rain to make you want to run along the beach and yell before you took refuge in the sea, or even if it had been a torrent, the kind you get on the Gulf that is like nothing so much as what happens when the bottom finally bursts out of a big paper bag suspended full of water. But it wasn't like any of those kinds of rain. It was as though the sky had sagged down as low as possible and there were a universal leaking of bilge down through the black, gummy, dispirited air.

So we put the top up on the roadster, getting well wet doing it, got in, and drove toward home. The light was blazing in my mother's place and on the gallery, and so we decided to go in there and make some coffee and sandwiches. It was still early, about nine-thirty. My mother, I remembered, had gone down the Row to play bridge with the Pattons and some fellow who was visiting them and was stuck on her. We wheeled up the drive and ground to a stop with a great crunching and spraying of shells and rain water. We ran up the right-hand sweep of the twin flights of steps leading to the gallery, then safe under the gallery roof began to stamp and shake the water from us like dogs. The running and stamping and the wet had made Anne's hair come loose. It was hanging down her back, with some odd wet strands plastered across her brow and one over her cheek to make her look like a child coming out of a bath. She laughed as she cocked her head to one side and shook it, the way girls do, to make the hair fall free. She ran her spread fingers through her hair like a big comb to catch the stray hairpins. A couple of them fell to the gallery floor. "I'm a fright," she said, "I'm an awful fright," and kept on cocking her head over and laughing and looking up at me sidewise with bright eyes. She was more like she had been before.

I said, yes, she was a fright, and we went on into the house.

I switched the light off in the big hall, but let the gallery lights stay on, then led the way back to the kitchen, through the dining room and pantry, off to the right of the hall. I put the coffee on to make, and got some food out of the icebox (that was back yonder before electric refrigerators or my mother would have had a brace of them big as a log cabin and surrounded at midnight by ladies with bare shoulders and tipsy men in dinner jackets, just like the ads). While I did the scullery work, Anne was braiding her hair. Apparently she was planning a pigtail on each side, for one was well under way by the time I had the grub laid out on the kitchen table. "Why don't you make the sandwiches and stop primping?" I said.

"All right," she said, "and you'll have to fix the hair."

So while she sat at the table and fixed the sandwiches, I finished the first pigtail. "There ought to be a ribbon on it to hold it together," I said, "or something." I was pressing the end between my fingers to keep it from coming unplaited. Then my eyes fell on a clean dish towel on the rack. I dropped the braid and went over to the towel and tore with the aid of a pocket knife two strips off the end. The dish towel was white with a red border. I came back, repaired the damage to the braid, and tied up the end with the piece of towel in a bowknot. "You'll look like a pickaninny," I said. She giggled and kept on spreading peanut butter.

I saw that the coffee was made, and turned off the gas. Then I began to work on the second pigtail. I leaned over and ran the silky stuff through my fingers, which were all tingling thumbs as rough as sandpaper, separated it into three skeins, and while I folded them over into place, one after another, breathed in the fresh meadowy smell the hair had because it was damp. I was thus occupied when the telephone rang. "Take this," I ordered Anne, "or it'll unravel," and thrust the end of the pigtail at her. Then I went out to the hall.

It was my mother. She and the Pattons and the fellow who was stuck on her, and God knew who else, were going to pile into the car and drive forty miles to La Grange, a joint in the next county, on the road to the city, where there were a few dice tables and a couple of roulette wheels and where the best people rubbed shoulders with the worst and inhaled a communal blue fog of throat-lacerating tobacco smoke and illicit alcohol fumes. She said she didn't know when she'd be in, but to leave the door open, for she'd forgotten her key. She didn't have to tell me to leave the door open, for nobody ever locked up in the Landing, anyway. She said not to worry, for she felt lucky, and laughed and hung up. Well, she needn't have told me not to worry, either. Not about her luck. She was lucky, all right. She got everything she wanted.

I hung up the receiver and looked up to see, in the light that came to the hall, from the door to the back passage, Anne standing a few feet from me, just tying the bow to the end of the second long pigtail. "It was my mother," I explained. "She and the Pattons are going to La Grange." Then added, "She won't be back till late."

As I said that last, I was suddenly aware of the emptiness of the house, the dark rooms around us, the weight of darkness stored above us, stuffing the rooms and the attic, spilling thickly but weightlessly down the stairs, and aware of the darkness outside. As I looked into Anne's face there wasn't a sound in the house. Outside there was the drip on leaves and on the roof, now subsiding. Then my heart took a big knock, and I felt the new blood coursing through me as though somebody had opened a sluice gate.

I was looking right into Anne's face, and doing so, I knew, and knew that she knew, that this was the moment the great current of the summer had been steadily moving toward all the time. I turned around and moved slowly up the hall toward the foot of the stairs. I couldn't tell at first whether she was following or not. Then I knew she was. I climbed the stairs, and knew she was following about four steps behind me.

At the head of the stairs, in the upstairs hall, I didn't even pause or look around. I moved up the hall, which was pitch dark, toward the door of my room. My hand touched the knob in the dark, and I pushed the door open and entered. There was a little light in the room, for the night had, apparently, cleared for the moment, and too, the glare of the gallery light below was reflected up from the wet leaves. I stood to one side, with my hand still on the knob of the door, while she walked into the room. She didn't even glance at me as she came in. She took about three steps into the room and stopped. I closed the door and moved toward the white-clothed narrow figure; but she did not turn around. I stood behind her drawing her shoulders back against me and folding my forearms over her bosom and putting my dry lips down against her hair. Meanwhile her arms hung loosely at her sides. We stood that way for a couple of minutes, like lovers in an advertisement watching a dramatic sunset or the ocean or Niagara Falls. But we weren't watching anything. We were standing in the middle of a bare, shadowy room (iron bed, old dresser, pine table, trunks and books and male gear—for I hadn't let my mother turn that room into a museum) and staring across the room out into the dark tops of trees which all at once began to stir with a wind off the Gulf and rattle in an increase of rain.

Then Anne lifted her arms and folded them before her so that one of her hands was on each of mine. "Jackie," she said in a low voice, which wasn't, however, a whisper, "Jackie-Bird, I came up here."

She had come, all right.

I began to undo the hooks and eyes down the back of the white dress. She stood absolutely still, as though good and obedient, with a pigtail hanging back over each shoulder. The fact that the light cloth was damp and clingy didn't make things any easier. I kept fumbling the God-damned hooks and eyes. Then I came to the sash. It was tied in a bow on the left side, I remember. I got that free, and it fell to the floor, and I began again on the dress. She was as patient, standing there with her arms at her side, as though I were a dress-maker and she were having a fitting. She didn't say anything except when I, in my clumsiness and confusion, tried to pull the dress down over her hips. "No," she said then, in the same low voice as before, "no, this way," and lifted her bare arms above her head. I noticed, even then, that she didn't let the fingers fall loose in the natural way, but held them together on each hand, and almost straight, as though she were lifting her arms for a dive and had stopped just before completing the preliminary posture. I drew the dress over her head and stood there with it clutched foolishly in my hands before I got the wit to lay it across a chair.

She was standing with her arms still up, and I took that as a sign the slip was to come off the same way the dress had. It came off the same way, and with my clumsy, nervous meticulousness I laid it across a chair, as though it might break. She lowered her arms to her sides and stood with the same passivity while I finished the task. While I unhooked the brassière, and lifted it forward so that it would fall down her motionless arms, and released the drawers and drew them down her legs, kneeling on the floor beside her, I was somehow so careful that my fingers never even brushed her skin. My breath was quick and the constriction in my throat and chest was like a knot, but my mind kept flying off to peculiar things—to a book I had started and never finished, to wondering whether I would go back to the dormitory that fall or take a room out, to an algebraic formula I remembered which kept running through my head, to a scene, just the corner of a field with a broken stile, which I tried desperately to locate out of my past. My mind would just take those crazy wild leaps and centrifugal plunges like an animal with one foot in a trap or a June bug on a string.

As I crouched there beside her, just as I had let the batiste drop about her feet, she slipped one foot from its pump—you know how girls do, pressing the heels together a little so that the feet can be drawn out—then the other. I rose to stand beside her, and experienced a kind of shock to find how small she was, standing flat on the floor without her heels. I had seen her that way a thousand times, in a bathing suit, standing barefooted on the sand or float. But it struck me now.

She stood there, as I rose, with her arms hanging loose as before, then she folded them across her breast and hunched her shoulders a little and gave a slight shiver, and I saw how with the drawing forward of the shoulders the shoulder blades suddenly seemed sharp and frail, with a pigtail hanging down across each one.

It was raining hard outside now, with violent gusts. I noticed that.

Her head was slightly inclined forward, and she apparently saw, or remembered, that she still had on her stockings. Turning from me a little, she leaned forward, and balancing herself on one foot and then the other, drew them off and let them fall with the sash and the little wispy pile of stuff there before her. Then she stood as before, hunched slightly forward, perhaps shivering, her knees slightly bent and pressed together.

While I stood there fumbling with the buttons on my shirt, tearing one loose because I couldn't seem to get it through the buttonhole (in a momentary lull of the wind and rain, it made a single *tick* when it struck the uncarpeted floor), and while my mind made the crazy June-bug leaps and plunges, she walked across to the iron bed and sat down, tentatively, close to the edge, her feet and knees pressed close, her arms still folded and her shoulders slightly hunched as before. She was looking up at me across the space, with a question, or appeal, in her eyes—I couldn't read them in the dimness.

Then, letting one hand drop to the bed for support, she leaned a little sideways, lifted her feet from the floor, still together, and with a gentle, curling motion, lay back on the white counterpane, then punctiliously straightened out and again folded her hands across her bosom, and closed her eyes.

And at the instant when she closed her eyes, as I stared at her, my mind took one of the crazy leaps and I saw her floating in the water, that day of the picnic three years before, with her eyes closed and the violent sky above and the white gull flashing high over, and that face and this face and that scene and this scene seemed to fuse, like superimposed photographs, each keeping its identity but without denying the other. And at that instant, as I stood there with the constriction in my throat that made me swallow hard and with my body tumescent, I looked at her there on the iron bed, then looked suddenly around the big, bare, shadowy room and heard the gusty rain and I knew that everything was wrong, completely wrong, how I didn't know, didn't try to know, and that this was somehow not what the summer had been driving toward. That I wasn't going to do it. "Anne," I said, hoarsely, "Anne—"

She didn't answer, but she opened her eyes, and looked at me.

"We oughtn't," I began, "we oughtn't—it wouldn't—it wouldn't be—it wouldn't be right." So I used the word *right*, which came to my lips to surprise me, for I hadn't ever thought of anything I had done with Anne Stanton or with any other woman or girl as being right or wrong, but as just something that happened, and hadn't ever

thought about right or wrong very much in connection with anything but had simply done the things people do and not done the
things people don't do. Which are the things people do and don't do.
And I remember now the surprise I felt when I heard that word
there in the air, like the echo of a word spoken by somebody else
God knows how many years before, and now unfrozen like a word
in Baron Munchausen's tale. I couldn't any more have touched her
then than if she had been my little sister.

She didn't answer then, but kept on looking at me, with an
expression I could not fathom, and as I looked at her I was over-
whelmed by a great, warm pity, like a flood in my bosom, and burst
out, "Anne—oh, Anne—" and felt the impulse to fling myself to my
knees beside the bed and seize her hand.

Now if I had done that, things might have developed differently
and more in the normal pattern, for it is probable that when a half-
clothed and healthy young man kneels beside a bed and seizes the
hand of an entirely unclothed and good-looking young girl, developments will follow the normal pattern sooner or later. And if I had
once touched her in the process of undressing her, or even if she had
spoken to me to say anything, to call me Jackie-Boy or tell me she
loved me or had giggled or seemed gay, or had even answered me,
saying anything whatsoever, when I looked at her lying there on the
bed and first cried out her name—if any of those things had happened things might have been different then and forever afterward.
But none of those things had happened, and I was not to follow the
wild impulse to throw myself on my knees by the bed and take her
hand to make the first trifling contact of flesh with flesh, which would
probably have been enough. For just as I burst out, "Anne—oh,
Anne—" there was the sound of tires on the drive, then the creaking
of brakes.

"They've come back, they've come back!" I exclaimed, and
Anne rose abruptly to a sitting position on the bed and looked wildly
at me.

"Grab your stuff," I ordered, "grab your stuff, and get to the
bathroom—you could have been in the bathroom!" I was cramming
my shirt in and was trying to buckle my belt all at once and was going
toward the door. "I'll be in the kitchen," I said, "I'll be fixing something to eat!"

Then I bolted from the room, and ran down the hall, trying to
run on tiptoe, and ran down the back stairs to the back passage and
then into the kitchen, where I put a match to the gas under the
coffeepot with trembling fingers just as the front screen door

slammed and people entered the hall. I sat down at the table and began to make sandwiches, waiting for my heart to stop pounding before I confronted my mother and the Pattons and whatever bastards they had with them.

When my mother came on back to the kitchen, right away, followed by her gang, there I was and there was a nice pile of toothsome sandwiches and they weren't going to La Grange because of the storm and kidded me about being a mind reader and having the sandwiches and coffee all ready for them, and I was charming and gracious to them all. Then Anne came down (she had done a good circumstantial job and flushed the toilet twice to advertise her whereabouts) and they kidded her about her pigtails and her pickaninny hair ribbons, and she didn't say anything but smiled shyly the way a nice well-bred young girl should when the grownups take amiable notice of her, and then she sat quietly and ate a sandwich and I couldn't read a thing from her face, not a thing.

Well, that was the way the summer ended. True, there was the rest of the night, with me lying on the iron bed and hearing the leaves drip and cursing myself for a fool and cursing my luck and trying to figure out what Anne had thought and trying to plan how I would get her off alone the next day—the last day. But then I would think how if I had gone on, it would have been worse, with my mother coming back and going upstairs with the ladies (as she had done), and with Anne and me trapped there in my room. And as that thought scared me into a cold sweat, I suddenly had the feeling of great wisdom: I had acted rightly and wisely. Therefore we had been saved. And so my luck became my wisdom (as the luck of the damned human race becomes its wisdom and gets into the books and is taught in schools), and then later my wisdom became my nobility, for in the end, a long time after, I got the notion that I had acted out of nobility. Not that I used that word to myself, but I skirted all around its edges and frequently, late at night or after a few drinks, thought better of myself for remembering my behavior on that occasion.

A BEAUTIFUL THING

Larry McMurtry

**The relationship of Sonny and Ruth is that of a sympathetic teenager
and a lonely middle-aged woman. Each, however, has a selfish reason
for wanting to share a sexual experience. For Sonny it was the first
time; it was an adventure to have slept with his coach's wife. "He
didn't know if he would tell anybody or not, but it was sort of a
feather in his cap, nonetheless." For Ruth, it was a bit more complicated; she wanted something beautiful to happen to her, something
her husband knew nothing about. The first encounter, however, is
a disappointment to her. She closed her eyes, supposing that Sonny
would know how to make her happy, his body pressed warmly
against hers. "It was only when she opened her eyes and looked at
him that she remembered how young he was and realized he didn't
know what to do." Paradoxically, rather than helping to minimize
their differences, the experience seems to intensify them.**

When Sonny kissed Mrs. Popper outside the Legion Hall it seemed
to him that a whole spectrum of delicious experience lay suddenly
within his grasp. No kisses had ever been so exciting and so full of
promise, neither for him nor for Ruth. She felt as if she were finally
about to discover something she had somehow missed discovering
twenty years before. Neither of them foresaw any great difficulties,
just the minor difficulty of keeping it all secret.

Both, in fact, were so excited that they longed to talk about it
to someone, but that they couldn't do. In Thalia sex was just not
talked about. Even Genevieve would go to considerable lengths to
keep from calling a spade a spade. Everything acknowledged the

existence of sex: babies were born now and then, and things to prevent them were sold at the drugstores and one or two of the filling stations. The men told dirty jokes and talked all the time about how they wished they had more pussy, but it didn't really seem to bother many of them so long as the football team was doing well. The kids were told as little about sex as possible and spent most of their time trying to find out more. The boys speculated a lot among themselves and got the nature of the basic act straight when they were fairly young, but some of the girls were still in the dark about it when they graduated from high school. Many girls simply refused to believe that the things the boys peed out of could have any part in the creation of babies. They knew good and well that God wouldn't have wanted any arrangement of His to be *that* nasty.

The only thing everyone agreed on was that the act itself could only be earthly bliss. Once the obstacle of virginity was done away with, mutual ecstasy would be the invariable result. One or two of the bolder girls knew differently, but they didn't want to be thought freaks so they kept quiet about their difficulties.

When Sonny and Ruth met again, the Tuesday after the dance, they both expected things to be simple and wonderful, and they were both disappointed. For one thing, they both felt compelled to go through with the unnecessary trip to the doctor; both of them were nervous and tense and they rode to Olney in silence. The dusty air had given Ruth a sniffle, and Sonny could see the bluish shadows under her eyes. The wait in Olney was short, but on the way back they found themselves even more at a loss for conversation than they had been coming. Ruth could not imagine what had possessed her to think she could bring off such a thing as a love affair. They each concluded that they were not as appealing in the daylight as they had been in the dark, so they sat looking out their separate windows at their separate sides of the road. There was little in the leafless winter landscape to cheer them.

It was only when Sonny drove the Chevrolet into the dimness of the garage, with Herman's lawn tools and hedge shears hanging neatly on the walls, that they regained some hope. They both realized they were about to miss the chance they had been counting on. Sonny reached for Ruth's hand and she quickly scooted over toward him and they kissed. The kiss was awkward but warm and they didn't think of moving apart—for several minutes they let their mouths and faces touch.

Both would have been just as happy to stay in the garage all afternoon, but they felt obligated to complete the experience, and for that they had to go in the house, where things were not so good. The wallpaper in the bedroom was light green, and blotched in places. It was the bedroom where Ruth and Herman had spent virtually all their married nights: on one wall there was a plaque Herman had been given for taking a troop of Boy Scouts to the National Jubilee. Two or three copies of *High School Athletics* lay on the bedside table.

"Are you sure he won't come?" Sonny asked. The room seemed full of the coach.

"You know he won't," Ruth said. "He's just starting basketball practice."

She took his hand again and they kissed standing up. Neither of them really believed what she said: as they kissed both of them kept imagining the coach walking in. They were so conscious of him they hardly felt the kiss, but Ruth was determined to go on however dangerous it was, even if Herman did walk in.

They were unable to think of a smooth way to undress—it would have been better to do it while they were still kissing, but neither of them were expert enough for that. Ruth had on a dress and a slip, both of which had to come off over her head. Sonny could not even get her bra unhooked with the dress still on. Both of them wished for something to say, something that would break the tension, but neither could think of anything. Finally they simply broke apart and hurried about their own undressing. Ruth got her dress off, but when she bent to pull the slip over her head one of the straps caught on a bobby pin—for an awkward moment she could not get the slip loose. Her face was hidden in the silk. Sonny moved to help her, but just as he did she tore it loose and looked up at him with a wry smile, as if to comment on her awkwardness. They took their undergarments off at the same time, both of them choked with embarrassment. Ruth glanced at Sonny's body, curious and a little frightened. He was two or three steps away from her and for a moment they did not know how to get to one another. Sonny was too self-conscious about his erection to move. Finally, with another wry smile, Ruth sat down on the bed and he sat down with her. When she lifted her arms to embrace him he saw the small scar on her breast. They fell over in an embrace but in a moment scrambled up again: the room was cold and they needed to be under the covers.

When they were covered and warm they felt better and kissed again with pleasure. They were amazed at the feel of one another's skin, but in a minute or two they began to be nervous again. It seemed to them they must have been lying there kissing for half an hour at least. Ruth touched her hand to Sonny's throat and chest now and then, but other than that she didn't move. He felt very unsure: it occurred to him that perhaps his experience was inadequate. There might be some way of doing it that was especially suitable to ladies, some way he knew nothing about.

Ruth had her eyes closed and was waiting trustfully for a beautiful thing to happen to her. She knew that Herman knew nothing about the beautiful thing, or that if he did he had no interest in giving it to her. But she supposed Sonny would know: she would only have to wait and receive it. His body was very warm against her. It was only when she opened her eyes and looked at him that she remembered how young he was and realized he didn't know what to do.

"It's all right," she said, opening her legs. Sonny gratefully moved above her, but there was another long moment of awkwardness when they tried to join. Sonny was not absolutely sure of the target, and when he found it Ruth could not at first accommodate him easily. When he moved she gasped and Sonny's face was so close to hers that he could not tell whether she felt pain or pleasure. She said nothing, so he kept moving—in a moment it became easier and pleasure made him move faster and more surely.

For Ruth the discomfort was only momentary, but even once it ceased she could not manage to cross over into pleasure. The bed had begun to squeak. As Sonny moved more confidently it squeaked louder, and Ruth could not help hearing it. She would never have imagined it could squeak so loudly. Soon the squeaking drove all hope of pleasure from her mind. The noise made her fearful that someone outside the house might hear it; anyone walking on the sidewalk in front of the house could hear it, she was sure.

In a few moments she was near panic: she was convinced that everyone in Thalia could hear the squeaking bedsprings. If all the cars stopped, if the housewives came to their doors and listened, they could all hear the squeaking bed and would know what she was doing. It was a horrible bed; she felt it had betrayed her. No one could receive a beautiful thing with such a squeaking going on beneath her. She tried to lay very still, but Sonny's movement went on, and the sound was constant. Finally she began to cry, and when the tears dripped down her cheeks and wet Sonny's neck he realized that something was wrong after all. He raised his head and saw that Ruth's eyes were flooded with tears. She was ashamed that she had stopped him and quickly hooked her arm over his neck so he wouldn't raise up and see her face again. Sonny felt she must want him to stop but his body didn't want to and in a moment he went on, hearing the springs only as a faint background to his pleasure. Soon he finished and lay still upon her.

As soon as the squeaking stopped Ruth felt better. She kept her arms around Sonny, holding him so he could not see her face and now and then wiping the tears out of her eyes with the back of one hand. Once Sonny became still it was very pleasant to have his body upon hers—he was so warm and young, almost like a child. She had always wanted a child more than anything, but Herman wouldn't hear of it—he didn't want the expense. On the rare occasions when he took his pleasure of her he was always careful to wear a condom, even though they made Ruth's bladder hurt. Having Sonny upon her was very different, and deeply pleasant. She ran her hands up and down his back, and when she felt composed again lifted her arms so he could raise his head.

"I'm sorry I cried," she said. "I guess I was just scared."

"Aw, he isn't going to come," Sonny said, no longer worried. "They're runnin' plays right now, I bet."

"No, not scared of that," Ruth said, touching his mouth softly with her fingers. "I was scared I could never do this, I guess. I wanted to be wholehearted about it, but I wasn't."

She was silent a moment. "Do you know what it means to be heartbroken?" she said. "It means your heart isn't whole, so you can't really do anything wholeheartedly."

Sonny wanted to leave, but he didn't think he should, quite so soon. Mrs. Popper was sad, but at least she seemed calm and she kept touching him softly with her hands. He kissed her lightly and her cheeks were warm; then he stretched and drew the covers back a little, so he could see more of her body. She was very slim and small-breasted, her arms a little too thin. When Ruth saw he was looking at her she grew frightened. She had never considered her body attractive, and she was afraid that if Sonny looked too long he would not want to be with her anymore. She turned on her side and curled toward him, her head on his thighs. Her shoulder bones stuck out, making her look even thinner. Sonny rubbed her back a minute and then got out of bed and quietly dressed. When he sat down on the edge of the bed to tell her good-bye she was on the verge of tears again.

"I was right the first time, wasn't I?" she said hopelessly. "I'm too old and ugly for a young man like you. I don't know how to do this anyway and maybe I'm too old to learn. I can't do anything without crying about it—how could you like me?"

"I like you," Sonny said awkwardly—actually he was not sure. All her crying upset him and made him nervous about himself, and she was certainly not as pretty as a movie star or as pretty as Jacy. Still, he did like her some. Since they hadn't got caught he had begun to feel elated about the whole thing. It was an adventure to have slept with somebody's wife. He didn't know if he would tell anybody or not, but it was sort of a feather in his cap, nonetheless.

Ruth sighed. "If you like me then you decide what to do about me," she said. "I'm not going to chase after you anymore. If you really like me you figure out how to come and see me—I sure don't want you to drive me to the doctor. I think right now you just like what you can do with me. That's fine, but now that you've found out women think you're good looking you'll probably want to go do it with somebody younger and prettier. I wouldn't blame you one bit."

Suddenly she wanted him to leave. She had become embarrassed about her body and didn't want him to see her naked anymore. She stayed curled up on the bed, her breasts and loins hidden from him.

"Track starts pretty soon," Sonny said. "I just won't go out. I can sneak up the alley and in the back door."

He sounded like he really wanted to, and Ruth changed back to hoping. What if he did only want her for sex? It was more than anyone else had ever wanted her for. Suddenly she felt like doing something a little wanton and she sat up and kissed him, her naked breasts against his shirt. Sonny liked that, and when he left he looked back through the doorway and saw her, still naked, bending over the bed to strip away the sheets. It would be well worth giving up track to come and see her, even though the coach would rage and storm at losing his only decent hurdler.

DON JUAN FROM THE PROVINCE

Stendhal

In this selection from Stendhal's *The Red and the Black,* we find the tutor of Madame de Rênal's children becoming tutored himself—in the art of seduction. Julien's tentative lovemaking wavers between the clumsy, impulsive blunderings of a country bumpkin and the shrewd maneuvering of a Napoleonic general, the latter contrived to disguise the former. As in the case of the protagonist in *Of Human Bondage,* Julien's fear of appearing inadequate causes the role of seducer to become a horrible burden for him. So great is his insecurity that he commits his plan for seduction to writing, and thus contemplates arousing "terrible remorse and everlasting ridicule if he deviated from the model he had set up for himself." The irony of the passage is that Julien's awkward scheming serves only to alienate Madame de Rênal, whereas she responded readily to his natural candor and charm. Julien's rigid sense of form so stifles the spontaneity of their relationship that neither enjoys the spoils of conquest.

A girl of sixteen had a rosy complexion, and she put on rouge.

—Polidori

As for Julien, Fouqué's offer had destroyed all his happiness; he was unable to decide on any course of action.

"Alas, I may be lacking in character," he thought. "I'd have been a bad soldier for Napoleon. But," he added, "my little intrigue with the lady of the house will at least distract me for a while."

Fortunately for him, even in this inconsequential train of thought his innermost feelings bore little relation to the flippancy of his tone. He was afraid of Madame de Rênal because of her pretty dress. That dress was, in his eyes, the advance guard of Paris. His pride was determined to leave nothing to chance or the inspiration of the moment. Using what he had learned from Fouqué's confessions and the little he had read about love in the Bible, he made highly detailed plans for his campaign. Since he was filled with anxiety, although he did not admit it to himself, he set down his plan in writing.

The next morning in the drawing room, Madame de Rênal was alone with him for a moment.

"Don't you have another name besides Julien?" she asked him.

Our hero did not know what answer to give to such a flattering question. This occurrence had not been foreseen in his plan. If he had not been so foolish as to make a plan, his quick mind would have served him well, and his surprise would only have made him more perceptive.

He behaved awkwardly, and believed himself to be more awkward than he really was. Madame de Rênal quickly forgave him for it. She saw it as the effect of a charming candor. And candor was the one thing she had found lacking in the young man whom everyone regarded as so brilliant.

"I don't trust your little tutor at all," Madame Derville had said to her several times. "It seems to me that he's always thinking and that he never does anything without a reason. He's crafty."

Julien was deeply humiliated by the misfortune of not having known what to reply to Madame de Rênal. "A man like me owes it to himself to make up for that failure," he thought, and, seizing the moment when they were going from one room to another, he felt it his duty to give her a kiss.

Nothing could have been less natural, less pleasant for both of them; and nothing could have been more imprudent. They just missed being seen. She thought he had gone mad. She was frightened and still more offended. His foolish behavior reminded her of Monsieur Valenod.

"What would happen to me," she asked herself, "if I were alone with him?" All her virtue returned, because her love was fading. She arranged to have one of her children always with her.

It was a tiresome day for Julien; he spent the whole of it clumsily carrying out his plan of seduction. Not once did he look at Madame de Rênal without a definite reason; however, he was not so foolish as to be unaware that he was not succeeding in even being pleasant, much less seductive.

Madame de Rênal could not get over her surprise at finding him so awkward and at the same time so bold. "It's the shyness of an intelligent man in love!" she finally said to herself with inexpressible joy. "Can it be possible that my rival has never loved him?"

After lunch, she went back into the drawing room to receive a visit from Monsieur Charcot de Maugiron, the subprefect. She began to work at a high little tapestry frame. Madame Derville was seated beside her. It was in this situation, and in the full light of day, that our hero saw fit to move his boot forward and press the pretty foot of Madame de Rênal, whose openwork stockings and attractive little Parisian shoes were obviously attracting the gaze of the gallant subprefect.

Madame de Rênal was horrified; she dropped her scissors, her ball of wool and her needles, and Julien's movement could have passed for a clumsy attempt to catch the scissors when he saw them fall. Fortunately these little scissors, made of English steel, broke when they struck the floor, and she profusely expressed her regret that he had not been sitting closer to her.

"You saw them falling before I did," she said, "so you could have caught them; but instead of that, your zeal succeeded only in giving me a violent kick."

All this deceived the sub-prefect, but not Madame Derville. "That handsome young man has a stupid way of going about things," she thought. The worldly wisdom of a provincial capital does not forgive mistakes of this kind.

Madame de Rênal found an opportunity to say to Julien, "I order you to be careful."

He realized his awkward blunder and it annoyed him. For a long time he debated with himself as to whether or not he ought to take offense at the words, "I order you." He was foolish enough to think, "She could say to me, 'I order you,' if it were a question of something to do with the children's education; but in responding to my love she should assume equality. It's impossible to love without equality." And he became lost in commonplace reflections on equality. He angrily repeated to himself the line from Corneille which Madame Derville had taught him a few days earlier: "Love creates equalities, it does not seek them."

Julien, stubbornly determined to play the part of a Don Juan even though he had never had a mistress in his life, behaved like an utter fool for the rest of the day. He had only one sensible thought: annoyed with himself and with Madame de Rênal, he was alarmed at the approach of evening, when he would be seated in the garden beside her in the dark. He told Monsieur de Rênal he was going to Verrières to see Father Chélan; he left after dinner and did not return until late that night.

In Verrières he found Father Chélan preparing to move out of his house; he had just been dismissed at last, and he was to be replaced by Father Maslon. Julien helped the kindly priest, and he conceived the idea of writing Fouqué a letter telling him that, while the irresistible vocation he felt for the sacred ministry had at first prevented him from accepting his generous offer, he had just seen such an example of injustice that it might be better for his salvation if he did not take holy orders.

Julien congratulated himself on his shrewdness in taking advantage of Father Chélan's dismissal to leave a door open for his return to business if, in his mind, dreary prudence should ever prevail over heroism.

If Julien had actually possessed a little of the shrewdness he so gratuitously attributed to himself, he might have congratulated himself the next day on the effect produced by his trip to Verrières. His absence had caused his blunders to be forgotten. He was again sullen all day. Toward evening a ridiculous idea came to him and, with unusual boldness, he communicated it to Madame de Rênal. They had scarcely sat down in the garden when, without waiting for adequate darkness, he put his lips to her ear and, at the risk of compromising her terribly, said to her, "Madame, tonight at two o'clock I will come to your room; there's something I must tell you."

He was trembling for fear his request might be granted; the role of a seducer was such a horrible burden for him that if he could have followed his inclination he would have withdrawn to his room for several days and never seen the two ladies again. He realized that, by his clever tactics of the preceding day, he had destroyed all the progress he had made two days before, and he was at his wits' end.

Madame de Rênal replied with genuine and by no means exaggerated indignation to the insolent declaration he had dared to make to her. He thought he could detect a note of scorn in her brief answer. He was certain that this answer, uttered in a very low tone, contained the words, "You ought to be ashamed!" On the pretext of having something to say to the children, he went off to their room.

When he returned, he sat down beside Madame Derville, very far from Madame de Rênal, thus eliminating all possibility of taking her hand. The conversation was serious and he acquitted himself quite well, except for a few moments of silence during which he racked his brain. "Why can't I think of some clever maneuver," he said to himself, "that will force her to show me those unmistakable signs of affection that made me think she was mine three days ago?"

He was extremely disconcerted by the almost hopeless situation in which he had placed himself. Nothing, however, would have embarrassed him as much as success.

When they separated at midnight, his pessimism convinced him that he had incurred Madame Derville's contempt and that Madame de Rênal's opinion of him was scarcely any better.

Feeling intensely irritated and deeply humiliated, he was unable to sleep. He was a thousand leagues away from any idea of giving up all pretense, all plans, and living with Madame de Rênal from day to day, contenting himself like a child with the happiness each day would bring. He exhausted his brain in devising shrewd maneuvers which he found absurd a moment later; in short, he was utterly miserable when the clock of the château struck two.

This sound aroused him as the crowing of the cock aroused Saint Peter. He knew that it was now time for him to carry out the most difficult undertaking of all. He had given no further thought to his insolent proposal from the time he had made it—it had been so badly received!

"I told her I'd come to her room at two o'clock," he said to himself as he stood up. "I may be inexperienced and crude, which is only natural for a peasant's son—Madame Derville has made that quite plain to me—but at least I won't be weak."

Julien was right to praise his own courage: he had never set himself a more painful task. When he opened his door he began to tremble so violently that his knees buckled and he was forced to lean against the wall.

He was in his stocking feet. He went to listen at Monsieur de Rênal's door and heard him snoring. He was bitterly disappointed. He no longer had any excuse for not going to her room. But what in the name of God would he do there? He had no plan, and even if he had had one, he was so overwrought that he would have been incapable of following it.

Finally, suffering a thousand times more intensely than if he had been going to his death, he entered the little corridor leading to

Madame de Rênal's room. He opened the door with a trembling hand, making a fearful noise in doing so.

There was a light in the room: a night lamp was burning below the mantelpiece; he had not expected this new mishap. When she saw him enter, Madame de Rênal quickly leapt out of bed. "Wretch!" she cried. There was a moment of disorder. Julien forgot his vain plans and became his natural self again; not to please such a charming woman appeared to him the greatest of misfortunes. His only reply to her reproaches was to throw himself at her feet and embrace her knees. As she spoke to him with extreme harshness, he burst into tears.

When he left her bedroom a few hours later, one could have said, in the language of novels, that he had nothing more to desire. He was indebted to the love he inspired, and to the unexpected effect produced on him by her seductive charms, for a victory to which all his awkward scheming would never have led him.

But, a victim of his grotesque pride even during the sweetest moments, he was still intent on playing the part of a man accustomed to subjugating women: he made incredibly concentrated efforts to destroy his natural charm. Instead of being attentive to the raptures he aroused, and to the remorse which made them more keenly felt, he constantly had the idea of *duty* before his eyes. He was afraid of terrible remorse and everlasting ridicule if he deviated from the ideal model he had set up for himself. In a word, what made Julien a superior person was precisely what prevented him from enjoying the happiness that lay at his feet. He was like a girl of sixteen who has a charming complexion and is foolish enough to put on rouge before going to a ball.

Mortally frightened by Julien's sudden appearance, Madame de Rênal was soon in the grip of cruel apprehensions. She was deeply moved by his tears and despair.

Even when she had nothing left to refuse him, she pushed him away from her with genuine indignation, then threw herself in his arms a moment later. There was no apparent purpose in this behavior. She believed herself to be damned without hope of remission, and she tried to shut out the vision of hell by showering Julien with ardent caresses. In short, nothing would have been lacking in our hero's happiness, not even the passionate responsiveness of the woman he had just seduced, if he had been capable of enjoying it. His departure ended neither her raptures, which took possession of her against her will, nor her struggles with the remorse that was piercing her heart.

"My God! Is this all there is to being happy, to being loved?" Such was Julien's first thought when he returned to his room. He was in that state of amazement and turbulent uneasiness into which a man falls when he has just obtained something he has desired for a long time: he has grown accustomed to desiring, but he no longer finds anything to desire and he has not yet acquired any memories. Like a soldier returning from a parade, Julien was attentively engaged in reviewing all the details of his conduct. "Did I fail in anything I owe to myself?" he thought. "Did I play my part well?"

And what part was he playing? That of a man accustomed to brilliant success with women.

THE SENIOR OUTING

Larry McMurtry

The senior outing was probably one of America's unspoken rituals of the 1940s and 1950s—a means of initiating thousands of young people from rural areas and small towns into the ways of the big city folk. The outing encouraged a break from small town mores, caused youth to experiment, to look at things differently, to behave differently toward each other. Duane and Jacy are no exception. The trip from Thalia, Texas, to San Francisco is filled with anticipation for these two teenagers. They "were full of secret plans about the Thing they were going to do." Again, the reality falls short of the ideal—a pattern which, concerning initial sexual experiences, seems to recur with predictable regularity. The cold, mechanical way in which Jacy submits to Duane is worth noting. The character of Jacy—her preoccupation with form rather than substance, her desire to make things "look good," her absolute inability to tolerate Duane's temporary inadequacy—suggests the archetypal bitch goddess of American womanhood. The character of Duane is equally curious, but in a different way. Driven by the need to prove his adequacy, Duane finally manages to have his moment of sexual satisfaction with Jacy. The act itself, as in many of the other selections, results in feelings quite opposite to those that were anticipated. For Duane, it is more like the winning of a footrace. For Jacy, it is a source of anger. "She didn't want to touch him again, ever, and it angered her to think that she would have to go on pretending to be his sweetheart for the rest of the trip."

They got to San Francisco in the middle of the night and checked into an expensive cheap motel on Van Ness Avenue, not far from the bay. Duane and Jacy were full of secret plans about the Thing they were going to do, and all the boys were itching to go bowling or to find whores. The first day there the room mothers kept them all herded together and saw to it that they rode a cable car, visited the Top of the Mark, and went across the Golden Gate bridge. All the Californians looked at them as if they were freaks, whereas it seemed to the kids it was the other way around. The room mothers were scandalized by the number of bars in the city and kept everyone in a tight group to protect them against lurking perverts.

The second day was unscheduled and most of the boys spent it on Market Street, looking at dirty magazines and talking to girls and sailors in the cheap sidewalk lunch counters. Sonny and three other boys wandered into a bar between Market and Mission and were met by a tall black-headed girl named Gloria who offered to let them take pictures of her naked. The bar itself was plastered with pictures of Gloria naked, a great inducement to photography. Unfortunately her fee for the privilege was twenty dollars and none of the boys could afford it.

The major event of the trip occurred on the afternoon of the second day in San Francisco when Jacy finally allowed Duane to seduce her. The girls were all supposed to accompany the room mothers to the De Young Museum that afternoon, but Jacy cleverly got out of it. She was rooming with an obliging little girl named Winnie Snips, and she got Winnie to tell the room mothers that she had taken to her bed with menstrual cramps. No one ever doubted the word of Winnie Snips. She was valedictorian, and just unpopular enough that she was glad to do anything anyone wanted of her.

After the girls and the room mothers left, Sonny stationed himself in the lobby of the motel so he could give the alarm if the party got back early. It was an ugly lobby full of postcard racks and it depressed him a little to sit in it. The only senior who bothered with postcards was Charlene Duggs who sent about a dozen a day to an airman boy friend of hers in Wichita Falls. She wanted everyone to know how much in love she was, but she didn't have much to say and just wrote "Gee, I miss you, Love and kisses, Charlene" on every card. When Sonny thought about Jacy he got even more depressed, but Duane was his friend and a scheme of such daring had to be supported.

As it turned out, Sonny's depression was nothing at all compared to the one Duane had to cope with in the seduction chamber upstairs.

The glorious moment had arrived, and was going to be just perfect: they could even see the bay and a part of Alcatraz through the window. "I love you," Duane said, as soon as they had kissed a few times. "I love you too," Jacy said, breathing heavily. It was the way things were done. Then she let Duane take absolutely all her clothes off, something she had never done before. For some reason, being naked with him was different than being naked around a bunch of Wichita kids. She caught him looking right at the place between her legs, and that seemed rather discourteous. Still, there was no backing out, so she stretched out on the bed while Duane undressed. He had been in a state of anticipatory erection for at least half of the 1,800-mile drive, and could hardly wait to get his socks off. They kissed again for a moment, but both supposed speed to be of the essence and Duane soon rolled on top. Jacy sucked in her breath, preparing to be painfully devirginized. For a moment or two she did feel something that was hard and slightly painful, but it wasn't nearly as painful as she had expected it to be and in a moment it ceased to be hard at all and became flexible and rather wiggly. It certainly wasn't hurting her, but it wasn't going in, either. It sort of tickled, and kept sliding off into her pubic hair. Curiosity got the better of her and she opened her eyes. Duane had a very strange look on his face. He was horrified at himself, unable to believe his member should betray him—not then, of all times.

"What's wrong, honey?" Jacy asked, wiggling slightly. She couldn't stand to be tickled.

"Um," Duane said, a little choked. "I don't know."

He held himself above her, embarrassed to death but hoping beyond hope that his body would come to its senses and enable him to go on. He hoped for two or three long minutes, while Jacy offered her intimate of intimates, but his body continued to register complete indifference. Duane didn't have the faintest idea what to do: no emergency had ever been more unlooked for.

After a time Jacy felt a rising sense of exasperation.

"Well get off a minute," she said. "You might get tired and fall on me."

Duane complied, too disgraced to venture speech. He sat hopelessly on the edge of the bed, looking out at the bay. Jacy sat up and shrugged her hair back across her shoulders. Obviously they were faced with a crisis. The situation had to be salvaged or they would be the laughing stock of the class. Suddenly she felt furious with Duane. She looked with vexation at the offending organ.

"It was Mexico," she said. "I hate you. No tellin' what you got down there. I don't know why I ever went with you."

"I don't know what happened," Duane said glumly. He got up and crept reluctantly back into his clothes, but Jacy stalked about the room, indignantly naked and not giving a damn.

"What'll we say," she said. "The whole class knows what we were going to do. I just want to cry. I think you're the meanest boy I ever saw and my mother was so right about you."

"I don't know what happened," Duane said again. He really didn't. He started for the door but Jacy stopped him.

"Don't go out there yet," she said. "We haven't had time to do it—Sonny would know. I don't want one soul to know."

Duane sat back down on the bed and Jacy went into the bathroom and cried a few real tears of anger. It seemed to her Duane had been a monster of thoughtlessness to put her in such a position. She didn't want to touch him again, ever, and it angered her to think she would have to go on pretending to be his sweetheart for the rest of the trip. It would never do to let the class think they had broken up over sex. In fact, she would have to be even more loving with him in public, so everyone would think they were having a warm, meaningful affair.

When she thought they had been in the room long enough she went out and told Duane to leave.

"You better not tell one soul, either," she said. "You just pretend it was wonderful. And wear your slacks when we go to supper tonight—I think we're going someplace nice."

She stood naked, hands on hips, conscious that her nudity embarrassed Duane a little, and thoroughly pleased that it did.

"Well, I'm sorry," he said again. "I don't know what happened."

"If you say that one more time I'll bite you," Jacy said.

When Winnie Snips and the other girls piled into the room an hour later, pale with curiosity, Jacy was sitting in a well-rumpled bed with only her pajama tops on, staring out at the bay. The evening fog was coming in.

"Oh, gee," Winnie said. "Tell us about it Jacy. What happened?"

Jacy looked languorously around at them, calm, replete, a little wasted even.

"I just can't describe it," she said. "I just can't describe it in words."

The very next day, to Duane's immense relief, the seduction happened after all. Jacy insisted he take her for a walk to show everyone how much they wanted to be alone, and while they were walking down Geary Street, holding hands in case anyone from the class should see them, Duane suddenly felt himself return. They were just outside a cheap hotel, and without hesitation he seized his chance.

"Come on," he said. He had Jacy in the lobby of the hotel before she even knew what he meant. An old lady in a blue-flowered silk bathrobe registered them without comment and took five dollars from Duane. In the creaky cage of an elevator he kissed Jacy hungrily and fondled her breast, conscious that all was still well below. Jacy was skeptical and didn't return the kiss, but there *was* something rather adventurous about being fondled in an elevator—Winnie Snips would faint if she heard of such a thing.

Their room was tiny, with green walls, an old fashioned bed, and a narrow window that looked across Geary Street to a one-story nightclub with a dead neon sign outside. Duane wasted absolutely no time—he was taking no chances with himself. He was out of his clothes by the time the door closed, and he tugged Jacy toward the bed, pulling rudely at her skirt. She shrugged loose and went to the window to undress at her own pace.

"If you can't wait you can jump out this window," she said. "I don't think it will work anyway."

Duane was not certain it would either, and waited nervously. The room was chill and Jacy had goose bumps on her breasts. As she lay down she looked at Duane casually—men were certainly strange. All she really expected was something tickly, but Duane surprised her horribly. He didn't tickle a bit, but instead he did something really painful. At first she was too startled to move, and then she yelled out loud. Someone in an adjoining room kicked the wall indignantly. "Quit, quit," she said—it was intolerable. Duane was much too thrilled to quit, but fortunately he didn't take long. Jacy was at her wit's end as it was.

She got gingerly out of bed, meaning to take a hot bath, and discovered that the little room didn't even have a bathroom in it, just a lavatory. "There must be one down the hall someplace," Duane said, but she wouldn't let him go look for it. She felt strange and wanted to leave. All the way back to the motel she kept glancing over her shoulder, expecting to see a trail of blood on the sidewalk behind her. Duane was walking happily along, infuriatingly proud of himself.

"Oh, quit prissing," Jacy said. "You needn't think I'm going to take you back just because of that. I don't think you did it right, anyway."

"Sure I did," Duane said, but he wasn't really positive, and he brooded about it during the remainder of the trip. They did it twice more, once in the motel in San Francisco and once in Flagstaff, Arizona, on the way home. Duane was confident he was doing it right, but for some reason Jacy didn't swoon with bliss. She only allowed it twice more because she thought Bobby Sheen would like it if she had a little more experience. The whole business was far from delightful, but she supposed that was probably because Duane was a roughneck. In Flagstaff it went on much too long and she got exasperated and told him off once and for all.

"You never will learn," she said. "I don't know why I went with you so long. I guess we have to keep on being sweethearts until we get home, but that's gonna be the end of it. We'll just have to think of something big to break up over."

Duane just couldn't understand it: he was more dejected and more in love than he ever had been. Jacy was bending over to slip her small breasts back into their brassiere cups; she had never looked more lovely, and he could not believe she was serious about breaking up. He tried to talk her out of it, but she went over to the motel dressing table and combed her hair thoroughly, looking at herself in the mirror and paying absolutely no attention to him.

The rest of the way home, across Arizona, New Mexico, Texas, he tried to think of ways to make her realize that they had to stay together. He was sure her disaffection would only be temporary. Jacy was thinking how glad she would be to get home. She had even decided there was no point in making a big production of breaking up: she was sick and tired of the seniors. As an audience they were not worth bothering about. When the bus finally pulled into Thalia late one June afternoon she didn't so much as tell Duane good-bye. She was tired and went right over to her parents' Cadillac while her father got her bags. Lois was watching her shrewdly.

"I see you got enough of him," she said quietly. "That's that."

"I'm just not interested in saying one word about it, if you don't mind," Jacy said.

Watching them drive away, Duane felt a little sick at his stomach. He realized Jacy had meant what she said: she was really done with him. It was very confusing to him because he had always thought you were supposed to get whoever you really loved. That was the way it worked in movies. It was all he could do to carry his suitcase to the pickup.

WAIT TO SEE IF IT'S A SURE THING, HONEY

Francie Schwartz

The following selection is important to this anthology for several reasons. It portrays the liberated consciousness of the contemporary female, and represents the writer's new freedom to treat sexual themes in a direct and candid manner. The thesis of this piece might well serve as the guiding credo for the Women's Liberation Movement: "I didn't want to be a housewife, and he wanted nothing more of me." Quite the opposite of the heroine, Alice Hindman, in Sherwood Anderson's "Adventure," who feels bound forever to her mate through the act of physical love, the narrator here enacts open contempt for wifely subordination, self-sacrifice and unquestioning fidelity. So strong, in fact, is her belief that subjugation to an unappreciative husband will impede her passionate quest for "independence, education, and youth," that she even rejects her unborn child. The blunt language of the story may shock and offend; yet it is a central part of the narrator's rebellion against the kind of romantic clichés with which such experiences are usually dealt. The narrator's tone may be cold and impersonal at times, and her attention to mundane practicalities emotionally sterile, but better this than the creation of false or ideal impressions of the significance of physical love through sentimental or euphemistic language. Perhaps the narrator's personal disillusionment causes her to over-react: to render in somewhat mechanical and trivial terms what, under normal circumstances, would be deeply intimate and fulfilling. Or perhaps the larger truth is that which is raised through the collective impact of this anthology: that meaning lies less in the act itself than in our perception of it.

I was sitting with a girlfriend neighbor in the recreation hall of the temple after a confirmation service, and when he walked in, though he was a good fifty feet away, I couldn't help staring. He was tall and lean, with olive brown skin and almond shaped eyes like an Arab prince.

"Who's that?" I whispered.

"Forget it, kid," replied Barbie. "That's Leon, and he's a *playboy*, and he's too old for you and you'll never get him anyway." I straightened up and leaning close to her ear said, "I've got news for you. I'm going to *marry* him."

She looked at me as if I were crazy and then shrugged, "Get outta my nose."

I watched him move through the crowd of kids, winking and flirting. He was obviously very popular with the girls. He danced close with a couple of them, and they both had the same starry-eyed look that you see in teenage movies and *Seventeen* magazine. It was disgusting. I wanted to run away to my room to plan my attack.

I knew that part of the secret of getting a boy to like you involved pretending you weren't interested. I also knew you had to wear mascara and not have any pimples. I wrote down clever things to say. I schemed. I was as patient as a nun. I even wrote his name in neat columns on notebook paper until I'd written it ten thousand times.

The problem was he was in an older group at the Temple, so I needed a liaison, and Barbie did fine, telling him hello from me every week for three months. Once I got to speak with him on the phone, but he didn't remember who I was. Shit! I wanted to cry.

We met finally at a Temple "youth group" party. I had spent an hour putting on eyeliner, mascara and lipstick. I wore all white, and glistened with anticipation. We danced together and afterwards he drove me home, saying, "See you next week."

We began to date, once a week. Very quickly he taught me how to kiss and we became a couple. I gave him a gold I.D. bracelet for his sixteenth birthday, and had it engraved with our secret expression: "G-R-R-R-R."

On the 4th of July we doubled with his best friend and the girl who had been chasing him until I got him. We became friends and made a foursome. Drive-in movies, beach parties, making out in the hills. Leon and Francie and Bill and Judy. Without pot or booze or much money we managed to have fun.

Marriage seemed so natural. I don't think I can remember him asking me formally; it was understood. We decided to wait until we were married before going "all the way" but what we did while we waited didn't satisfy either of us. We'd sit in the car, parked near my parent's house, rolling back and forth over each other. I would not be content giving less than he, so each time his strong brown hands came a little closer to the ultimate destination in some untouched zone, I'd let go just a little more.

We wanted to "go all the way" but we couldn't get married, so we decided to sanctify the act with a ceremony of our own.

We married ourselves, soberly and intensely, one night in February on a beach at the L.A. County Line. We drove in silence, a Bible and a prayer book lying between us on the seat. Tucked inside the Holy Book was a contract Leon had composed himself, with my approval, and a cigar band to be used as the ring.

When we arrived we climbed down the rocky cliff to the beach and laid out our ritual objects of love. We recited the words of the contract and the sensual verses of Solomon. We lay down together, closer than before, more to keep warm than for passion's sake, touching the tears on each other's cheeks.

"My wife," Leon sighed to me.

"My husband," I replied, loving the sound of it, and loving him with fierce intensity.

There was nothing more to say, and we walked slowly back to the car, puzzled at our own seriousness.

We wanted to sleep in each other's arms and wake next to each other. That was impossible, of course, because he had to get back to his parent's house and I had to get back to mine. So the moment we had been waiting for didn't actually arrive until months later in the summer. My mother and father were sleeping in their part of the house, and Leon and I were left alone.

His skin felt warm from the beach sun.

"I want to touch you all over. Can we?"

"I'm afraid."

"I am too," I admitted, "but I want you so much I'll go mad if I can't feel all of you next to me."

"Please be careful."

There was only a sigh when I pressed by body next to his, and the electricity of skin touching skin for the first time. My belly felt the pressure of his enormous erection and my breasts swelled against the strength of his chest. I had to touch more of him, so without prompting, I moved closer and guided his virgin penis between my thighs. Before either of us could stop we were in a different realm: I gave my love a cherry in about thirty seconds.

It was the most gorgeous feeling I could imagine, having my insides full of that strength, even if it was for less than a minute.

We hardly had time to talk about it, because both of us were worried about staining my mother's new couch. We ran to the kitchen for a dishtowel and some soap and hurried back looking for the tiny red rose.

While we were cleaning up I had jumped into my panties and they too were stained, so we put them in a paper sack for him to throw out on his way home.

Six months before we were legally married, Leon told me I wasn't satisfying him. I was terrified of losing him and this was my first reminder that the world is run by the ones with penises. Hadn't I "gone all the way"?

We took Tuesday afternoons off from school for fucking, although I insisted that we call it making love. It was in his mother's musty old beach house in Santa Monica.

After the first time, Leon lay with his face turned away from me, staring out at the window. I panicked, thinking I had failed to satisfy him again, and whispered, "Forget the rubbers this time," caressing him until he was bigger and harder than ever before. He thrust into me silently and with determination, until finally we forgot where each left off and the other began.

We conceived a child, and both of us knew it. I felt flooded and alive, my womb bathed in his potent life. Neither of us dared speak about it until much later, when it began to screw up our plans. All I knew is that I had given him what he wanted, regardless of my own future.

I had just graduated from high school when my breasts began to show the first signs of pregnancy. I wanted to learn a profession and started art courses at the Chouinard Institute in February, 1962.

That was the dream-like year when we all felt protected by a gorgeous President who was as handsome as a movie star. There didn't seem to be any reason why everything should not turn out all right.

Leon had been at the school for two years and had been awarded a working scholarship, which meant he spent extra hours designing and mounting exhibitions for the school's tiny lobby. The guy who'd won it the year before had broken up with his wife because he was never home.

The first thing that Leon said when I hinted that I might be pregnant was, "I've got to refuse the scholarship."

"Please wait and see if it's a sure thing, honey. It might just be a late period. You know how irregular I am and my mother had two miscarriages when she was young."

"But if I accept and then you have the baby, I'll have to drop out and get a night job. *Then* how would the school feel about me? They would never take me back again."

"Look, if I'm going to have a baby, that doesn't mean you have to screw up your education. I can drop out, and work now, and save up some money, and then . . ."

"No, Francie, you aren't going to work. You're going to be my wife, and have my children, and that's all that matters. I'll figure something out. But I can't take the scholarship. You know what happened to Jim and his wife last year. I can't take that chance."

"Dummy, it's not going to happen to us. I love you."

"I love you, too, but please don't think about taking a job. You should stay in school as long as possible. Just don't take sculpture or anything heavy like that."

I was getting angry. "I don't even know for sure I'm pregnant! Look, we'll go to the doctor next week. The wedding is only two months away. Let me worry about it, and you just take that scholarship. You're not dropping out, and that's that."

"We'll see."

We did see. The doctor made Leon and my mother wait outside, while he draped a sheet over my knees and stuck two rubber-gloved fingers up my vagina. He felt the cervix, soft and enlarged, and without hesitation said, "Yup, for sure."

I had to be alone for a few minutes to cry by myself, and so the doctor left me with my feet in the stirrups to wonder what was going to happen. I was pregnant after all. I would never finish college, never become anybody important. I'd end up just like my mother, cleaning the house all day. I'd be subjugating myself to a husband who would never understand what I'd given up.

When Leon came into the room and kissed my belly, things seemed better. I felt fulfilled and pleased with myself. My mother reeked with understanding, even though she was crying.

I knew I couldn't tell my father, but I hadn't expected the reaction of Leon's parents. It was out of a soap opera. They were sitting in their strange living room when we arrived to see them, looking haggard but straining to look relaxed. They kissed and hugged me and I could see that Leon's mother was ready to cry at the slightest opportunity. She wanted us to have a "quiet little civil ceremony," on account of the child.

"You have to think of the boy," her husband added.

When I said I still wanted a wedding I'd dreamed of for three years, his mother broke down and shouted, "No, you can't do this to us. The shame . . ."

Leon looked at me, totally helpless. He said nothing. As far as his parents were concerned he had absolutely no guts.

"Let's get out of here, Leon," I said, and he got up and followed me silently out. I felt like hitting him.

The whole fight was absurd, and useless, because a few weeks later the baby died. My father sat beside me on the bed as I lay there in pain, bleeding onto the sheets. "Maybe it's good that this is happening. You've learned a lesson," he said. There was no time to figure out that statement, because I was screaming in pain.

I was driven to the hospital where a doctor knocked me out. When I awoke, filled with sterile packing, I felt emptier than I had ever felt in my life. They said it would have been a little boy. I wondered whether I hadn't secretly wished to lose him, so I could get back my independence, my education, my youth.

The woman in the bed next to mine was in to have her fourth child. She looked at me with a leer.

"You ever lost a kid before, honey?"

"No, this is the first."

"I bet you're not even married. Hell, you'll have another. Don't worry."

"I'm not."

I was feeling totally wasted by the loss of the baby and she was reassuring me that I'd have another. I never wanted to fuck again. I wanted to be little and pure and free.

Leon and his parents filed through the room, expressed their sympathies and regrets, and showered me with flowers and apologies for the upset they had created. They felt guilty, I suppose. But I didn't care. As the days went by, and I looked forward to my flat tummy coming back, and my white-veiled wedding, I smirked inwardly at the thought of my restored freedom. And I began to doubt my husband-to-be. I didn't want to be a housewife, and he wanted nothing more of me.

The wedding was charming, middle-class and Jewish. We were given hundreds of gifts.

I remember noticing through my triple veil that my father was crying and that my mother wasn't.

We spent two days honeymooning in San Francisco. At night we made love, trying to get back the freshness that had gone with the baby. All we could celebrate was that at last, we were *sleeping* together, and the magic of that wore off when we returned to L.A. for summer school.

At school I felt older and wiser. Chouinard was definitely funky. It had a WPA facade, paint spattered floors and four hundred students up to their elbows in paint, plaster or charcoal. I loved every minute. In the morning I studied Dada, Expressionism, the Renaissance, the Archaic Greek snake goddesses. We studied Nietzsche, Marx, Plato and Sartre in philosophy, Shaw and Shakespeare in literature. At lunch we used to play bridge on the patio, do research in the tiny library and bitch about the grading system. There were no fraternities, no athletics and no political groups. Just the free exploration of creativity in all its exhilarating forms. Everything was very loose.

Leon was busy with his work and I soon discovered the surprising truth about him: he was pretty dull. He didn't see many people, but he didn't seem to mind whether or not I did. He still thought I was the little girl he'd picked up in the Temple Youth Group.

Then something political happened, and I found myself on the opposite side from my husband. The Board of Trustees at Chouinard, backed by the Disney Foundation, had fired a "radical" drawing and print instructor. The man had been busted by the police for a La Cienega exhibit of erotic drawings of his Japanese wife, and now he'd been victimized at the school.

He didn't fit in with the Disney plan for a new super-art-university in the hills outside of L.A. They didn't want to spoil the image they were planning to create with their millions. They began to cut down hard on the variety of departments at the school. There would be no Advertising or Illustration or Fashion or Design at their superschool.

They wanted the school to produce chic art-gallery bullshit. I demonstrated in the lobby with a bunch of students protesting the policy and the firings. We sat on the floor and drew until CBS News showed up, and then debated angrily with the administrators.

Leon thought I was absurd to sign the petitions and go to the meetings. He was totally absorbed in the Design Lab and the working scholarship.

Nights at home, I'd cook dinner, do dishes, nap, then work until midnight while he slept on the balcony he'd built. We'd moved out of a tiny apartment in the hills and were living in a store. It was an immense womb, with a tiny window in front, and a frosted one in back. He'd put in plumbing and straw matting on the floor, and we had the furniture my parents had given us when they moved back to Allentown. My father's transfer meant more money for the whole family, and gave my sister, Harrie, a chance to start college and become the center of attention for a change.

I was suddenly alone, living two lives, one for my husband, one for myself. I found myself wondering if it had ever been this way for my mother.

I suppose part of the reason it was so bad at home was that Leon refused to talk about anything controversial. Even politics.

If I was under pressure, he's show me his answer and expect me to accept it blindly. If I disputed the peaceful surface of our life, he'd go for a long walk, not returning until I was too exhausted to even try to talk, much less fight.

His answer to the problem was simple and obscene. "Let's make love every night for the next month," he said, as if he were prescribing a pill.

"Are you serious? Do you think that's going to solve our problem?"

"It's better than fighting. Non-verbal communication is better."

I was furious and insulted. "No, you're wrong. I need to talk things out, even if we fight. We can't cover it up with orgasms. It's not going to work, and I think it's phony."

He went for a walk.

He complained about my cooking.

He complained that I didn't call his mother enough.

He complained that he didn't like my father's advice about insurance.

He complained that I resented him helping me with my design homework.

He was going sour, and I didn't care. There had to be something better than this drudgery.

I gave a party, and he hated every minute of it.

I learned to play chess, and he wouldn't play with me.

I tried to get along with his mother, but every time she came over, she brought sickening bags of Jewish food, and kept commenting how thin her son looked.

How could I let him cover his beautiful chin with that beard? Didn't I realize he was beginning to look like a beatnik?

I didn't know what to do. Was it my fault? Was I supposed to stop growing, stop exploring for my husband's sake? Was I wrong to care more about my work than whether or not dinner was the way Leon wanted it?

I began looking for an escape.

FOUR
Guilt

I went to the Garden of Love,
And saw what I never had seen:
A Chapel was built in the midst,
Where I used to play on the green.

And the gates of this Chapel were shut,
And "Thou shalt not" writ over the door:
So I turned to the Garden of Love
That so many sweet flowers bore;

And I saw it was filled with graves,
And tomb-stones where flowers should be;
And Priests in black gowns were walking their rounds,
And binding with briars my joys and desires.

THE GARDEN OF LOVE
William Blake

ADVENTURE

Sherwood Anderson

Winesburg, Ohio, from which this story is taken, is perhaps the most famous study of inhibition and abnormal relationships in all of American fiction. Helping lead the fight against narrow, puritanical restraints in the treatment of sexual themes, Sherwood Anderson detested the repressive, warping effects of puritanism in American small town life, and dared treat his subject in a truthful, direct manner. "Adventure" is a story of tragic human waste, of pathetic self-effacement, misplaced loyalty to an abstract moral concept, and the unbearable loneliness and frustration it brings. The romantic euphoria that envelops Ned Currie and Alice Hindman after lovemaking, and causes them to pledge eternal fidelity, soon dissipates for Ned. But Alice believes herself to be bound forever by their act. Lacking the modern consciousness of a woman's right to seek her own ends in life, she sees herself belonging only to Ned and is thus led into a dull, uneventful life of waiting, until finally she is threatened with a frigid spinsterhood. At age twenty-seven, Alice has become a suppressed volcano of frustrations, thwarted passions, and bitterness, and is hopelessly neurotic in her loneliness. Betrayed "by her desire to have something beautiful come into her rather narrow life," she turns first to religion, and then to the realm of grotesque fantasy fulfillment. Perhaps the major value of this story for the purposes of this anthology is that the author demonstrates that social or moral deviates are not evil or reprehensible, but are emotional invalids, warped by their contact with organized society and its rigid moral conventions.

Alice Hindman, a woman of twenty-seven when George Willard was a mere boy, had lived in Winesburg all her life. She clerked in Winney's Dry Goods Store and lived with her mother, who had married a second husband.

Alice's step-father was a carriage painter, and given to drink. His story is an odd one. It will be worth telling some day.

At twenty-seven Alice was tall and somewhat slight. Her head was large and overshadowed her body. Her shoulders were a little stooped and her hair and eyes brown. She was very quiet but beneath a placid exterior a continual ferment went on.

When she was a girl of sixteen and before she began to work in the store, Alice had an affair with a young man. The young man, named Ned Currie, was older than Alice. He, like George Willard, was employed on the *Winesburg Eagle* and for a long time he went to see Alice almost every evening. Together the two walked under the trees through the streets of the town and talked of what they would do with their lives. Alice was then a very pretty girl and Ned Currie took her into his arms and kissed her. He became excited and said things he did not intend to say and Alice, betrayed by her desire to have something beautiful come into her rather narrow life, also grew excited. She also talked. The outer crust of her life, all of her natural diffidence and reserve, was torn away and she gave herself over to the emotions of love. When, late in the fall of her sixteenth year, Ned Currie went away to Cleveland where he hoped to get a place on a city newspaper and rise in the world, she wanted to go with him. With a trembling voice she told him what was in her mind. "I will work and you can work," she said. "I do not want to harness you to a needless expense that will prevent your making progress. Don't marry me now. We will get along without that and we can be together. Even though we live in the same house no one will say anything. In the city we will be unknown and people will pay no attention to us."

Ned Currie was puzzled by the determination and abandon of his sweetheart and was also deeply touched. He had wanted the girl to become his mistress but changed his mind. He wanted to protect and care for her. "You don't know what you're talking about," he said sharply; "you may be sure I'll let you do no such thing. As soon as I get a good job I'll come back. For the present you'll have to stay here. It's the only thing we can do."

On the evening before he left Winesburg to take up his new life in the city, Ned Currie went to call on Alice. They walked about through the streets for an hour and then got a rig from Wesley

Moyer's livery and went for a drive in the country. The moon came up and they found themselves unable to talk. In his sadness the young man forgot the resolutions he had made regarding his conduct with the girl.

They got out of the buggy at a place where a long meadow ran down to the bank of Wine Creek and there in the dim light became lovers. When at midnight they returned to town they were both glad. It did not seem to them that anything that could happen in the future could blot out the wonder and beauty of the thing that had happened. "Now we will have to stick to each other, whatever happens we will have to do that," Ned Currie said as he left the girl at her father's door.

The young newspaper man did not succeed in getting a place on a Cleveland paper and went west to Chicago. For a time he was lonely and wrote to Alice almost every day. Then he was caught up by the life of the city; he began to make friends and found new interests in life. In Chicago he boarded at a house where there were several women. One of them attracted his attention and he forgot Alice in Winesburg. At the end of a year he had stopped writing letters, and only once in a long time, when he was lonely or when he went into one of the city parks and saw the moon shining on the grass as it had shone that night on the meadow by Wine Creek, did he think of her at all.

In Winesburg the girl who had been loved grew to be a woman. When she was twenty-two years old her father, who owned a harness repair shop, died suddenly. The harness maker was an old soldier, and after a few months his wife received a widow's pension. She used the first money she got to buy a loom and became a weaver of carpets, and Alice got a place in Winney's store. For a number of years nothing could have induced her to believe that Ned Currie would not in the end return to her.

She was glad to be employed because the daily round of toil in the store made the time of waiting seem less long and uninteresting. She began to save money, thinking that when she had saved two or three hundred dollars she would follow her lover to the city and try if her presence would not win back his affections.

Alice did not blame Ned Currie for what had happened in the moonlight in the field, but felt that she could never marry another man. To her the thought of giving to another what she still felt could belong only to Ned seemed monstrous. When other young men tried to attract her attention she would have nothing to do with them. "I am his wife and shall remain his wife whether he comes back or not," she whispered to herself, and for all of her willingness to support herself could not have understood the growing modern idea of a woman's owning herself and giving and taking for her own ends in life.

Alice worked in the dry goods store from eight in the morning until six at night and on three evenings a week went back to the store to stay from seven until nine. As time passed and she became more and more lonely she began to practice the devices common to lonely people. When at night she went upstairs into her own room she knelt on the floor to pray and in her prayers whispered things she wanted to say to her lover. She became attached to inanimate objects, and because it was her own, could not bear to have anyone touch the furniture of her room. The trick of saving money, begun for a purpose, was carried on after the scheme of going to the city to find Ned Currie had been given up. It became a fixed habit, and when she needed new clothes she did not get them. Sometimes on rainy afternoons in the store she got out her bank book and, letting it lie open before her, spent hours dreaming impossible dreams of saving money enough so that the interest would support both herself and her future husband.

"Ned always liked to travel about," she thought. "I'll give him the chance. Some day when we are married and I can save both his money and my own, we will be rich. Then we can travel together all over the world."

In the dry goods store weeks ran into months and months into years as Alice waited and dreamed of her lover's return. Her employer, a grey old man with false teeth and a thin grey mustache that drooped down over his mouth, was not given to conversation, and sometimes, on rainy days and in the winter when a storm raged in Main Street, long hours passed when no customers came in. Alice arranged and rearranged the stock. She stood near the front window where she could look down the deserted street and thought of the evenings when she had walked with Ned Currie and of what he had said. "We will have to stick to each other now." The words echoed and re-echoed through the mind of the maturing woman. Tears came into her eyes. Sometimes when her employer had gone out and she was alone in the store she put her head on the counter and wept. "Oh, Ned, I am waiting," she whispered over and over, and all the time the creeping fear that he would never come back grew stronger within her.

In the spring when the rains have passed and before the long hot days of summer have come, the country about Winesburg is delightful. The town lies in the midst of open fields, but beyond the fields are pleasant patches of woodlands. In the wooded places are many little cloistered nooks, quiet places where lovers go to sit on Sunday afternoons. Through the trees they look out across the fields and see farmers at work about the barns or people driving up and down on the roads. In the town bells ring and occasionally a train passes, looking like a toy thing in the distance.

For several years after Ned Currie went away Alice did not go into the wood with other young people on Sunday, but one day after he had been gone for two or three years and when her loneliness seemed unbearable, she put on her best dress and set out. Finding a little sheltered place from which she could see the town and a long stretch of the fields, she sat down. Fear of age and ineffectuality took possession of her. She could not sit still, and arose. As she stood looking out over the land something, perhaps the thought of never ceasing life as it expresses itself in the flow of the seasons, fixed her mind on the passing years. With a shiver of dread, she realized that for her the beauty and freshness of youth had passed. For the first time she felt that she had been cheated. She did not blame Ned Currie and did not know what to blame. Sadness swept over her. Dropping to her knees, she tried to pray, but instead of prayers words of protest came to her lips. "It is not going to come to me. I will never find happiness. Why do I tell myself lies?" she cried, and an odd sense of relief came with this, her first bold attempt to face the fear that had become a part of her everyday life.

In the year when Alice Hindman became twenty-five two things happened to disturb the dull uneventfulness of her days. Her mother married Bush Milton, the carriage painter of Winesburg, and she herself became a member of the Winesburg Methodist Church. Alice joined the church because she had become frightened by the loneliness of her position in life. Her mother's second marriage had emphasized her isolation. "I am becoming old and queer. If Ned comes he will not want me. In the city where he is living men are perpetually young. There is so much going on that they do not have time to grow old," she told herself with a grim little smile, and went resolutely about the business of becoming acquainted with people. Every Thursday evening when the store had closed she went to a prayer meeting in the basement of the church and on Sunday evening attended a meeting of an organization called The Epworth League.

When Will Hurley, a middle-aged man who clerked in a drug store and who also belonged to the church, offered to walk home with her she did not protest. "Of course I will not let him make a practice of being with me, but if he comes to see me once in a long time there can be no harm in that, " she told herself, still determined in her loyalty to Ned Currie.

Without realizing what was happening, Alice was trying feebly at first, but with growing determination, to get a new hold upon life. Beside the drug clerk she walked in silence, but sometimes in the darkness as they went stolidly along she put out her hand and touched softly the folds of his coat. When he left her at the gate before her mother's house she did not go indoors, but stood for a moment by the door. She wanted to call to the drug clerk, to ask him to sit with her in the darkness on the porch before the house, but was afraid he would not understand. "It is not him that I want," she told herself; "I want to avoid being so much alone. If I am not careful I will grow unaccustomed to being with people."

During the early fall of her twenty-seventh year a passionate restlessness took possession of Alice. She could not bear to be in the company of the drug clerk, and when, in the evening, he came to walk with her she sent him away. Her mind became intensely active and when, weary from the long hours of standing behind the counter in the store, she went home and crawled into bed, she could not sleep. With staring eyes she looked into the darkness. Her imagination, like a child awakened from long sleep, played about the room. Deep within her there was something that would not be cheated by phantasies and that demanded some definite answer from life.

Alice took a pillow into her arms and held it tightly against her breasts. Getting out of bed, she arranged a blanket so that in the darkness it looked like a form lying between the sheets and, kneeling beside the bed, she caressed it, whispering words over and over, like a refrain. "Why doesn't something happen? Why am I left here alone?" she muttered. Although she sometimes thought of Ned Currie, she no longer depended on him. Her desire had grown vague. She did not want Ned Currie or any other man. She wanted to be loved, to have something answer the call that was growing louder and louder within her.

And then one night when it rained Alice had an adventure. It frightened and confused her. She had come home from the store at nine and found the house empty. Bush Milton had gone off to town and her mother to the house of a neighbor. Alice went upstairs to her room and undressed in the darkness. For a moment she stood by the window hearing the rain beat against the glass and then a strange desire took possession of her. Without stopping to think of what she intended to do, she ran downstairs through the dark house and out into the rain. As she stood on the little grass plot before the house and felt the cold rain on her body a mad desire to run naked through the streets took possession of her.

She thought that the rain would have some creative and wonderful effect on her body. Not for years had she felt so full of youth and courage. She wanted to leap and run, to cry out, to find some other lonely human and embrace him. On the brick sidewalk before the house a man stumbled homeward. Alice started to run. A wild, desperate mood took possession of her. "What do I care who it is. He is alone, and I will go to him," she thought; and then without stopping to consider the possible result of her madness, called softly. "Wait!" she cried. "Don't go away. Whoever you are, you must wait."

The man on the sidewalk stopped and stood listening. He was an old man and somewhat deaf. Putting his hand to his mouth, he shouted. "What? What say?" he called.

Alice dropped to the ground and lay trembling. She was so frightened at the thought of what she had done that when the man had gone on his way she did not dare get to her feet, but crawled on hands and knees through the grass to the house. When she got to her own room she bolted the door and drew her dressing table across the doorway. Her body shook as with a chill and her hands trembled so that she had difficulty getting into her nightdress. When she got into bed she buried her face in the pillow and wept brokenheartedly. "What is the matter with me? I will do something dreadful if I am not careful," she thought, and turning her face to the wall, began trying to force herself to face bravely the fact that many people must live and die alone, even in Winesburg.

BENJAMIN'S AFFAIR

Charles Webb

As in several of the selections in this anthology, the affair of Benjamin and Mrs. Robinson is that of a young, naive man and an older, more experienced woman. While Sonny's and Ruth's affair (in "The Beautiful Thing") is set in a small Texas town, Benjamin and Mrs. Robinson are from the affluent Waspish suburbs of Southern California. Benjamin is the son of a wealthy lawyer, Mrs. Robinson the wife of the law partner of Benjamin's father. Prior to the affair, Benjamin has looked upon Mrs. Robinson as a close relative, never as a possible mistress. And, ironically, it is Mrs. Robinson's daughter whom Benjamin really loves. The relationship of Benjamin and Mrs. Robinson is incestuous, in spirit if not in reality. As you read "Benjamin's Affair," note how it reflects "The American business ethic," a combinaton of conventional religion and hard work, nominally adhered to by members of the affluent, uppermiddle class. Benjamin and Mrs. Robinson break one of the rules of that ethic. And ultimately, if the rules are taken seriously, someone must pay—in guilt, in auguish, in pain, or in economic deprivation.

Two days after he got home from the trip Benjamin decided to begin his affair with Mrs. Robinson. He ate dinner with his parents in the evening, then went up to his room to take a shower and shave. When he had shined his best pair of shoes and dressed in a suit and tie he returned downstairs and told his parents he was going to a concert in Los Angeles. He showed them the article in the morning newspa-

per announcing the concert. Then he climbed into his car and drove
to the Hotel Taft.

The Hotel Taft was on a hill in one of the better sections of town.
A wide street curved up past large expensive homes until it neared
the top of the hill, then there was an archway over the street with
a sign on the archway reading Taft Hotel and as it passed under the
archway the street turned into the entranceway of the hotel. Benjamin drove slowly under the archway, then up the long driveway
until he came to the building itself. He had to slow his car and wait
in a line while other cars, most of them driven by chauffeurs, stopped
by the entrance of the building for a doorman to open the door for
their passengers. When Benjamin was beside the entrance an attendant appeared at his car and pulled open the door.

"Thank you," Benjamin said as he climbed out.

Others the same age as Benjamin were walking across a broad
pavilion leading to the doors of the hotel. A few of the boys were
wearing suits but most were wearing summer tuxedos with black
pants and white coats. A girl who had on a shiny white dress and a
white orchid on one of her wrists walked arm-in-arm with her escort
up to the door and in. Benjamin followed. Just inside the door a man
smiled at Benjamin and pointed across the lobby of the hotel.

"Main ballroom," he said.

"What?"

"Are you with the Singleman party?"

"No," Benjamin said.

"I beg your pardon."

He nodded at the man, then walked into the large lobby, looking
around him at the main desk and at the telephone booths against one
wall and at the several elevators standing open with their operators
in front of them. He walked slowly across the thick white carpet of
the lobby to the door where the others had gone and for a long time
stood looking into the ballroom. There were tables around the sides
of the room covered with white tablecloths and in the center of each
table was a small sign with a number on it. Some of the couples were
wandering around the room looking for their tables and others were
already seated talking together or leaning over the backs of their
chairs to talk to someone at the next table. Just inside the door of
the ballroom two women and a man were standing in a line. Each
time a girl and her escort walked through the door the two women
and the man smiled and shook their hands. Then the man reached
into his pocket for a sheet of paper and told them where to sit.

"I'm Mrs. Singleman," the woman closest to the door said to Benjamin after he had stood to watch several couples go in.

"Oh," Benjamin said. "Well I'm not—" She was holding out her hand to him. He looked at it a moment, then shook it. "I'm pleased to meet you," he said, "But I'm—"

"What is your name," she said.

"My name's Benjamin Braddock. But I'm—"

"Benjamin?" she said. "I'd like you to know my sister, Miss De-Witte."

Miss DeWitte, wearing a large purple corsage on one of her breasts, stepped forward smiling and extended her hand.

"Well I'm glad to meet you," Benjamin said, shaking it, "but I'm afraid—"

"And that's Mr. Singleman," Mrs. Singleman said, nodding at her husband.

"How are you, Ben," Mr. Singleman said, shaking his hand. "Let's see if we can't find you a table here."

"Well that's very kind of you," Benjamin said. "But I'm not with the party."

"What?"

"I'm—I'm here to meet a friend." He nodded and walked back past them and into the lobby.

Across from the ballroom was a bar with a sign over its door reading The Verandah Room. Benajmin walked across the lobby and under the sign and into the bar. He found an empty table in one of the corners of the room beside a large window that stretched across the entire length of the wall and overlooked the grounds of the hotel.

Although he seldom smoked Benjamin bought a package of cigarettes when he ordered his first drink and smoked several of them as he drank. He kept his face to the window, sometimes watching the reflection of people as they came in through the door of the bar and found tables, but usually looking through the glass at the lighted walks and the trees and the shrubbery outside.

After several drinks he gave the waitress a tip and left the bar for the telephone booths in the lobby. He looked up the Robinsons' telephone number, memorized it and closed himself into a booth. For a long time he sat with the receiver in one hand and a coin in the other but without dropping it into the machine. Finally he returned the receiver to its hook and lighted another cigarette. He sat smoking it inside the closed booth and frowning down at one of the booth's walls. Then he ground it out under his foot and walked out of the booth and into the one beside it to call Mrs. Robinson.

"I don't quite know how to put this," he said when she answered the phone.

"Benjamin?"

"I say I don't quite know how to put this," he said again, "but I've been thinking about that time after the party. After the graduation party."

"You have."

"Yes," he said. "And I wondered—I wondered if I could buy you a drink or something."

A boy wearing a summer tuxedo closed himself into the booth beside Benjamin. Benjamin listened to him drop his coin into the telephone and dial.

"Shall I meet you somewhere?" Mrs. Robinson said.

"Well," Benjamin said, "I don't know. I mean I hope you don't think I'm out of place or anything. Maybe I could—maybe I could buy you a drink and we could just talk. Maybe—"

"Where are you," she said.

"The Taft Hotel."

"Do you have a room there?"

"What?"

"Did you get a room?"

"Oh no," Benjamin said. "No. I mean—look, don't come if you— if you're busy. I don't want to—"

"Will you give me an hour?"

"What?"

"An hour?"

"Oh," Benjamin said. "Well. I mean don't feel you have to come if you don't—in fact maybe some other—"

"I'll be there in an hour," Mrs. Robinson said. She hung up the phone.

Exactly an hour later she arrived. She had on a neat brown suit and white gloves and a small brown hat. Benjamin was sitting at the corner table looking out the window at the grounds of the hotel and didn't see her until she was standing directly across the table from him.

"Hello Benjamin."

"Oh," Benjamin said. He rose quickly from the chair, jarring the table with his leg. "Hello. Hello."

"May I sit down?"

"Of course," Benjamin said. He hurried around the table and held the chair for her as she sat.

"Thank you."

Benjamin watched her remove the two white gloves and drop them into a handbag she had set on the floor. Then he cleared his throat and returned to his chair.

"How are you," Mrs. Robinson said.

"Very well. Thank you." He looked down at a point in the center of the table.

It was quiet for several moments.

"May I have a drink?" Mrs. Robinson said.

"A drink," he said. "Of course." He looked up for the waitress. She was on the other side of the room taking an order. Benjamin whistled softly and motioned to her but she turned and walked in the other direction. "She didn't see me," he said, rising from his chair and jarring the table. "I'll—"

Mrs. Robinson reached across the table and rested her hand on his wrist. "There's time," she said.

Benjamin nodded and sat down. He kept his eyes on the waitress as she made her way to the bar and placed an order with the bartender. As she turned around and waited for him to fill it Benjamin waved his arm through the air.

"She saw me," he said.

"Good," Mrs. Robinson said.

They drank quietly, Benjamin smoking cigarettes and looking out the window, sometimes drumming his fingers on the surface of the table.

"You've been away," Mrs. Robinson said.

"What?"

"Weren't you away for a while?"

"Oh," Benjamin said. "The trip. I took a trip."

"Where did you go," Mrs. Robinson said, taking a sip of her martini.

"Where did I go?"

"Yes."

"Where did I go," Benjamin said. "Oh. North. I went north."

"Was it fun?"

Benjamin nodded. "It was," he said. "Yes."

Mrs. Robinson sat quietly a few moments, smiling across the table at him.

"Darling?" she said.

"Yes?"

"You don't have to be so nervous, you know."

"Nervous," Benjamin said. "Well I am a bit nervous. I mean it's—it's pretty hard to be suave when you're . . ." He shook his head.

Mrs. Robinson sat back in her chair and picked up her drink again. "Tell me about your trip," she said.

"Well," Benjamin said. "There's not much to tell."

"What did you do," she said

"What did I do," Benjamin said. "Well I fought a fire."

"Oh?"

"Yes. The big forest fire up there. You might have—you might have read about it in the newspaper."

She nodded.

"It was quite exciting," Benjamin said. "It was quite exciting to be right up there in the middle of it. They had some Indians too."

"Did you put it out?"

"What?"

"Did you get the fire out all right?"

"Oh," Benjamin said. "Well there were some others fighting it too. There were—yes. It was under control when I left."

"Good," she said.

Benjamin picked up his glass and quickly finished the drink. "Well," he said. "I'll buy you another."

Mrs. Robinson held up her glass. It was still nearly full.

"Oh," Benjamin said. He nodded.

"Benjamin?"

"What."

"Will you please try not to be so nervous?"

"I am trying!"

"All right," she said.

Benjamin shook his head and turned to look out the window again.

"Did you get us a room?" Mrs. Robinson said.

"What?"

"Have you gotten us a room yet?"

"I haven't. No."

"Do you want to?"

"Well," Benjamin said. "I don't—I mean I could. Or we could just talk. We could have another drink and just talk. I'd be perfectly happy to—"

"Do you want me to get it?"

"You?" he said, looking up at her. "Oh no. No. I'll get it." He began nodding.

"Do you want to get it now?" she said.

"Now?"

"Yes."

"Well," he said. "I don't know."

"Why don't you get it."

"Why don't I get it now? Right now?"

"Why don't you."

"Well," Benjamin said. "I will then." He rose from the table. "I'll get it right now then." He walked a few steps away, stopped, then turned around and came back. "Mrs. Robinson, I'm sorry to be so awkward about this but—"

"I know," she said.

Benjamin shook his head and walked across the Verandah Room. He stood for several moments in the doorway looking at the clerk behind the main desk, then finally pushed his hands down into his pockets and walked across the thick white carpet.

"Yes sir?" the clerk said.

"A room. I'd like a room, please."

"A single room or a double room," the clerk said.

"A single," Benajmin said. "Just for myself, please."

The clerk pushed a large book across the counter at him. "Will you sign the register, please?" There was a pen on the counter beside the book. Benajmin picked it up and quickly wrote down his name. Then he stopped and continued to stare at the name he had written as the clerk slowly pulled the register back to his side.

"Is anything wrong, sir?"

"What? No. Nothing."

"Very good, sir," the clerk said. "We have a single room on the fifth floor. Twelve dollars. Would that be suitable?"

"Yes," Benjamin said, nodding. "That would be suitable." He reached for his wallet.

"You can pay when you check out, sir."

"Oh," Benjamin said. "Right. Excuse me."

The clerk's hand went under the counter and brought up a key. "Do you have any luggage?" he said.

"What?"

"Do you have any luggage?"

"Luggage," Benjamin said. "Yes. Yes I do."

"Where is it."

"What?"

"Where is your luggage."

"Well it's in the car," Benjamin said. He pointed across the lobby. "It's out there in the car."

"Very good, sir," the clerk said. He held the key up in the air and looked around the lobby. "I'll have a porter bring it in."

"Oh no," Benjamin said.

"Sir?"

"I mean I'd—I'd rather not go to the trouble of bringing it all in. I just have a toothbrush. I can get it myself. If that's all right."

"Of course."

Benjamin reached for the key.

"I'll have a porter show you the room."

"Oh," Benjamin said, withdrawing his hand. "Well actually I'd just as soon find it myself. I just have the toothbrush to carry up and I think I can handle it myself."

"Whatever you say, sir." The man handed him the key.

"Thank you."

Benjamin walked across the lobby and out through the front doors of the hotel. He watched the doorman open the doors of several cars and a taxi that drove up, then he turned around and went back inside. As he passed the clerk he stopped and patted one of the pockets of his coat.

"Got it," he said.

"Sir?"

"The toothbrush. I got the toothbrush all right."

"Oh. Very good, sir."

Benjamin nodded. "Well," he said. "I guess I'll stop in the bar a minute before going up."

"You do whatever you like, sir."

"Thank you."

Benjamin returned to the Verandah Room. Mrs. Robinson looked up to smile at him when he came to the table.

"Well," Benjamin said. "I did it. I got it."

"You got us a room."

"Yes."

He reached into his pocket for the key. "It's on the fifth floor," he said, squinting at the number on the key. "Five hundred and ten it is."

"Shall we go up?" Mrs. Robinson said.

"Oh," Benjamin said, frowning. "Well I'm afraid there's a little problem."

"Oh?"

"I got a single."

Mrs. Robinson nodded. "That's all right," she said.

"Well that's all right," Benjamin said. "But the man at the desk. The clerk. He seemed—he seemed like he might be a little suspicious."

"Oh," she said. "Well do you want to go up alone first?"

"I think I'd better," Benjamin said. "And also—also I was wondering if you could wait. Till he's talking to someone. So he—I mean I signed my own name by mistake and I—"

"I'll be careful," Mrs. Robinson said.

"I know," Benjamin said. "But I don't know what their policy is here. I wouldn't—"

"Benjamin?"

"What."

"Will you try and relax please?"

"Well I'm trying," Benjamin said. "It's just that this clerk—he gave me a funny look."

"I'll be up in ten minutes," Mrs. Robinson said.

"Ten minutes," Benjamin said. "Right. I mean—right." He nodded and hurried away from the table.

In ten minutes Mrs. Robinson knocked on the door of the room. Benjamin had just drawn two large curtains over the window. He hurried across the carpet and pulled open the door for her. They stood looking at each other for a moment, then Benjamin began nodding.

"I see—I see you found it all right," he said.

She smiled at him and walked into the room, looking at a television set in the corner, then at the bed. She removed the small round hat from the top of her head and set it down on a writing desk against one of the walls.

"Well," Benjamin said. He nodded but didn't say anything more.

Mrs. Robinson walked slowly back to where he was standing. "Well?" she said, looking up into his face.

Benjamin waited a few moments, then brought one of his hands up to her shoulder. He bent his face down, cleared his throat, and kissed her. Then he lifted his face back up and nodded again. "Well," he said again, removing his hand from her shoulder.

Mrs. Robinson returned to the writing table and looked down at her hat. "Benjamin?"

"Yes?"

"I'll get undressed now," she said, running one of her fingers around the edge of the hat. "Is that all right?"

"Sure," Benjamin said. "Fine. Do you—do you—"

"What?"

"I mean do you want me to just stand here?" he said. "I don't—I don't know what you want me to do."

"Why don't you watch," she said.

"Oh. Sure. Thank you."

He watched her unbutton the three buttons on the front of her suit, then reach up to unbutton the top button on her blouse. She smiled at him as she moved her hand slowly down the front of her blouse, then leaned for support on the writing table and reached down to remove her shoes.

"Will you bring me a hanger?" she said.

"What?"

She straightened up and frowned at him. "Benjamin, if you want another drink we'll go down and have one."

"Oh no," Benjamin said. "A hanger. I'll get a hanger." He hurried to the closet and opened its door. "A wood one?" he said.

"What?"

"Do you want a wood one?"

"A wood one would be fine," she said.

"Right," Benjamin said. He reached into the closet for a wooden hanger and carried it across the room to her.

"Thank you," she said, taking it.

"You're welcome," Benjamin said. He walked back to the door. He slid his hands into his pockets and watched her as she removed the jacket of her suit, then the blouse she was wearing and hung them on the hanger.

Suddenly Benjamin began shaking his head. He pulled his hands up out of his pockets and opened his mouth to say something but then closed it again. "Mrs. Robin—?"

"What?"

"Nothing."

She frowned at him.

"Nothing," Benjamin said. "Nothing. Do you need another hanger."

"No," she said. She looked at him a moment longer, then pushed her skirt down around her legs, stepped out of it and folded it. "Would it be easier for you in the dark?" she said, draping the skirt through the hanger and over the wooden bar.

"No."

"You're sure."

"I'm sure. Yes."

"Hang this up please?" she said. Benajmin walked across the room to take the hanger from her and carried it to the closet. When he had hung it up and turned around she had let a half-slip she was wearing drop to the floor and was stepping out of it. She slid a girdle and the stockings fastened to it down around her legs and onto the floor. "Will you undo my bra?" she said, turning around.

"Your—your—"

"Will you?"

Benjamin looked at her a moment longer, then suddenly began shaking his head. He rushed to one of the walls of the room. "No!" he said.

"What?"

"Mrs. Robinson! Please! I can't!"

"What?"

"I cannot do this!"

Mrs. Robinson watched him for a moment, then turned and walked slowly to the bed. She seated herself and moved back to sit with her back against the board at the head of the bed. She crossed her legs in front of her and reached behind her back to unhook the bra. "You don't want to do it," she said.

"I want to but I can't!" he said to the wall. "Now I'm just—I'm sorry I called you up but I—"

"Benjamin?"

"I mean don't you see?" he said, turning around. "Don't you see that this is the worst thing I could possibly do? The very worst thing in the world?"

"Is it?"

He shook his head. "Now I feel awful about this," he said. "About having you come up here like this. But I—I just—Mrs. Robinson, I like being with you. It's not that. I mean maybe we—maybe we could do something else together. Could we—could we go to a movie? Can I take you to a movie?"

She frowned at him. "Are you trying to be funny?" she said.

"No!No! But I don't know what to say! Because I've got you up here and I—"

"And you don't know what to do."

"Well I know I can't do this!"

"Why not."

"For God's sake why do you think, Mrs. Robinson."

She shrugged. "I suppose you don't find me particularly desirable," she said.

"Oh no," Benjamin said, taking a step toward the bed. "No. That has nothing to do with it."

"You don't have to—"

"Look," Benjamin said. "Mrs. Robinson. I think—I think you're the most attractive woman of all my parents' friends. I mean that. I find you desirable. But I— For God's sake can you imagine my parents?" He held his arms up beside him.

"What?"

"Can you imagine what they'd say if they just saw us here in this room right now?"

"What would they say," she said.

"I have no idea, Mrs. Robinson. But for God's sake. They've brought me up. They've made a good life for me. And I think they deserve better than this. I think they deserve a little better than jumping into bed with the partner's wife."

She nodded.

"So it's nothing to do with you. But I respect my parents. I appreciate what they've—"

"Benjamin?" she said, looking up at him.

"What."

"Would you think I was being forward if I asked you a rather personal question?"

"Oh no," Benjamin said. "You can ask me anything you want. I'd be happy to—"

"Are you a virgin?" she said.

"What?"

"You don't have to tell me if you don't want."

Benjamin frowned at her. "Am I a virgin." he said.

She nodded.

Benjamin continued to frown at her and finally she smiled. "All right," she said. "You don't have to tell me."

"Well what do you think," he said.

"I don't know," she said. "I guess you probably are."

"Come on," Benjamin said.

"Well aren't you?"

"Of course I'm not."

"It's nothing you should be ashamed of, Benjamin," she said, dropping her bra beside her on the bed.

"What?"

She folded her arms over her breasts and leaned her head back against the wall. "I mean I wish you'd just admit to me you're a little bit frightened of being with a woman instead of . . ."

"What?"

"I wish you'd just tell me you don't think you'd be able to go through with it rather than. . . "

Benjamin shook his head. "Look," he said. " You're missing the point."

"I don't think so."

"Well you are," he said. "The point is that I come from a family where we trust each other."

Mrs. Robinson brought her head up and smiled slightly. "Come on," she said.

"What?"

"Now look," she said. "I'm sure there isn't a man living who wasn't a little scared his first time."

"But it's not!"

"Benjamin there's no reason to be scared of me."

"Do you really believe that?" he said, taking another step toward the bed. "Do you really believe I've never done this thing before?"

"Well," she said, "I think it's pretty obvious you haven't. You don't have the slightest idea what to do. You're nervous and awkward. You can't even—"

"Oh my God,"Benjamin said.

"I mean just because you might be inadequate in one way doesn't—"

"Inadequate?!"

She nodded, then it was quiet. Benjamin stared at her as she frowned down at one of her breasts. "Well," she said finally, straightening up and putting one foot down on the floor. "I guess I'd better be—"

"Stay on that bed," Benjamin said. He removed his coat quickly and dropped it on the floor. Then he began unbuttoning his shirt. He walked to the bed to sit down beside her, then reached behind her head to remove several bobby pins. Mrs. Robinson shook her head and her hair fell down around her shoulders. Benjamin finished taking off his shirt and dropped it on the floor. Then he put his arms around her and eased her down onto her back on the bed. He kissed her and kicked off his shoes at the same time. Mrs. Robinson put her hands up at the sides of his head and then moved her fingernails up through his hair and finally wrapped both her arms around him and pressed him down against her until he could feel her breasts flattening underneath his chest and the muscles trembling in her arms. She pulled her mouth away from his and pushed it against his neck, then pushed one of her hands down between them to the buckle of his belt.

"Please," she said.

Benjamin raised his head up several inches to look at her face. Her eyes were closed and her mouth was partly open.

"Please," she said again.

Benjamin reached for the lamp on the table beside them. "Inadequate," he said, turning it off. "That's good. That's really pretty—"

"Please!"

He let her unbuckle his belt and push his pants down around his legs, then climbed on top of her and started the affair.

THE MAIDEN

Thomas Hardy

It was noted in the preface to this book that until recently the writer's attempt to deal freely and frankly with sexual themes has been severely curtailed by social and moral taboos. Perhaps nowhere in literary history have such prohibitions been so strongly enforced as in Victorian England, and Hardy's *Tess of the d' Urbervilles* is a perfect case in point. The seduction scene in this passage is so indistinct, so clouded over with fanciful metaphors and euphemisms, that nothing physical seems to happen. At the key moment, the author's voice veils the physical details of the scene by inviting the reader to engage in speculative philosophical abstractions. Yet Tess carries away from the experience feelings of everlasting moral and social disgrace. In the chapter that follows her undoing, we find her weighed down with the crushing horror of the act, filled with thoughts of treachery, retribution, and doom. Hardy writes: "The familiar green world . . . was terribly beautiful to Tess today, for since her eyes last fell upon it she had learnt that the serpent hisses where the sweet birds sing, and her views of life had been totally changed for her by the lesson."

Every village has its idiosyncrasy, its constitution, often its own code of morality. The levity of some of the younger women in and about Trantridge was marked, and was perhaps symptomatic of the choice spirit who ruled The Slopes in that vicinity. The place had also a more abiding defect; it drank hard. The staple conversation on the farms around was on the uselessness of saving money; and smock-frocked arithmeticians, leaning on their ploughs or hoes, would enter into calculations of great nicety to prove that parish relief was a fuller provision for a man in his old age than any which could result from savings out of their wages during a whole lifetime.

The chief pleasure of these philosophers lay in going every Saturday night, when work was done, to Chaseborough, a decayed market-town two or three miles distant; and, returning in the small hours of the next morning, to spend Sunday in sleeping off the dyspeptic effects of the curious compounds sold to them as beer by the monopolizers of the once independent inns.

For a long time Tess did not join in the weekly pilgrimages. But under pressure from matrons not much older than herself—for a field-man's wages being as high at twenty-one as at forty, marriage was early here—Tess at length consented to go. Her first experience of the journey afforded her more enjoyment than she had expected, the hilariousness of the others being quite contagious after her monotonous attention to the poultry-farm all the week. She went again and again. Being graceful and interesting, standing moreover on the momentary threshold of womanhood, her appearance drew down upon her some sly regards from loungers in the streets of Chaseborough; hence, though sometimes her journey to the town was made independently, she always searched for her fellows at nightfall, to have the protection of their companionship homeward.

This had gone on for a month or two when there came a Saturday in September, on which a fair and a market coincided; and the pilgrims from Trantridge sought double delights at the inns on that account. Tess's occupations made her late in setting out, so that her comrades reached the town long before her. It was a fine September evening, just before sunset, when yellow lights struggle with blue shades in hair-like lines, and the atmosphere itself forms a prospect without aid from more solid objects, except the innumerable winged insects that dance in it. Through this low-lit mistiness Tess walked leisurely along.

She did not discover the coincidence of the market with the fair till she had reached the place; by which time it was close upon dusk. Her limited marketing was soon completed; and then as usual she began to look about for some of the Trantridge cottagers.

At first she could not find them, and she was informed that most of them had gone to what they called a private little jig at the house of a hay-trusser and peat-dealer who had transactions with their farm. He lived in an out-of-the-way nook of the townlet, and in trying to find her course thither her eyes fell upon Mr. d'Urberville standing at a street corner.

'What—my Beauty? You here so late?' he said.

She told him that she was simply waiting for company home-ward.

'I'll see you again,' said he over her shoulder as she went on down the back lane.

Approaching the hay-trussers she could hear the fiddled notes of a reel proceeding from some building in the rear; but no sound of dancing was audible—an exceptional state of things for these parts, where as a rule the stamping drowned the music. The front door being open she could see straight through the house into the garden at the back as far as the shades of night would allow; and nobody appearing to her knock she traversed the dwelling and went up the path to the outhouse whence the sound had attracted her.

It was a windowless erection used for storage, and from the open door there floated into the obscurity a mist of yellow radiance, which at first Tess thought to be illuminated smoke. But on drawing nearer she perceived that it was a cloud of dust, lit by candles within the outhouse, whose beams upon the haze carried forward the outline of the doorway into the wide night of the garden.

When she came close and looked in she beheld indistinct forms racing up and down to the figure of the dance, the silence of their footfalls arising from their being overshoe in 'scroff'—that is to say, the powdery residiuum from the storage of peat and other products, the stirring of which by their turbulent feet created the nebulosity that involved the scene. Through this floating, fusty débris of peat and hay, mixed with the perspirations and warmth of the dancers, and forming together a sort of vegeto-human pollen, the muted fiddles feebly pushed their notes, in marked contrast to the spirit with which the measure was trodden out. They coughed as they danced, and laughed as they coughed. Of the rushing couples there could barely be discerned more than the high lights—the indistinct-ness shaping them to satyrs clasping nymphs—a multiplicity of Pans whirling a multiplicity of Syrinxes; Lotis attempting to elude Pria-pus,[1] and always failing.

At intervals a couple would approach the doorway for air, and the haze no longer veiling their features, the demigods resolved themselves into the homely personalities of her own next-door neigh-

[1]Syrinx, a nymph pursued by Pan, turned into an armful of reeds when she was caught. Lotis, another nymph, in a similar situation turned into a lotus plant. Priapus, a Roman god of male generative power, was worshipped in orgiastic rites. "Sileni" (below): plural of Silenus, the name of a son of Pan who became a fat old satyr, fond of drink.

bours. Could Trantridge in two or three short hours have metamorphosed itself thus madly!

Some Sileni of the throng sat on benches and hay-trusses by the wall; and one of them recognized her.

'The maids don't think it respectable to dance at "The Flower-de-Luce"' he explained. 'They don't like to let everybody see which be their fancy-men. Besides, the house sometimes shuts up just when their jints begin to get greased. So we come here and send out for liquor.'

'But when be any of you going home?' asked Tess with some anxiety.

'Now—a'most directly. This is all but the last jig.'

She waited. The reel drew to a close, and some of the party were in the mind for starting. But others would not, and another dance was formed. This surely would end it, thought Tess. But it merged in yet another. She became restless and uneasy; yet, having waited so long, it was necessary to wait longer; on account of the fair the roads were dotted with roving characters of possibly ill intent; and, though not fearful of measurable dangers, she feared the unknown. Had she been near Marlott she would have had less dread.

'Don't ye be nervous, my dear good soul,' expostulated, between his coughs, a young man with a wet face, and his straw hat so far back upon his head that the brim encircled it like the nimbus of a saint. 'What's yer hurry? To-morrow is Sunday, thank God, and we can sleep it off in church-time. Now, have a turn with me?'

She did not abhor dancing, but she was not going to dance here. The movement grew more passionate: the fiddlers behind the luminous pillar of cloud now and then varied the air by playing on the wrong side of the bridge or with the back of the bow. But it did not matter; the panting shapes spun onwards.

They did not vary their partners if their inclination were to stick to previous ones. Changing partners simply meant that a satisfactory choice had not as yet been arrived at by one or other of the pair, and by this time every couple had been suitably matched. It was then that the ecstasy and the dream began, in which emotion was the matter of the universe, and matter but an adventitious intrusion likely to hinder you from spinning where you wanted to spin.

Suddenly there was a dull thump on the ground: a couple had fallen, and lay in a mixed heap. The next couple, unable to check its progress, came toppling over the obstacle. An inner cloud of dust rose around the prostrate figures amid the general one of the room, in which a twitching entanglement of arms and legs was discernible.

'You shall catch it for this, my gentleman, when you get home!' burst in female accents from the human heap—those of the unhappy partner of the man whose clumsiness had caused the mishap; she happened also to be his recently married wife, in which assortment there was nothing unusual at Trantridge as long as any affection remained between wedded couples; and, indeed, it was not uncustomary in their later lives, to avoid making odd lots of the single people between whom there might be a warm understanding.

A loud laugh from behind Tess's back, in the shade of the garden, united with the titter within the room. She looked round, and saw the red coal of a cigar: Alec d'Urberville was standing there alone. He beckoned to her, and she reluctantly retreated towards him.

'Well, my Beauty, what are you doing here?'

She was so tired after her long day and her walk that she confided her trouble to him—that she had been waiting ever since he saw her to have their company home, because the road at night was strange to her. 'But it seems they will never leave off, and I really think I will wait no longer.'

'Certainly do not. I have only a saddle-horse here to-day; but come to "The Flower-de-Luce," and I'll hire a trap, and drive you home with me.'

Tess, though flattered, had never quite got over her original mistrust of him, and, despite their tardiness, she preferred to walk home with the work-folk. So she answered that she was much obliged to him, but would not trouble him. 'I have said that I will wait for 'em, and they will expect me to now.'

'Very well, Miss Independence. Please yourself. . . . Then I shall not hurry . . . My good Lord, what a kick-up they are having there!'

He had not put himself forward into the light, but some of them had perceived him, and his presence led to a slight pause and a consideration of how the time was flying. As soon as he had re-lit a cigar and walked away the Trantridge people began to collect themselves from amid those who had come in from other farms, and prepared to leave in a body. Their bundles and baskets were gathered up, and half an hour later, when the clock-chime sounded a quarter past eleven, they were straggling along the lane which led up the hill towards their homes.

It was a three-mile walk, along a dry white road, made whiter tonight by the light of the moon.

Tess soon perceived as she walked in the flock, sometimes with this one, sometimes with that, that the fresh night air was producing staggerings and serpentine courses among the men who had partak-

en too freely; some of the more careless women also were wandering
in their gait—to wit, a dark virago, Car Darch, dubbed Queen of
Spades, till lately a favourite of d'Urberville's; Nancy, her sister, nick-
named the Queen of Diamonds; and the young married woman who
had already tumbled down. Yet however terrestrial and lumpy their
appearance just now to the mean unglamoured eye, to themselves
the case was different. They followed the road with a sensation that
they were soaring along in a supporting medium, possessed of original and profound thoughts, themselves and surrounding nature
forming an organism of which all the parts harmoniously and joyous-
ly interpenetrated each other. They were as sublime as the moon and
stars above them, and the moon and stars were as ardent as they.

Tess, however, had undergone such painful experiences of this
kind in her father's house, that the discovery of their condition spoilt
the pleasure she was beginning to feel in the moonlight journey. Yet
she stuck to the party, for reasons above given.

In the open highway they had progressed in scattered order; but
now their route was through a field-gate, and the foremost finding
a difficulty in opening it they closed up together.

This leading pedestrian was Car the Queen of Spades, who carried a wicker-basket containing her mother's groceries, her own
draperies, and other purchases for the week. The basket being large
and heavy, Car had placed it for convenience of porterage on the
top of her head, where it rode on in jeopardized balance as she
walked with arms akimbo.

'Well—whatever is that a-creeping down thy back, Car Darch?'
said one of the group suddenly.

All looked at Car. Her gown was a light cotton print, and from
the back of her head a kind of rope could be seen descending to some
distance below her waist, like a Chinaman's queue.

' 'Tis her hair falling down,' said another.

No; it was not her hair: it was a black stream of something oozing
from her basket, and it glistened like a slimy snake in the cold still
rays of the moon.

' 'Tis treacle,' said an observant matron.

Treacle it was. Car's poor old grandmother had a weakness for
the sweet stuff. Honey she had in plenty out of her own hives, but
treacle was what her soul desired, and Car had been about to give
her a treat of surprise. Hastily lowering the basket the dark girl found
that the vessel containing the syrup had been smashed within.

By this time there had arisen a shout of laughter at the extraordinary appearance of Car's back, which irritated the dark queen into

getting rid of the disfigurement by the first sudden means available, and independently of the help of the scoffers. She rushed excitedly into the field they were about to cross, and flinging herself flat on her back upon the grass, began to wipe her gown as well as she could by spinning horizontally on the herbage and dragging herself over it upon her elbows.

The laughter rang louder; they clung to the gate, to the posts, rested on their staves, in the weakness engendered by their convulsions at the spectacle of Car. Our heroine, who had hitherto held her peace, at this wild moment could not help joining in with the rest.

It was a misfortune—in more ways than one. No sooner did the dark queen hear the soberer richer note of Tess among those of the other work-people than a long smouldering sense of rivalry inflamed her to madness. She sprang to her feet and closely faced the object of her dislike.

'How darest th' laugh at me, hussy!' she cried.

'I couldn't really help it when t'others did,' apologized Tess, still tittering.

'Ah, th'st think th' beest everybody, dostn't, because th' beest first favourite with He just now! But stop a bit, my lady, stop a bit! I'm as good as two of such! Look here—here's at 'ee!'

To Tess's horror the dark queen began stripping off the bodice of her gown—which for the added reason of its ridiculed condition she was only too glad to be free of—till she had bared her plump neck, shoulders, and arms to the moonshine, under which they looked as luminous and beautiful as some Praxitclean[2] creation, in their possession of the faultless rotundities of a lusty country girl. She closed her fists and squared up at Tess.

The rather too inclusive speech brought down a torrent of vituperation from other quarters upon fair Tess's unlucky head, particularly from the Queen of Diamonds, who having stood in the relations to d'Urberville that Car had also been suspected of, united with the latter against the common enemy. Several other women also chimed in, with an animus which none of them would have been so fatuous as to show but for the rollicking evening they had passed. Thereupon, finding Tess unfairly browbeaten, the husbands and lovers tried to

---

[2] Praxiteles was a Greek sculptor of the fourth century B.C.

make peace by defending her; but the result of that attempt was directly to increase the war.

Tess was indignant and ashamed. She no longer minded the loneliness of the way and the lateness of the hour; her one object was to get away from the whole crew as soon as possible. She knew well enough that the better among them would repent of their passion next day. They were all now inside the field, and she was edging back to rush off alone when a horseman emerged almost silently from the corner of the hedge that screened the road, and Alec d'Urberville looked round upon them.

'What the devil is all this row about, work-folk?' he asked.

The explanation was not readily forthcoming; and, in truth, he did not require any. Having heard their voices while yet some way off he had ridden creepingly forward, and learnt enough to satisfy himself.

Tess was standing apart from the rest, near the gate. He bent over towards her. 'Jump up behind me,' he whispered, 'and we'll get shot of the screaming cats in a jiffy!'

She felt almost ready to faint, so vivid was her sense of the crisis. At almost any other moment of her life she would have refused such proffered aid and company, as she had refused them several times before; and now the loneliness would not of itself have forced her to do otherwise. But coming as the invitation did at the particular juncture when fear and indignation at these adversaries could be transformed by a spring of the foot into a triumph over them, she abandoned herself to her impulse, climbed the gate, put her toe upon his instep, and scrambled into the saddle behind him. The pair were speeding away into the distant gray by the time that the contentious revellers became aware of what had happened.

The Queen of Spades forgot the stain on her bodice, and stood beside the Queen of Diamonds and the new-married, staggering young woman—all with a gaze of fixity in the direction in which the horse's tramp was diminishing into silence on the road.

'What be ye looking at?' asked a man who had not observed the incident.

'Ho-ho-ho!' laughed dark Car.

'Hee-hee-hee!' laughed the tippling bride, as she steadied herself on the arm of her fond husband.

'Heu-heu-heu!' laughed dark Car's mother, stroking her moustache as she explained laconically: 'Out of the frying-pan into the fire!'

Then these children of the open air, whom even excess of alcohol could scarce injure permanently, betook themselves to the fieldpath; and as they went there moved onward with them, around the shadow of each one's head, a circle of opalized light, formed by the moon's rays upon the glistening sheet of dew. Each pedestrian could see no halo but his or her own, which never deserted the headshadow, whatever its vulgar unsteadiness might be; but adhered to it, and persistently beautified it; till the erratic motions seemed an inherent part of the irradiation, and the fumes of their breathing a component of the night's mist; and the spirit of the scene, and of the moonlight, and of Nature, seemed harmoniously to mingle with the spirit of wine.

The twain cantered along for some time without speech, Tess as she clung to him still panting in her triumph, yet in other respects dubious. She had perceived that the horse was not the spirited one he sometimes rode, and felt no alarm on that score, though her seat was precarious enough despite her tight hold of him. She begged him to slow the animal to a walk, which Alec accordingly did.

'Neatly done, was it not, dear Tess?' he said by and by.

'Yes!' said she. 'I am sure I ought to be much obliged to you.'

'And are you?'

She did not reply.

'Tess, why do you always dislike my kissing you?'

'I suppose—because I don't love you.'

'You are quite sure?'

'I am angry with you sometimes!'

'Ah, I half feared as much.' Nevertheless, Alec did not object to that confession. He knew that anything was better than frigidity. 'Why haven't you told me when I have made you angry?'

'You know very well why. Because I cannot help myself here.'

'I haven't offended you often by love-making?'

'You have sometimes.'

'How many times?'

'You know as well as I—too many times.'

'Every time I have tried?'

She was silent, and the horse ambled along for a considerable distance, till a faint luminous fog, which had hung in the hollows all the evening, became general and enveloped them. It seemed to hold the moonlight in suspension, rendering it more pervasive than in clear air. Whether on this account, or from absent-mindedness, or from sleepiness, she did not perceive that they had long ago passed the point at which the lane to Trantridge branched from the highway, and that her conductor had not taken the Trantridge track.

She was inexpressibly weary. She had risen at five o'clock every morning of that week, had been on foot the whole of each day, and on this evening had in addition walked the three miles to Chaseborough, waited three hours for her neighbours without eating or drinking, her impatience to start them preventing either; she had then walked a mile of the way home, and had undergone the excitement of the quarrel, till, with the slow progress of their steed, it was now nearly one o'clock. Only once, however, was she overcome by actual drowsiness. In that moment of oblivion her head sank gently against him.

D'Urberville stopped the horse, withdrew his feet from the stirrups, turned sideways on the saddle, and enclosed her waist with his arm to support her.

This immediately put her on the defensive, and with one of those sudden impulses of reprisal to which she was liable she gave him a little push from her. In his ticklish position he nearly lost his balance and only just avoided rolling over into the road, the horse, though a powerful one, being fortunately the quietest he rode.

'That is devilish unkind!' he said. 'I mean no harm—only to keep you from falling.'

She pondered suspiciously; till, thinking that this might after all be true, she relented, and said quite humbly, 'I beg your pardon, sir.'

'I won't pardon you unless you show some confidence in me. Good God!' he burst out, 'what am I, to be repulsed so by a mere chit like you? For near three mortal months have you trifled with my feelings, eluded me, and snubbed me; and I won't stand it!'

'I'll leave you to-morrow, sir.'

'No, you will not leave me to-morrow! Will you, I ask once more, show your belief in me by letting me clasp you with my arm? Come, between us two and nobody else, now. We know each other well; and you know that I love you, and think you the prettiest girl in the world, which you are. Mayn't I treat you as a lover?'

She drew a quick pettish breath of objection, writhing uneasily on her seat, looked far ahead, and murmured, 'I don't know—I wish—how can I say yes or no when—'

He settled the matter by clasping his arm round her as he desired, and Tess expressed no further negative. Thus they sidled slowly onward till it struck her they had been advancing for an unconscionable time—far longer than was usually occupied by the short journey from Chaseborough, even at this walking pace, and that they were no longer on hard road, but in a mere trackway.

'Why, where be we?' she exclaimed.

'Passing by a wood.'

'A wood—what wood? Surely we are quite out of the road?'

'A bit of The Chase—the oldest wood in England. It is a lovely night, and why should we not prolong our ride a little?'

'How could you be so treacherous!' said Tess, between archness and real dismay, and getting rid of his arm by pulling open his fingers one by one, though at the risk of slipping off herself. 'Just when I've been putting such trust in you, and obliging you to please you, because I thought I had wronged you by that push! Please set me down, and let me walk home.'

'You cannot walk home, darling, even if the air were clear. We are miles away from Trantridge, if I must tell you, and in this growing fog you might wander for hours among these trees.'

'Never mind that,' she coaxed. 'Put me down, I beg you. I don't mind where it is; only let me get down, sir, please!'

'Very well, then, I will—on one condition. Having brought you here to this out-of-the-way place, I feel myself responsible for your safe-conduct home, whatever you may yourself feel about it. As to your getting to Trantridge without assistance, it is quite impossible; for, to tell the truth, dear, owing to this fog, which so disguises everything, I don't quite know where we are myself. Now, if you will promise to wait beside the horse while I walk through the bushes till I come to some road or house, and ascertain exactly our whereabouts, I'll deposit you here willingly. When I come back I'll give you full directions, and if you insist upon walking you may; or you may ride—at your pleasure.'

She accepted these terms, and slid off on the near side, though not till he had stolen a cursory kiss. He sprang down on the other side.

'I suppose I must hold the horse?' said she.

'Oh no; it's not necessary,' replied Alec, patting the panting creature. "He's had enough of it for to-night.'

He turned the horse's head into the bushes, hitched him on to a bough, and made a sort of couch or nest for her in the deep mass of dead leaves.

'Now, you sit there,' he said. 'The leaves have not got damp as yet. Just give an eye to the horse—it will be quite sufficient.'

He took a few steps away from her, but, returning, said, 'By the bye, Tess, your father has a new cob to-day. Somebody gave it to him.'

'Somebody? You!'

D'Urberville nodded.

'O how very good of you that is!' she exclaimed, with a painful sense of the awkwardness of having to thank him just then.

'And the children have some toys.'

'I didn't know—you ever sent them anything!' she murmured, much moved. 'I almost wish you had not—yes, I almost wish it!'

'Why, dear?'

'It—hampers me so.'

'Tessy—don't you love me ever so little now?'

'I'm grateful,' she reluctantly admitted. 'But I fear I do not—' The sudden vision of his passion for herself as a factor in this result so distressed her that, beginning with one slow tear, and then following with another, she wept outright.

'Don't cry, dear, dear one! Now sit down here, and wait till I come.' She passively sat down amid the leaves he had heaped, and shivered slightly. 'Are you cold?' he asked.

'Not very—a little.'

He touched her with his fingers, which sank into her as into down. 'You have only that puffy muslin dress on—how's that?'

'It's my best summer one. 'Twas very warm when I started, and I didn't know I was going to ride, and that it would be night.'

'Nights grow chilly in September. Let me see.' He pulled off a light overcoat that he had worn, and put it round her tenderly. 'That's it—now you'll feel warmer,' he continued. 'Now, my pretty, rest there; I shall soon be back again.'

Having buttoned the overcoat round her shoulders he plunged into the webs of vapour which by this time formed veils between the trees. She could hear the rustling of the branches as he ascended the adjoining slope, till his movements were no louder than the hopping of a bird, and finally died away. With the setting of the moon the pale light lessened, and Tess became invisible as she fell into reverie upon the leaves where he had left her.

In the meantime Alec d'Urberville had pushed on up the slope to clear his genuine doubt as to the quarter of The Chase they were in. He had, in fact, ridden quite at random for over an hour, taking any turning that came to hand in order to prolong companionship with her, and giving far more attention to Tess's moonlit person than to any wayside object. A little rest for the jaded animal being desirable, he did not hasten his search for landmarks. A clamber over the hill into the adjoining vale brought him to the fence of a highway whose contours he recognized, which settled the question of their whereabouts. D'Urberville thereupon turned back; but by this time the moon had quite gone down, and partly on account of the fog The Chase was wrapped in thick darkness, although morning was not far off. He was obliged to advance with outstretched hands to avoid contact with the boughs, and discovered that to hit the exact spot from which he had started was at first entirely beyond him. Roaming up and down, round and round, he at length heard a slight movement of the horse close at hand; and the sleeve of his overcoat unexpectedly caught his foot.

'Tess!' said d'Urberville.

There was no answer. The obscurity was now so great that he could see absolutely nothing but a pale nebulousness at his feet, which represented the white muslin figure he had left upon the dead leaves. Everything else was blackness alike. D'Urberville stooped; and heard a gentle regular breathing. He knelt and bent lower, till her breath warmed his face, and in a moment his cheek was in contact with hers. She was sleeping soundly, and upon her eyelashes there lingered tears.

Darkness and silence ruled everywhere around. Above them rose the primeval yews and oaks of The Chase, in which were poised gentle roosting birds in their last nap; and about them stole the hopping rabbits and hares. But, might some say, where was Tess's guardian angel? where was the providence of her simple faith? Perhaps, like that other god of whom the ironical Tishbite spoke, he was talking, or he was pursuing, or he was in a journey, or he was sleeping and not to be awaked.[3]

Why it was that upon this beautiful feminine tissue, sensitive as gossamer, and practically blank as snow as yet, there should have been traced such a coarse pattern as it was doomed to receive; why so often the coarse appropriates the finer thus, the wrong man the woman, the wrong woman the man, many thousand years of analytical philosophy have failed to explain to our sense of order. One may, indeed, admit the possibility of a retribution lurking in the present catastrophe. Doubtless some of Tess d'Urberville's mailed ancestors rollicking home from a fray had dealt the same measure even more ruthlessly towards peasant girls of their time. But though to visit the

[3] I Kings xviii:27: "Elijah mocked them, and said, Cry aloud: for he is a god: either he is talking, or he is pursuing, or he is in a journey, or peradventure he sleepeth, and must be awaked."

sins of the fathers upon the children may be a morality good enough
for divinities,[4] it is scorned by average human nature; and it therefore does not mend the matter.

As Tess's own people down in those retreats are never tired of
saying among each other in their fatalistic way: 'It was to be.' There
lay the pity of it. An immeasurable social chasm was to divide our
heroine's personality thereafter from that previous self of hers who
stepped from her mother's door to try her fortune at Trantridge
poultry-farm.

[4] Exodus .xx:5: "I the Lord thy God am a jealous God, visiting the iniquity
of the fathers upon the children unto the third and fourth generation of them
that hate me."

FIVE
Exploration

Like untuned golden strings all women are,
Which Long time lie untouched, will harshly jar.
Vessels of brass, oft handled, brightly shine;
What difference betwixt the richest mine
And basest mold, but use? for both, not used,
Are of like worth. Then treasure is abused,
When misers keep it; being put to loan,
In time it will return us two for one.
Rich robes themselves and others do adorn;
Neither themselves nor others, if not worn.
Who builds a palace, and rams up the gate,
Shall see it ruinous and desolate.

from HERO AND LEANDER
Christopher Marlowe

PICNIC

Carson McCullers

Taken from a classic American novel set in the rural South during the late 1930s, this excerpt deals with the first sexual encounter of Mick, a tomboyish teenager, and her friend Harry. The two start out on borrowed bikes to swim and have a picnic lunch at a creek that runs through a lonely stretch of backwoods Georgia. This "loss of innocence" of these two young people alone in an idyllic setting is poignant and not without humor, but it is also tinged with complications and fear. It's interesting to speculate on the extent to which the two experience change or growth as a result of the encounter. Once again, the author's focus is on the effects of this experience on the people involved; the ways in which they change, and whether or not they grow as a result.

She and Harry had talked about so many things lately. Nearly every day they walked home from school together. They talked about God. Sometimes she would wake up in the night and shiver over what they had said. Harry was a Pantheist. That was a religion, the same as Baptist or Catholic or Jew. Harry believed that after you were dead and buried you changed to plants and fire and dirt and clouds and water. It took thousands of years and then finally you were a part of all the world. He said he thought that was better than being one single angel. Anyhow it was better than nothing.

Harry threw the newspaper into his hall and then came over. 'It's hot like summer,' he said. 'And only March.'

'Yeah. I wish we could go swimming.'

'We would if there was any place.'

'There's not any place. Except that country club pool.'

'I sure would like to do something—to get out and go some-where.'

'Me too,' she said. 'Wait! I know one place. It's out in the country about fifteen miles. It's a deep, wide creek in the woods. The Girl Scouts have a camp there in the summer-time. Mrs. Wells took me and George and Pete and Sucker swimming there one time last year.'

'If you want to I can get bicycles and we can go tomorrow. I have a holiday one Sunday a month.'

'We'll ride out and take a picnic dinner,' Mick said.

'O.K. I'll borrow the bikes.'

It was time for him to go to work. She watched him walk down the street. He swung his arms. Halfway down the block there was a bay tree with low branches. Harry took a running jump, caught a limb, and chinned himself. A happy feeling came in her because it was true they were real good friends. Also he was handsome. Tomorrow she would borrow Hazel's blue necklace and wear the silk dress. And for dinner they would take jelly sandwiches and Nehi. Maybe Harry would bring something queer, because they ate orthodox Jew. She watched him until he turned the corner. It was true that he had grown to be a very good-looking fellow.

Harry in the country was different from Harry sitting on the back steps reading the newspapers and thinking about Hitler. They left early in the morning. The wheels he borrowed were the kind for boys—with a bar between the legs. They strapped the lunches and bathing-suits to the fenders and were gone before nine o'clock. The morning was hot and sunny. Within an hour they were far out of town on a red clay road. The fields were bright green and the sharp smell of pine trees was in the air. Harry talked in a very excited way. The warm wind blew into their faces. Her mouth was very dry and she was hungry.

'See that house up on the hill there? Less us stop and get some water.'

'No, we better wait. Well water gives you typhoid.'

'I already had typhoid. I had pneumonia and a broken leg and a infected foot.'

'I remember.'

'Yeah,' Mick said. 'Me and Bill stayed in the front room when we had typhoid fever and Pete Wells would run past on the sidewalk holding his nose and looking up at the window. Bill was very embarrassed. All my hair came out so I was bald-headed.'

'I bet we're at least ten miles from town. We've been riding an hour and a half—fast riding, too.'

'I sure am thirsty,' Mick said. 'And hungry. What you got in that sack for lunch?'

'Cold liver pudding and chicken salad sandwiches and pie.'

'That's a good picnic dinner.' She was ashamed of what she had brought. 'I got two hard-boiled eggs—already stuffed—with separate little packages of salt and pepper. And sandwiches—blackberry jelly with butter. Everything wrapped in oil paper. And paper napkins.'

'I didn't intend for you to bring anything,' Harry said. 'My Mother fixed lunch for both of us. I asked you out here and all. We'll come to a store soon and get cold drinks.'

They rode half an hour longer before they finally came to the filling-station store. Harry propped up the bicycles and she went in ahead of him. After the bright glare the store seemed dark. The shelves were stacked with slabs of white meat, cans of oil, and sacks of meal. Flies buzzed over a big, sticky jar of loose candy on the counter.

'What kind of drinks you got?' Harry asked.

The storeman started to name them over. Mick opened the ice box and looked inside. Her hands felt good in the cold water. 'I want a chocolate Nehi. You got any of them?'

'Ditto,' Harry said. 'Make it two.'

'No, wait a minute. Here's some ice-cold beer. I want a bottle of beer if you can treat as high as that.'

Harry ordered one for himself, also. He thought it was a sin for anybody under twenty to drink beer—but maybe he just suddenly wanted to be a sport. After the first swallow he made a bitter face. They sat on the steps in front of the store. Mick's legs were so tired that the muscles in them jumped. She wiped the neck of the bottle with her hand and took a long, cold pull. Across the road there was a big empty field of grass, and beyond that a fringe of pine woods. The trees were every color of green—from a bright yellow-green to a dark color that was almost black. The sky was hot blue.

'I like beer,' she said. 'I used to sop bread down in the drops our Dad left. I like to lick salt out my hand while I drink. This is the second bottle to myself I've ever had.'

'The first swallow was sour. But the rest tastes good.'

The storeman said it was twelve miles from town. They had four more miles to go. Harry paid him and they were out in the hot sun again. Harry was talking loud and he kept laughing without any reason.

'Gosh, the beer along with this hot sun makes me dizzy. But I sure do feel good,' he said.

'I can't wait to get in swimming.'

There was sand in the road and they had to throw all their weight on the pedals to keep from bogging. Harry's shirt was stuck to his back with sweat. He still kept talking. The road changed to red clay and the sand was behind them. There was a slow colored song in her mind—one Portia's brother used to play on his harp. She pedaled in time to it.

Then finally they reached the place she had been looking for. 'This is it! See that sign that says PRIVATE? We got to climb the bob-wire fence and then take that path there—see!'

The woods were very quiet. Slick pine needles covered the ground. Within a few minutes they had reached the creek. The water was brown and swift. Cool. There was no sound except from the water and a breeze singing high up in the pine trees. It was like the deep, quiet woods made them timid, and they walked softly along the bank beside the creek.

'Don't it look pretty.'

Harry laughed. 'What makes you whisper? Listen here!' He clapped his hand over his mouth and gave a long Indian whoop that echoed back at them. 'Come on. Let's jump in the water and cool off.'

'Aren't you hungry?'

'O.K. Then we'll eat first. We'll eat half the lunch now and half later on when we come out.'

She unwrapped the jelly sandwiches. When they were finished Harry balled the papers neatly and stuffed them into a hollow tree stump. Then he took his shorts and went down the path. She shucked off her clothes behind a bush and struggled into Hazel's bathing-suit. The suit was too small and cut her between the legs.

'You ready?' Harry hollered.

She heard a splash in the water and when she reached the bank Harry was already swimming. 'Don't dive yet until I find out if there are any stumps or shallow places,' he said. She just looked at his head bobbing in the water. She had never intended to dive, anyway. She couldn't even swim. She had been in swimming only a few times in her life—and then she always wore water-wings or stayed out of parts that were over her head. But it would be sissy to tell Harry. She was embarrassed. All of a sudden she told a tale:

'I don't dive any more. I used to dive, high dive, all the time. But once I busted my head open, so I can't dive any more.' She thought for a minute. 'It was a double jack-knife dive I was doing. And when I came up there was blood all in the water. But I didn't think anything about it and just began to do swimming tricks. These people were hollering at me. Then I found out where all this blood in the water was coming from. And I never have swam good since.'

Harry scrambled up the bank. 'Gosh! I never heard about that.'

She meant to add on to the tale to make it sound more reasonable, but instead she just looked at Harry. His skin was light brown and the water made it shining. There were hairs on his chest and legs. In the tight trunks he seemed very naked. Without his glasses his face was wider and more handsome. His eyes were wet and blue. He was looking at her and it was like suddenly they got embarrassed.

'The water's about ten feet deep except over on the other bank, and there it's shallow.'

'Less us get going. I bet that cold water feels good.'

She wasn't scared. She felt the same as if she had got caught at the top of a very high tree and there was nothing to do but just climb down the best way she could—a dead-calm feeling. She edged off the bank and was in the ice-cold water. She held to a root until it broke in her hands and then she began to swim. Once she choked and went under, but she kept going and didn't lose any face. She swam and reached the other side of the bank where she could touch bottom. Then she felt good. She smacked the water with her fists and called out crazy words to make echoes.

'Watch here!'

Harry shimmied up a tall, thin little tree. The trunk was limber and when he reached the top it swayed down with him. He dropped into the water.

'Me too! Watch me do it!'

'That's a sapling.'

She was as good a climber as anybody on the block. She copied exactly what he had done and hit the water with a hard smack. She could swim, too. Now she could swim O.K.

They played follow the leader and ran up and down the bank and jumped in the cold brown water. They hollered and jumped and climbed. They played around for maybe two hours. Then they were standing on the bank and they both looked at each other and there didn't seem to be anything new to do. Suddenly she said:

'Have you ever swam naked?'

The woods was very quiet and for a minute he did not answer. He was cold. His titties had turned hard and purple. His lips were purple and his teeth chattered. 'I—I don't think so.'

This excitement was in her, and she said something she didn't mean to say. 'I would if you would. I dare you to.'

Harry slicked back the dark, wet bangs of his hair. 'O.K.'

They both took off their bathing-suits. Harry had his back to her. He stumbled and his ears were red. Then they turned toward each other. Maybe it was half an hour they stood there—maybe not more than a minute.

Harry pulled a leaf from a tree and tore it to pieces. 'We better get dressed.'

All through the picnic dinner neither of them spoke. They spread the dinner on the ground. Harry divided everything in half. There was the hot, sleepy feeling of a summer afternoon. In the deep woods they could hear no sound except the slow flowing of the water and the songbirds. Harry held his stuffed egg and mashed the yellow with his thumb. What did that make her remember? She heard herself breathe.

Then he looked up over her shoulder. 'Listen here. I think you're so pretty, Mick. I never did think so before. I don't mean I thought you were very ugly—I just mean that—'

She threw a pine cone in the water. 'Maybe we better start back if we want to be home before dark.'

'No,' he said. 'Let's lie down. Just for a minute.'

He brought handfuls of pine needles and leaves and gray moss. She sucked her knee and watched him. Her fists were tight and it was like she was tense all over.

'Now we can sleep and be fresh for the trip home.'

They lay on the soft bed and looked up at the dark-green pine clumps against the sky. A bird sang a sad, clear song she had never heard before. One high note like an oboe—and then it sank down five tones and called again. The song was sad as a question without words.

'I love that bird,' Harry said. 'I think it's a vireo.'

'I wish we was at the ocean. On the beach and watching the ships far out on the water. You went to the beach one summer—exactly what is it like?'

His voice was rough and low. 'Well—there are the waves. Sometimes blue and sometimes green, and in the bright sun they look glassy. And on the sand you can pick up these little shells. Like the kind we brought back in a cigar box. And over the water are these white gulls. We were at the Gulf of Mexico—these cool bay breezes blew all the time and there it's never baking hot like it is here. Always——'

'Snow,' Mick said. 'That's what I want to see. Cold, white drifts of snow like in pictures. Blizzards. White, cold snow that keeps falling soft and falls on and on and on through all the winter. Snow like in Alaska.'

They both turned at the same time. They were close against each other. She felt him trembling and her fists were tight enough to crack. 'Oh, God,' he kept saying over and over. It was like her head was broke off from her body and thrown away. And her eyes looked up straight into the blinding sun while she counted something in her mind. And then this was the way.

This was how it was.

They pushed the wheels slowly along the road. Harry's head hung down and his shoulders were bent. Their shadows were long and black on the dusty road, for it was late afternoon.

'Listen here,' he said.

'Yeah.'

'We got to understand this. We got to. Do you—any?'

'I don't know. I reckon not.'

'Listen here. We got to do something. Let's sit down.'

They dropped the bicycles and sat by a ditch beside the road. They sat far apart from each other. The late sun burned down on their heads and there were brown, crumbly ant beds all around them.

'We got to understand this,' Harry said.

He cried. He sat very still and the tears rolled down his white face. She could not think about the thing that made him cry. An ant stung her on the ankle and she picked it up in her fingers and looked at it very close.

'It's this way,' he said. 'I never had even kissed a girl before.'

'Me neither. I never kissed any boy. Out of the family.'

'That's all I used to think about—was to kiss this certain girl. I used to plan about it during school and dream about it at night. And then once she gave me a date. And I could tell she meant for me to kiss her. And I just looked at her in the dark and I couldn't. That was all I had thought about—to kiss her—and when the time came I couldn't.'

She dug a hole in the ground with her finger and buried the dead ant.

'It was all my fault. Adultery is a terrible sin any way you look at it. And you were two years younger than me and just a kid.'

'No, I wasn't. I wasn't any kid. But now I wish I was, though.'

'Listen here. If you think we ought to we can get married—secretly or any other way.'

Mick shook her head. 'I didn't like that. I never will marry with any boy.'

'I never will marry either. I know that. And I'm not just saying so—it's true.'

His face scared her. His nose quivered and his bottom lip was mottled and bloody where he had bitten it. His eyes were bright and wet and scowling. His face was whiter than any face she could remember. She turned her head from him. Things would be better if only he would just quit talking. Her eyes looked slowly around her—at the streaked red-and-white clay of the ditch, at a broken whiskey bottle, at a pine tree across from them with a sign advertising for a man for county sheriff. She wanted to sit quietly for a long time and not think and not say a word.

'I'm leaving town. I'm a good mechanic and I can get a job some other place. If I stayed home Mother could read this in my eyes.'

'Tell me. Can you look at me and see the difference?'

Harry watched her face a long time and nodded that he could. Then he said:

'There's just one more thing. In a month or two I'll send you my address and you write and tell me for sure whether you're all right.'

'How you mean?' she asked slowly.

He explained to her. 'All you need to write is "O.K." and then I'll know.'

They were walking home again, pushing the wheels. Their shadows stretched out giant-sized on the road. Harry was bent over like an old beggar and kept wiping his nose on his sleeve. For a minute there was a bright, golden glow over everything before the sun sank down behind the trees and their shadows were gone on the road before them. She felt very old, and it was like something was heavy inside her. She was a grown person now, whether she wanted to be or not.

They had walked the sixteen miles and were in the dark alley at home. She could see the yellow light from their kitchen. Harry's house was dark—his mother had not come home. She worked for a tailor in a shop on a side street. Sometimes even on Sunday. When

you looked through the window you could see her bending over the
machine in the back or pushing a long needle through the heavy
pieces of goods. She never looked up while you watched her. And
at night she cooked these orthodox dishes for Harry and her.

'Listen here——' he said.

She waited in the dark, but he did not finish. They shook hands
with each other and Harry walked up the dark alley between the
houses. When he reached the sidewalk he turned and looked back
over his shoulder. A light shone on his face and it was white and hard.
Then he was gone.

ENCOUNTER ON A ROOFTOP

William Melvin Kelley

Even though the young third grader's encounter with sex in this story occurs before the time of puberty, it has a deep and lasting effect on him. "As time went by, I came to understand how rare and wonderful an experience it has been," he says. The boy's inquisitive probings and pinchings of the slightly amused, slightly stimulated lady on the rooftop are seen as the natural, healthy explorations of an alert and imaginative mind. The lesson in the mysteries of sex provided by the willing lady sunbather compensates for the refusal of his friend to make such information available to him. Once again we have a case in which religious upbringing—which brings about an association of sex with sin—confounds an otherwise naturally instructive experience. The incident occurs in the context of Stinger's reference to "Adam and Eve and the Garden of Eden and the first sin and all that noise," which leaves the protagonist mightily afraid of offending both God and Father Cassidy.

Whenever I get to thinking about the evil in the world, I always think about my friend, Stinger Riley. This is not because Stinger is evil, although there are a lot of people who have said so. It's just because he seems to have had it all figured out from the beginning, from the time we were in the third grade and had to go around on Wednesday afternoons with the rest of the Catholic kids for religious instructions at the nuns' high school. Stinger always went through the motions with the rest of us, but I could tell that he wasn't having any. He didn't even believe in God. And, because I didn't give him credit for an overdose of brains, I used to think he came by this attitude out of plain badness. But gradually, as we got older and moved into high school, I became aware that Stinger lived by a set of fairly sophisticated truths: that men are born savages, are selfish and prone to what is called evil; that they are sometimes idealists and invent gods; that they get scared and invent redeemers and heavens; that they are sadistic and invent devils and hells; and that they are damned fools and spend their lives trying to reconcile good and evil, gods and men, life and death. But I wasn't convinced that he had thought these things out, consciously and systematically, until one day just a couple of years ago when we were walking around Central Park Reservoir and he got off the one and only theological disquisition of his life. And it ran something like this:

"You know how it is, Bas, when you try to figure out life and what the hell we're doing here. Maybe you start off thinkin' about what a bunch of bastards people are, and just how in hell they got that way. I mean, were they always such bastards? And this gets you to thinkin' about Adam and Eve and the Garden of Eden and the first sin and all that noise, and that's where the cheese gets bindin'. Because you've got to decide which side you're on. And it's easy to get on God's side. All you've got to say is that He's a great guy and gave people free will just to be big about it, and that sin and evil got into things because people used their free will the wrong way. And that's okay and explains why people are such nasty bastards. But then, Bas, you are just figurin' you've got it knocked when you remember about hurricanes, clap, mosquitoes, cancer, earthquakes, piss-ants, volcanoes, and tidal waves, and these are a blow in the ass. Because nobody's free will invented them. So you think about it some more, taking it from all sides and finin' it all down to the short hair, and it gets to look like God ain't so good after all, or maybe He just ain't. And that's when you decide that there's evil in the world just because there is, and that people are nasty bastards just because that's what most of them naturally are."

Now, I'm not trying to tell you that Stinger did this sort of thinking in the third grade, but I insist that he did have it figured out vaguely, working from an instinctive awareness that the body, not the soul, was the basic reality and that it held all the important secrets. For, all his life, he has acted with a certain consistency, without tensions or guilt. He goes along enjoying what he sees and whatever is offered. He takes the good with the bad, deciding which is which for himself, and he scratches it where it itches if it itches at all. He's the happiest man I know.

I didn't meet Stinger until I was skipped into the third grade in January of my second year in school. We sat side by side then, and so we were more or less thrown together. And we became friends right away. Stinger got his nickname on account of his dexterity with a three-inch hatpin and, as far as I know, I was the only one in the third grade who was spared the rigors of his steel. He was a hell-raiser, impulsive and without inhibition. I was quiet, generally cautious, and given even that early to calculating odds and consequences. But we had a profound regard for one another's talents. Stinger was in awe, for example, of the ease with which I learned, concluding that I must be genius if I could skip a whole year of schooling. I was equally in awe of his gift for social relations, his ability to charm everybody with far less effort than it took me to tell someone my name. It wasn't this clear to us in the third grade, of course, and it was to be some time before I realized that Stinger's great talent was a simple matter of sex.

Everybody else said sex was evil. Stinger didn't think so, and, being a year older than I and precocious anyway, he was concerned with it from the very beginning. One result was that I got curious about this great evil pretty early. But I had no talent for it, and I didn't begin to understand for a long, long time. And this was not really Stinger's fault; he did try. I made inquiry once about why it was necessary for girls and boys to have separate toilets, and Stinger did the best he could with it. But I received the information with such apparent confusion and lack of comprehension that he soon gave it up as a bad job. We remained friendly, but he developed a certain respect or delicacy with regard to me that seemed to preclude any inclination on his part either to ridicule my ignorance or dispel any of it.

It didn't help any that at this time Stinger and I were being forced to undergo training as altar boys at the parish church. I took it seriously and Stinger didn't, but this doesn't mean that I was pious. The ceremonies of the Church didn't mean any more to me than to Stinger. But the Church and Father Cassidy scared me, and I had a great fear of offending either one of them. I would serve Father Cassidy's Mass in the winter, when the air was cold in the church and the pews were almost empty, and I would ring the bell at the elevation of the Host and, looking at its whiteness, begin to imagine that I had committed all manner of terrible sins. I would quake until the ordeal was over, and scurry out of the church, and from under Father Cassidy's hard eyes, as fast as I could get rid of my surplice.

Stinger was not so troubled. His only comment on the Mass was that it took too damned long and that all the kneeling made his knees hurt. He used to yawn, wiggle, belch, and scratch throughout the ceremony, and when I would tell him to be careful, he'd say that God wasn't watching. I would insist that God most assuredly was watching, but this never seemed to worry him. Sometimes I would tell him about the fires of purgatory, and he could begin to wince and look worried, but it had no lasting effect.

And Stinger mistook my fear for piety and, typically, respected it as such. So I got no lessons in sex that I didn't ask for and sometimes not even then. And I guess things would have stayed that way for a long time had it not been for the lady on the roof. I met this lady during the summer between the third and fourth grades. And when I told Stinger about her the following fall, he thought it was the greatest story he had every heard, and he had me tell it to him over and over again. And it changed everything between Stinger and me, because, after the lady on the roof, I was adjudged fully qualified to receive even the most delicate sexual information. This despite the fact that even after Stinger's patient explanations, I still had no clear idea as to what the lady had been up to, if indeed, as Stinger darkly hinted, she had been up to anything. You have got to judge for yourself.

I remember it was a hot day and Sean, my grandfather, was cleaning the hallway on the fifth floor. I was sitting on the steps watching him. He was mopping, bent over, the sweat dripping from his forehead onto the wet floor. I was watching the drops of sweat, waiting in fascination until the black, soggy mass of the mop swept over them and they disappeared without a trace.

Every few minutes he would stop and take a red bandanna from his pocket. He would wipe his face and tell me that it was pretty damned hot. I already knew this but didn't say so.

After a while he stopped mopping and said that he had to help the man with the ashes from the hot-water heater and that I should wait for him until he got back. Then he walked by me and down the stairs. I sat there and listened to his footsteps until he was all the way down into the cellar.

I waited and waited and the time went by very slowly. I got hot and itchy and tired. So I got up and walked down the hall to where the stairs went up to the roof. The door at the top of the stairs was propped open and a slow breeze was coming through. I sat down on the bottom step and it was much cooler there.

And I sat for what seemed like another hour at least, but Sean did not come, and I began to get hot again, so I moved up the stairs a couple of steps. Later I moved up a couple more. This went on, it getting hotter and hotter and the breeze feeling nicer and nicer as I got nearer the top, until I was sitting on the top step.

There I could lean back and look right out onto the roof. It was the first time I had seen it, being under positive assurance from Sean that if I ever went out on it I would invariably fall off the edge and get all smashed to a bloody pulp on the sidewalk. I remember this and it worried me. So I leaned back and looked for the edge of the roof, trying to see around the big red chimney that was opposite the door. And I saw a bare foot sticking out from behind the chimney.

It looked like a big foot and there was a little chain, like the one on my Blessed Virgin medal, around the ankle. I watched this foot awhile. The toes were pointing downward toward the roof. Several times the foot went up in the air and in behind the chimney. But it always came down again. I got to wondering where the other one was. I thought that maybe it was a one-legged man. Then I saw the toes of the other foot right against the chimney sticking out a little beyond it.

So I started to slither out a little further to see what else there was, still on my back and pushing myself with my legs, and I banged my head against the open roof door. It hurt, but I did not cry out. I rubbed my head with my eyes closed tight. Then I thought that since I was all the way out on the roof now anyway, I might just as well stand up and take a good look.

So I got up quietly and looked around. I couldn't see much of anything except the sky and other roofs and New Jersey way over on the other side of the river. But I could see the edge of the roof. It was a good block away. I decided I could walk over to the chimney without running the risk of falling off. I was wearing sneakers and made no noise. I eased my way around the side of the chimney where I had seen the feet. I got right up to the corner. The toes of one foot were still sticking out from behind it a little. I leaned forward around the toes and took a look.

The feet belonged to a lady who was lying on her stomach on a white blanket, and her hair was long and brown and hung down over her shoulders. And she had no clothes on.

I pulled my head back again and thought about this for a minute. I guessed that she lived in one of the apartments in the building. I

also guessed that she did not have much sense. Nobody else I knew
went around with no clothes on, and Sean had told me that you could
get locked up for not covering your parts in public. I decided I would
tell this lady a few things. I stepped out from behind the chimney.

"Hey, lady," I said. I almost whispered because I was scared. She
did not move, so I reached over and tapped her near foot.

"Hey, lady," I said again.

This time she whirled around and grabbed for a towel that was
lying near her head. I recognized her as a lady who lived on the
fourth floor. I did not know her name. She stopped as soon as she
saw me. She dropped the towel over her bottom and smiled. It was
a nice smile, as though I had done something only a little wrong.

"Don't ever sneak up on anybody like that, Bascomb," she said.

"I wasn't sneaking. How did you know my name is Bascomb?"

"Oh, I find out all kinds of things." And she turned her head
around again and brushed her hair back and began to look at a
magazine propped up in front of her. I stood there looking, but she
appeared to have forgotten me.

"Hey, lady," I said. I walked around and stood by her side.
"Don't you know you can get locked up for not covering your parts
in public?"

She laughed out loud and turned to look at me. I remember that
her teeth were very even and straight and looked snowwhite against
her tanned face.

"What do you know about parts?" She spoke as she laughed. Her
eyes flashed in the sunlight.

"My grandfather told me. Sean, I mean."

"Your grandfather!" She jumped and stopped laughing and
reached for a bathrobe that was folded up alongside of her. "Where's
your grandfather?"

"He's downstairs."

"How far down?"

"All the way down into the cellar."

"Good." She put the robe down. "What does your grandfather
say?"

"He says you can get locked up for not covering your parts in
public."

"He's right."

"So then, why don't you cover them?"

"Well, they are covered." She readjusted the towel without looking back. "Can you see anything?"

I made a short inspection. "Not now, I guess. But when I came up here first I could see your backside, and if I'd been a cop I'd have run you in."

"What for?" Now she was laughing again. I began to figure that she was really dumb. Somebody was going to lock her up for sure.

"For not covering your parts in public, that's what for."

"Well, I'm not in public, am I?"

This one stopped me for a minute. But only for a minute.

"I'm here and I'm public," I told her shortly.

"Oh no," she said quickly, shaking her head and making her hair slide back and forth across her bare shoulders. "You're strictly private. You're a friend of mine."

"How can I be a friend of yours if I don't even know your name?"

"How will it be if I tell you my name?"

"All right, I guess."

"Okay. My name is Lilly Vale. Now are we friends?"

"I guess so." I knew I had been trapped but it was too late. And I hated to see the law in point lose its effect by my rapid transition from public to private. But I did not see how I could get around it now. So I went back to my question. She was looking at her magazine again.

"What are you doing up here, lady?"

"Why don't you call me Lilly?"

"Lilly."

"I'm taking a sunbath."

"A sunbath?"

"That's right."

"Is it like a water bath any?"

"Sure."

"Do you scrub?"

"Oh no. You just lie here."

"Don't use soap?"

"No soap."

"And no water?"

"No water."

This, I decided, was the way to take a bath. I would have to tell Sean about it. And it cleared up a few things for me.

"Is that why you've got no clothes on, because you're taking a bath?"

"That's right."

"Is it fun?"

"Oh sure."

"How long do you have to lie there before you are clean?"

"Not too long. Matter of fact, I'm done on this side now." She looked back at her legs. Then she reached down and secured the towel around her bottom, turned over, and sat up. And for the first time I saw her breasts. I stood fascinated by them as she reached for a bottle of sun oil and rubbed it on them and on her shoulders, arms, and stomach. When she had finished, she lay back and put one arm over her eyes. Her breasts stood straight up, like the tops of two fire hydrants.

"Hey, lady." I spoke softly. "What are those?"

"What are what?" she said gently, not moving.

"These things." I bent down and touched the near breast. She jumped a little. Then she peeked out at me from under her arm.

"Oh, you've seen things like those before." She smiled.

"No, I haven't."

"Why, sure. Haven't you seen your mother's?"

"My mother hasn't got any."

"Sure she has."

"I never saw any."

"Well, she has. You look next time."

"Next time what?"

"How should I know? Just next time. Next time you take a bath with her."

"I don't take any baths with her."

"Didn't you ever?"

"No. I took a bath with my brother Tim once."

"Well, that isn't the same thing."

"He took up all the room."

"Do you always take a bath alone?"

"Yes. But Sean scrubs me."

"Your grandfather? Doesn't your mother take care of you?"

"No. She takes care of my father and my brother Tim."

"Oh." Then she turned away and closed her eyes and said something about a strange family.

"Hey, lady."

"Why don't you call me Lilly like I told you?"

"I forgot."

"Suppose I called you 'boy'?"

"I am a boy."

"I know. But you've got a name. Don't you like to be called by your name?"

"I guess so."

"Well, I like to be called by mine."

"All right. Lilly."

"That's better."

"Well, can I?"

"Can you what?"

"Can I touch them?"

"Touch what?" Then she saw where I was looking. She rose on one elbow. "You mean my . . . Oh no! That wouldn't be nice."

"Why wouldn't it be nice?"

"It just wouldn't. I mean, little boys just don't go around touching ladies' things."

"I'm not a little boy. I'm eight."

"Oh, I didn't mean it that way. Big boys don't go around feeling them either."

"Why don't they?"

"Well, because. Because it's bad, that's all. Bad."

"What do you mean, bad?"

"How should I know what I mean?"

"Bad like a sin?"

"Sure. I guess so. Bad like a sin." Then she smiled and lay back on her blanket. "Though I guess it depends on who does it and all."

"Would it be a sin if I did it?"

She closed her eyes and still smiled and said something about the mouths of babes and how she would be hung for a liar. Then she laughed out loud, causing her breasts to shake.

"How old did you say you were?" she asked.

"Eight."

"And you never, I mean, nobody's ever told you about girls?"

"Sean told me about girls. He said they have all got empty heads. He's going to tell me more about them someday, he said."

"I'd like to hear that." And she laughed again.

"And my best friend Stinger told me too."

"What did he tell you?"

"He said girls go to the toilet different."

"Do you know why?"

"No."

"Aren't you curious?"

'What's that?"

"I mean don't you want to know why girls go to the toilet different?"

"Girls do everything different. I don't care."

"Well, I'll be damned." She shook her head back and forth.

"So then would it be a sin if I touched them?"

"You really want to touch them, don't you?"

"Yes. Really."

"Well, after everybody else that's touched them, I don't see why I should draw the line with you."

"Can I do it now?"

"Sure. Go ahead."

So I knelt down beside her and took the point of the near breast between my fingers. Then I squeezed.

"Does that hurt?" I asked. It was a clinical question.

"No." She spoke softly, her arm over her eyes. "Feels fine. What's it feel like to you?"

"Feels like Sean's nose."

She roared with laughter. I let go for a minute so I could watch them. They were very pretty. Like jello.

"What are these things for?" I asked.

"Well, let's see. They're for little babies to play with."

"Have you got any little babies?"

"Nope."

"So then who plays with yours?"

"Oh, you'd be surprised. Only big babies play with mine." I thought about this for a minute. But I did not know what to say, so I leaned over and started to feel them again.

"What do you call them?" I asked.

"Oh, different things. Anything from louse to a son of a . . . Oh! You mean—my things!"

"Yes, these things."

"Oh sure. Well, most people just call them—call them knobs."

"Knobs? Like on a radio?"

"Sure. That's it."

"They're pretty big knobs."

"Thanks, kid. I like them that way."

"Can I feel them all over?"

"Haven't you had enough?"

"No."

"How come you talk so nice? Now come you never say 'yeah' and 'naw' like other kids?"

"Because Sean says he will paddle my backside if I do."

This made her laugh again.

Then I could feel them getting harder, and I saw that the tips were sharper now and standing up, and that they looked bigger all over.

"They're getting big," I said solemnly.

"Yes, they are." But she did not look.

"How big do they get?"

"Oh, that's as big as they get. You're doing a fine job."

Then, all at once, there were voices and footsteps in the hallway below. Not wanting to, but thinking of Sean and of getting caught on the roof, I lifted my hands from Lilly's breasts.

"Don't stop," she said.

"I think I have to go now."

"Why do you have to go?" She raised her arm from her eyes and looked at me. Then she heard the voices too. Her face became tense at once. "Is that your grandfather?"

I listened. I did not hear Sean. "No, I don't think it is. It sounds like two ladies."

Lilly smiled. "That's good."

"I think I'd better go now." I spoke uneasily and began to move away, inching backward on my knees.

"What's your hurry, Bascomb?" She lifted herself to one elbow. "It isn't your grandfather."

"Yes. But I think I better go anyway."

"Don't you want to touch them any more?"

"No. I don't. Thank you."

Then I started to stand up. Lilly reached out and took me by the wrist.

"Now just a minute." She spoke gently. I tried to pull away but her grip was too strong.

"Let me go," I said.

"If I let go now, do you promise you won't tell anybody about what you've done? Not even your grandfather?"

"I promise."

Then she let go of my wrist and I backed away, still on my knees. She turned and reached for her bathrobe. The towel had fallen away from her hips. I could see her whole body. And her belly was very white down near where her legs began. I watched her as she put on the robe, her body all tan except for the white patch on her belly. Then she noticed me watching her.

"Okay, free show's over. Get along now."

"Yes. I'm going." I got up and walked over by the chimney and looked back at her. She was standing up now, combing her long brown hair with swift, hard strokes, and it shimmered in the sunlight. She was looking out and down in the direction of the Hudson River.

"Good-by, Lilly," I said quietly.

"Good-by," she said over her shoulder, and she half turned, causing the robe to fall away from her breasts, and they were pretty in the sun.

"Thanks for letting me feel your knobs, Lilly."

"Oh sure, kid, sure. Any time. Any time you got the price."

Her voice didn't carry in the breeze, and she turned away from me as she spoke, but I am fairly sure that those were her words. And I thought about them as I walked down the stairs and wondered what she meant by the price. I decided that she must have meant that the next time I felt her knobs it was going to cost me something.

But I never felt Lilly's knobs again. She moved out shortly after the incident, and I watched her walking down West 107th Street, carrying her straw suitcase. When she turned the corner onto Broadway I hollered to her and waved. But she didn't hear me, and I felt bad about it because she looked lonely.

As I said, this story made a great impression on Stinger. As time went by, I came to understand how rare and wonderful an experience it had been, but I don't think I ever got quite the kick out of it that Stinger did. Its value to me was in the fact that it served to put Stinger in a mood for talking about sex, and I listened to whatever he had to say with great eagerness, feeding an insatiable curiosity.

DARKER THAN THE SWOON OF SIN, SOFTER THAN SOUND OR ODOUR

James Joyce

In *A Portrait of the Artist as a Young Man,* Joyce is concerned with tracing the emotional and psychological events that led him to his vocation of artist. The environment he presents us with is stifling, cramped, and stultifying, one whose victims are inartistic, indecisive, and inactive. There is a world outside the Dublin cosmos, however, which these haunted people aspire to—one of glamour and freedom of spirit and movement, but their efforts to cross over into that larger world are doomed to failure. In the following passage, young Stephen Dedalus seeks escape from the inhibiting life around him through abandonment in an ecstasy of sin. His idealistic formulations of an encounter with a prostitute symbolize his longings for beauty and purity and gentleness, which he mistakenly feels he has realized. He sublimates the experience as ideal and pure and emotionally securing, when it is his brutish environment that has triumphed over his ideals.

Stephen's mother and his brother and one of his cousins waited at the corner of quiet Foster Place while he and his father went up the steps and along the colonnade where the highland sentry was parading. When they had passed into the great hall and stood at the counter Stephen drew forth his orders on the governor of the bank of Ireland for thirty and three pounds; and these sums, the moneys of his exhibition and essay prize, were paid over to him rapidly by the teller in notes and in coin respectively. He bestowed them in his pockets and feigned composure and suffered the friendly teller, to whom his father chatted, to take his hand across the broad counter and wish him a brilliant career in after life. He was impatient of their voices and could not keep his feet at rest. But the teller still deferred the serving of others to say he was living in changed times and that there was nothing like giving a boy the best education that money could buy. Mr Dedalus lingered in the hall gazing about him and up at the roof and telling Stephen, who urged him to come out, that they were standing in the house of commons of the old Irish parliament.

—God help us! he said piously, to think of the men of those times, Stephen, Hely Hutchison and Flood and Henry Grattan and Charles Kendal Bushe, and the noblemen we have now, leaders of the Irish people at home and abroad. Why, by God, they wouldn't be seen dead in a tenacre field with them. No, Stephen, old chap, I'm sorry to say that they are only as I roved out one fine May morning in the merry month of sweet July.

A keen October wind was blowing round the bank. The three figures standing at the edge of the muddy path had pinched cheeks and watery eyes. Stephen looked at his thinly clad mother and remembered that a few days before he had seen a mantle priced at twenty guineas in the windows of Barnardo's.

—Well that's done, said Mr Dedalus.

—We had better go to dinner, said Stephen. Where?

—Dinner? said Mr Dedalus. Well, I suppose we had better, what?

—Some place that's not too dear, said Mrs Dedalus.

—Underdone's?

—Yes. Some quiet place.

—Come along, said Stephen quickly. It doesn't matter about the dearness.

He walked on before them with short nervous steps, smiling. They tried to keep up with him, smiling also at his eagerness.

—Take it easy like a good young fellow, said his father. We're not out for the half mile, are we?

For a swift season of merrymaking the money of his prizes ran through Stephen's fingers. Great parcels of groceries and delicacies and dried fruits arrived from the city. Every day he drew up a bill of fare for the family and every night led a party of three or four to the theatre to see *Ingomar* or *The Lady of Lyons*. In his coat pockets he carried squares of Vienna chocolate for his guests while his trousers' pockets bulged with masses of silver and copper coins. He bought presents for everyone, overhauled his room, wrote out resolutions, marshalled his books up and down their shelves, pored upon all kinds of price lists, drew up a form of commonwealth for the household by which every member of it held some office, opened a loan bank for his family and pressed loans on willing borrowers so that he might have the pleasure of making out receipts and reckoning the interests on the sums lent. When he could do no more he drove up and down the city in trams. Then the season of pleasure came to an end. The pot of pink enamel paint gave out and the wainscot of his bedroom remained with its unfinished and illplastered coat.

His household returned to its usual way of life. His mother had no further occasion to upbraid him for squandering his money. He too returned to his old life at school and all his novel enterprises fell to pieces. The commonwealth fell, the loan bank closed its coffers and its books on a sensible loss, the rules of life which he had drawn about himself fell into desuetude.

How foolish his aim had been! He had tried to build a breakwater of order and elegance against the sordid tide of life without him and to dam up, by rules of conduct and active interests and new filial relations, the powerful recurrence of the tides within him. Useless. From without as from within the water had flowed over his barriers: their tides began once more to jostle fiercely above the crumbled mole.

He saw clearly too his own futile isolation. He had not gone one step nearer the lives he had sought to approach nor bridged the restless shame and rancour that divided him from mother and brother and sister. He felt that he was hardly of the one blood with them but stood to them rather in the mystical kinship of fosterage, fosterchild and fosterbrother.

He burned to appease the fierce longings of his heart before which everything else was idle and alien. He cared little that he was in mortal sin, that his life had grown to be a tissue of subterfuge and falsehood. Beside the savage desire within him to realise the enormities which he brooded on nothing was sacred. He bore cynically with the shameful details of his secret riots in which he exulted to defile with patience whatever image had attracted his eyes. By day and by night he moved among distorted images of the outer world. A figure that had seemed to him by day demure and innocent came towards him by night through the winding darkness of sleep, her face transfigured by a lecherous cunning, her eyes bright with brutish joy. Only the morning pained him with its dim memory of dark orgiastic riot, its keen and humiliating sense of transgression.

He returned to his wanderings. The veiled autumnal evenings led him from street to street as they had led him years before along the quiet avenues of Blackrock. But no vision of trim front gardens or of kindly lights in the windows poured a tender influence upon him now. Only at times, in the pauses of his desire, when the luxury that was wasting him gave room to a softer languor, the image of Mercedes traversed the background of his memory. He saw again the small white house and the garden of rosebushes on the road that led to the mountains and he remembered the sadly proud gesture of refusal which he was to make there, standing with her in the moonlit garden after years of estrangement and adventure. At those moments the soft speeches of Claude Melnotte rose to his lips and eased his unrest. A tender premonition touched him of the tryst he had then looked forward to and, in spite of the horrible reality which lay between his hope of then and now, of the holy encounter he had then imagined at which weakness and timidity and inexperience were to fall from him.

Such moments passed and the wasting fires of lust sprang up again. The verses passed from his lips and the inarticulate cries and the unspoken brutal words rushed forth from his brain to force a passage. His blood was in revolt. He wandered up and down the dark slimy streets peering into the gloom of lanes and doorways, listening eagerly for any sound. He moaned to himself like some baffled prowling beast. He wanted to sin with another of his kind, to force another being to sin with him and to exult with her in sin. He felt some dark presence moving irresistibly upon him from the darkness, a presence subtle and murmurous as a flood filling him wholly with itself. Its murmur besieged his ears like the murmur of some multitude in sleep; its subtle streams penetrated his being. His hands clenched convulsively and his teeth set together as he suffered the agony of its penetration. He stretched out his arms in the street to hold fast the frail swooning form that eluded him and incited him: and the cry that he had strangled for so long in his throat issued from his lips. It broke from him like a wail of despair from a hell of sufferers and

died in a wail of furious entreaty, a cry for an iniquitous abandonment, a cry which was but the echo of an obscene scrawl which he
had read on the oozing wall of a urinal.

He had wandered into a maze of narrow and dirty streets. From
the foul laneways he heard bursts of hoarse riot and wrangling and
the drawling of drunken singers. He walked onward, undismayed,
wondering whether he had strayed into the quarter of the jews.
Women and girls dressed in long vivid gowns traversed the street
from house to house. They were leisurely and perfumed. A trembling
seized him and his eyes grew dim. The yellow gasflames arose before
his troubled vision against the vapoury sky, burning as if before an
altar. Before the doors and in the lighted halls groups were gathered
arrayed as for some rite. He was in another world: he had awakened
from a slumber of centuries.

He stood still in the middle of the roadway, his heart clamouring
against his bosom in a tumult. A young woman dressed in a long pink
gown laid her hand on his arm to detain him and gazed into his face.
She said gaily:

—Good night, Willie dear!

Her room was warm and lightsome. A huge doll sat with her legs
apart in the copious easychair beside the bed. He tried to bid his
tongue speak that he might seem at ease, watching her as she undid
her gown, noting the proud conscious movements of her perfumed
head.

As he stood silent in the middle of the room she came over to
him and embraced him gaily and gravely. Her round arms held him
firmly to her and he, seeing her face lifted to him in serious calm
and feeling the warm calm rise and fall of her breast, all but burst
into hysterical weeping. Tears of joy and relief shone in his delighted
eyes and his lips parted though they would not speak.

She passed her tinkling hand through his hair, calling him a little
rascal.

—Give me a kiss, she said.

His lips would not bend to kiss her. He wanted to be held firmly
in her arms, to be caressed slowly, slowly, slowly. In her arms he felt
that he had suddenly become strong and fearless and sure of himself.
But his lips would not bend to kiss her.

With a sudden movement she bowed his head and joined her
lips to his and he read the meaning of her movements in her frank
uplifted eyes. It was too much for him. He closed his eyes, surrender-
ing himself to her, body and mind, conscious of nothing in the world
but the dark pressure of her softly parting lips. They pressed upon

his brain as upon his lips as though they were the vehicle of a vague speech; and between them he felt an unknown and timid pressure, darker than the swoon of sin, softer than the sound or odour.

THE SIEGE OF MISS WILKINSON'S VIRTUE

W. Somerset Maugham

As in the selections from Stendhal and Joyce, the protagonist of Maugham's *Of Human Bondage* is convinced that he is the world's most foolish, inexperienced, and romantically inept young man. Having become convinced by a steady diet of romantic novels that the key to self-possession and worldly knowledge lies in the seduction of an older woman more experienced and sophisticated than himself, Philip Carey falls easy prey to the coquettish flirtations of Miss Wilkinson, whose life she assures him (through provocative tales of a recent love affair) is the "very soul of romance." Philip's confusion is that Miss Wilkinson, who is thirty-seven "if she is a day," bears scant resemblance to the beautiful fictional seductresses who have fed his romantic expectations. But so strong is his conviction, or delusion, that she provides the threshold to a fuller, more secure world, and so important to his vanity is it that he not prove inadequate in her eyes, that the learns to play "the most thrilling game" of his life. He is finally propelled to her bedroom not as an act of love, nor one of consuming passion, but insincerely, in pursuit of an idea he feels he is obligated to fulfill.

Philip cound not get Miss Wilkinson's story out of his head. It was
clear enough what she meant even though she cut it short, and he
was a little shocked. That sort of thing was all very well for married
women, he had read enough French novels to know that in France
it was indeed the rule, but Miss Wilkinson was English and unmarried; her father was a clergyman. Then it struck him that the art-
student probably was neither the first nor the last of her lovers, and
he gasped: he had never looked upon Miss Wilkinson like that; it
seemed incredible that anyone should make love to her. In his in-
genuousness he doubted her story as little as he doubted what he
read in books, and he was angry that such wonderful things never
happened to him. It was humiliating that if Miss Wilkinson insisted
upon his telling her of his adventures in Heidelberg he would have
nothing to tell. It was true that he had some power of invention, but
he was not sure whether he could persuade her that he was steeped
in vice; women were full of intuition, he had read that, and she might
easily discover that he was fibbing. He blushed scarlet as he thought
of her laughing up her sleeve.

Miss Wilkinson played the piano and sang in a rather tired voice;
but her songs, Massenet, Benjamin Goddard, and Augusta Holmès,
were new to Philip; and together they spent many hours at the piano.
One day she wondered if he had a voice and insisted on trying it.
She told him he had a pleasant baritone and offered to give him
lessons. At first with his usual bashfulness he refused, but she insisted,
and then every morning at a convenient time after breakfast she
gave him an hour's lesson. She had a natural gift for teaching, and
it was clear that she was an excellent governess. She had method and
firmness. Though her French accent was so much part of her that
it remained, all the mellifluousness of her manner left her when she
was engaged in teaching. She put up with no nonsense. Her voice
became a little peremptory, and instinctively she suppressed inatten-
tion and corrected slovenliness. She knew what she was about and
put Philip to scales and exercises.

When the lesson was over she resumed without effort her seductive smiles, her voice became again soft and winning, but Philip
could not so easily put away the pupil as she the pedagogue; and this
impression conflicted with the feelings her stories had aroused in
him. He looked at her more narrowly. He liked her much better in
the evening than in the morning. In the morning she was rather
lined and the skin of her neck was just a little rough. He wished she
would hide it, but the weather was very warm just then and she wore
blouses which were cut low. She was very fond of white; in the

morning it did not suit her. At night she often looked very attractive, she put on a gown which was almost a dinner dress, and she wore a chain of garnets round her neck; the lace about her bosom and at her elbows gave her a pleasant softness, and the scent she wore (at Blackstable no one used anything but *Eau de Cologne,* and that only on Sundays or when suffering from a sick headache) was troubling and exotic. She really looked very young then.

Philip was much exercised over her age. He added twenty and seventeen together, and could not bring them to a satisfactory total. He asked Aunt Louisa more than once why she thought Miss Wilkinson was thirty-seven: she didn't look more than thirty, and everyone knew that foreigners aged more rapidly than English women; Miss Wilkinson had lived so long abroad that she might almost be called a foreigner. He personally wouldn't have thought her more than twenty-six.

"She's more than that," said Aunt Louisa.

Philip did not believe in the accuracy of the Careys' statements. All they distinctly remembered was that Miss Wilkinson had not got her hair up the last time they saw her in Lincolnshire. Well, she might have been twelve then: it was so long ago and the Vicar was always so unreliable. They said it was twenty years ago, but people used round figures, and it was just as likely to be eighteen years, or seventeen. Seventeen and twelve were only twenty-nine, and hang it all, that wasn't old, was it? Cleopatra was forty-eight when Antony threw away the world for her sake.

It was a fine summer. Day after day was hot and cloudless; but the heat was tempered by the neighbourhood of the sea, and there was a pleasant exhilaration in the air, so that one was excited and not oppressed by the August sunshine. There was a pond in the garden in which a fountain played; water lilies grew in it and gold fish sunned themselves on the surface. Philip and Miss Wilkinson used to take rugs and cushions there after dinner and lie on the lawn in the shade of a tall hedge of roses. They talked and read all the afternoon. They smoked cigarettes, which the Vicar did not allow in the house; he thought smoking a disgusting habit, and used frequently to say that it was disgraceful for anyone to grow a slave to a habit. He forgot that he was himself a slave to afternoon tea.

One day Miss Wilkinson gave Philip *La Vie de Bohème.* She had found it by accident when she was rummaging among the books in the Vicar's study. It had been bought in a lot with something Mr. Carey wanted and had remained undiscovered for ten years.

Philip began to read Murger's fascinating, ill-written, absurd masterpiece, and fell at once under its spell. His soul danced with joy at that picture of starvation which is so good-humoured, of squalor which is so picturesque, of sordid love which is so romantic, of bathos which is so moving. Rodolphe and Mimi, Musette and Schaunard! They wander through the gray streets of the Latin Quarter, finding refuge now in one attic, now in another, in their quaint costumes of Louis Philippe, with their tears and their smiles, happy-go-lucky and reckless. Who can resist them? It is only when you return to the book with a sounder judgment that you find how gross their pleasures were, how vulgar their minds; and you feel the utter worthlessness, as artists and as human beings, of that gay procession. Philip was enraptured.

"Don't you wish you were going to Paris instead of London?" asked Miss Wilkinson, smiling at his enthusiasm.

"It's too late now even if I did," he answered.

During the fortnight he had been back from Germany there had been much discussion between himself and his uncle about his future. He had refused definitely to go to Oxford, and now that there was no chance of his getting scholarships even Mr. Carey came to the conclusion that he could not afford it. His entire fortune had consisted of only two thousand pounds, and though it had been invested in mortgages at five per cent, he had not been able to live on the interest. It was now a little reduced. It would be absurd to spend two hundred a year, the least he could live on at a university, for three years at Oxford which would lead him no nearer to earning his living. He was anxious to go straight to London. Mrs. Carey thought there were only four professions for a gentleman, the Army, the Navy, the Law, and the Church. She had added medicine because her brother-in-law practised it, but did not forget that in her young days no one ever considered the doctor a gentleman. The first two were out of the question, and Philip was firm in his refusal to be ordained. Only the law remained. The local doctor had suggested that many gentlemen now went in for engineering, but Mrs. Carey opposed the idea at once.

"I shouldn't like Philip to go into trade," she said.

"No, he must have a profession," answered the Vicar.

"Why not make him a doctor like his father?"

"I should hate it," said Philip.

Mrs. Carey was not sorry. The Bar seemed out of the question, since he was not going to Oxford, for the Careys were under the impression that a degree was still necessary for success in that calling;

and finally it was suggested that he should become articled to a solicitor. They wrote to the family lawyer, Albert Nixon, who was co-executor with the Vicar of Blackstable for the late Henry Carey's estate, and asked him whether he would take Philip. In a day or two the answer came back that he had not a vacancy, and was very much opposed to the whole scheme; the profession was greatly overcrowded, and without capital or connections a man had small chance of becoming more than a managing clerk; he suggested, however, that Philip should become a chartered accountant. Neither the Vicar nor his wife knew in the least what this was, and Philip had never heard of anyone being a chartered accountant; but another letter from the solicitor explained that the growth of modern businesses and the increase of companies had led to the formation of many firms of accountants to examine the books and put into the financial affairs of their clients an order which old-fashioned methods had lacked. Some years before a Royal Charter had been obtained, and the profession was becoming every year more respectable, lucrative, and important. The chartered accountants whom Albert Nixon had employed for thirty years happened to have a vacancy for an articled pupil, and would take Philip for a fee of three hundred pounds. Half of this would be returned during the five years the articles lasted in the form of salary. The prospect was not exciting, but Philip felt that he must decide on something, and the thought of living in London over-balanced the slight shrinking he felt. The Vicar of Blackstable wrote to ask Mr. Nixon whether it was a profession suited to a gentleman; and Mr. Nixon replied that, since the Charter, men were going into it who had been to public schools and a university; moreover, if Philip disliked the work and after a year wished to leave, Herbert Carter, for that was the accountant's name, would return half the money paid for the articles. This settled it, and it was arranged that Philip should start work on the fifteenth of September.

"I have a full month before me," said Philip.

"And then you go to freedom and I to bondage," returned Miss Wilkinson.

Her holidays were to last six weeks, and she would be leaving Blackstable only a day or two before Philip.

"I wonder if we shall ever meet again," she said.

"I don't know why not."

"Oh, don't speak in that practical way. I never knew anyone so unsentimental."

Philip reddened. He was afraid that Miss Wilkinson would think him a milksop: after all she was a young woman, sometimes quite pretty, and he was getting on for twenty; it was absurd that they should talk of nothing but art and literature. He ought to make love to her. They had talked a good deal of love. There was the art-student in the Rue Bréda, and then there was the painter in whose family she had lived so long in Paris: he had asked her to sit for him, and had started to make love to her so violently that she was forced to invent excuses not to sit to him again. It was clear enough that Miss Wilkinson was used to attentions of that sort. She looked very nice now in a large straw hat: it was hot that afternoon, the hottest day they had had, and beads of sweat stood in a line on her upper lip. He called to mind Fräulein Cäcilie and Herr Sung. He had never thought of Cäcilie in an amorous way, she was exceedingly plain; but now, looking back, the affair seemed very romantic. He had a chance of romance too. Miss Wilkinson was practically French, and that added zest to a possible adventure. When he thought of it at night in bed, or when he sat by himself in the garden reading a book, he was thrilled by it; but when he saw Miss Wilkinson it seemed less picturesque.

At all events, after what she had told him, she would not be surprised if he made love to her. He had a feeling that she must think it odd of him to make no sign: perhaps it was only his fancy, but once or twice in the last day or two he had imagined that there was a suspicion of contempt in her eyes.

"A penny for your thoughts," said Miss Wilkinson, looking at him with a smile.

"I'm not going to tell you," he answered.

He was thinking that he ought to kiss her there and then. He wondered if she expected him to do it; but after all he didn't see how he could without any preliminary business at all. She would just think him mad, or she might slap his face; and perhaps she would complain to his uncle. He wondered how Herr Sung had started with Fräulein Cäcilie. It would be beastly if she told his uncle: he knew what his uncle was, he would tell the doctor and Josiah Graves; and he would look a perfect fool. Aunt Louisa kept on saying that Miss Wilkinson was thirty-seven if she was a day; he shuddered at the thought of the ridicule he would be exposed to; they would say she was old enough to be his mother.

"Twopence for your thoughts," smiled Miss Wilkinson.

"I was thinking about you," he answered boldly.

That at all events committed him to nothing.

"What were you thinking?"

"Ah, now you want to know too much."

"Naughty boy!" said Miss Wilkinson.

There it was again! Whenever he had succeeded in working himself up she said something which reminded him of the governess. She called him playfully a naughty boy when he did not sing his exercises to her satisfaction. This time he grew quite sulky.

"I wish you wouldn't treat me as if I were a child."

"Are you cross?"

"Very."

"I didn't mean to."

She put out her hand and he took it. Once or twice lately when they shook hands at night he had fancied she slightly pressed his hand, but this time there was no doubt about it.

He did not quite know what he ought to say next. Here at last was his chance of an adventure, and he would be a fool not to take it; but it was a little ordinary, and he had expected more glamour. He had read many descriptions of love, and he felt in himself none of that uprush of emotion which novelists described; he was not carried off his feet in wave upon wave of passion; nor was Miss Wilkinson the ideal: he had often pictured to himself the great violet eyes and the alabaster skin of some lovely girl, and he had thought of himself burying his face in the rippling masses of her auburn hair. He could not imagine himself burying his face in Miss Wilkinson's hair, it always struck him as a little sticky. All the same it would be very satisfactory to have an intrigue, and he thrilled with the legitimate pride he would enjoy in his conquest. He owed it to himself to seduce her. He made up his mind to kiss Miss Wilkinson; not then, but in the evening; it would be easier in the dark, and after he had kissed her the rest would follow. He would kiss her that very evening. He swore an oath to that effect.

He laid his plans. After supper he suggested that they should take a stroll in the garden. Miss Wilkinson accepted, and they sauntered side by side. Philip was very nervous. He did not know why, but the conversation would not lead in the right direction; he had decided that the first thing to do was to put his arm round her waist; but he could not suddenly put his arm round her waist when she was talking of the regatta which was to be held next week. He led her artfully into the darkest parts of the garden, but having arrived there his courage failed him. They sat on a bench, and he had really made up his mind that here was his opportunity when Miss Wilkinson said she was sure there were earwigs and insisted on moving. They walked round the garden once more, and Philip promised himself he would take the plunge before they arrived at that bench again;

but as they passed the house, they saw Mrs. Carey standing at the door.

"Hadn't you young people better come in? I'm sure the night air isn't good for you."

"Perhaps we had better go in," said Philip. "I don't want you to catch cold."

He said it with a sigh of relief. He could attempt nothing more that night. But afterwards, when he was alone in his room, he was furious with himself. He had been a perfect fool. He was certain that Miss Wilkinson expected him to kiss her, otherwise she wouldn't have come into the garden. She was always saying that only Frenchmen knew how to treat women. Philip had read French novels. If he had been a Frenchman he would have seized her in his arms and told her passionately that he adored her; he would have pressed his lips on her *nuque*. He did not know why Frenchmen always kissed ladies on the *nuque*. He did not himself see anything so very attractive in the nape of the neck. Of course it was much easier for Frenchmen to do these things; the language was such an aid; Philip could never help feeling that to say passionate things in English sounded a little absurd. He wished now that he had never undertaken the siege of Miss Wilkinson's virtue; the first fortnight had been so jolly, and now he was wretched; but he was determined not to give in, he would never respect himself again if he did, and he made up his mind irrevocably that the next night he would kiss her without fail.

Next day when he got up he saw it was raining, and his first thought was that they would not be able to go into the garden that evening. He was in high spirits at breakfast. Miss Wilkinson sent Mary Ann in to say that she had a headache and would remain in bed. She did not come down till tea-time, when she appeared in a becoming wrapper and a pale face; but she was quite recovered by supper, and the meal was very cheerful. After prayers she said she would go straight to bed, and she kissed Mrs. Carey. Then she turned to Philip.

"Good gracious!" she cried. "I was just going to kiss you too."

"Why don't you?" he said.

She laughed and held out her hand. She distinctly pressed his.

The following day there was not a cloud in the sky, and the garden was sweet and fresh after the rain. Philip went down to the beach to bathe and when he came home ate a magnificent dinner. They were having a tennis party at the vicarage in the afternoon and Miss Wilkinson put on her best dress. She certainly knew how to wear her clothes, and Philip could not help noticing how elegant she looked beside the curate's wife and the doctor's married daughter.

There were two roses in her waistband. She sat in a garden chair by
the side of the lawn, holding a red parasol over herself, and the light
on her face was very becoming. Philip was fond of tennis. He served
well and as he ran clumsily played close to the net: notwithstanding
his clubfoot he was quick, and it was difficult to get a ball past him.
He was pleased because he won all his sets. At tea he lay down at
Miss Wilkinson's feet, hot and panting.

"Flannels suit you," she said. "You look very nice this afternoon."

He blushed with delight.

"I can honestly return the compliment. You look perfectly rav-
ishing."

She smiled and gave him a long look with her black eyes.

After supper he insisted that she should come out.

"Haven't you had enough exercise for one day?"

"It'll be lovely in the garden tonight. The stars are all out."

He was in high spirits.

"D'you know, Mrs. Carey has been scolding me on your account?" said Miss Wilkinson, when they were sauntering through the
kitchen garden. "She says I mustn't flirt with you."

"Have you been flirting with me? I hadn't noticed it."

"She was only joking."

"It was very unkind of you to refuse to kiss me last night."

"If you saw the look your uncle gave me when I said what I did!"

"Was that all that prevented you?"

"I prefer to kiss people without witnesses."

"There are no witnesses now."

Philip put his arm round her waist and kissed her lips. She only
laughed a little and made no attempt to withdraw. It had come quite
naturally. Philip was very proud of himself. He said he would, and
he had. It was the easiest thing in the world. He wished he had done
it before. He did it again.

"Oh, you mustn't," she said.

"Why not?"

"Because I like it," she laughed.

Next day after dinner they took their rugs and cushions to the
fountain, and their books; but they did not read. Miss Wilkinson made
herself comfortable and she opened the red sun-shade. Philip was
not at all shy now, but at first she would not let him kiss her.

"It was very wrong of me last night," she said. "I couldn't sleep, I felt I'd done so wrong."

"What nonsense!" he cried. "I'm sure you slept like a top."

"What do you think your uncle would say if he knew?"

"There's no reason why he should know."

He leaned over her, and his heart went pit-a-pat.

"Why d'you want to kiss me?"

He knew he ought to reply: "Because I love you." But he could not bring himself to say it.

"Why do you think?" he asked instead.

She looked at him with smiling eyes and touched his face with the tips of her fingers.

"How smooth your face is," she murmured.

"I want shaving awfully," he said.

It was astonishing how difficult he found it to make romantic speeches. He found that silence helped him much more than words. He could look inexpressible things. Miss Wilkinson sighed.

"Do you like me at all?"

"Yes, awfully."

When he tried to kiss her again she did not resist. He pretended to be much more passionate than he really was, and he succeeded in playing a part which looked very well in his own eyes.

"I'm beginning to be rather frightened of you," said Miss Wilkinson.

"You'll come out after supper, won't you?" he begged.

"Not unless you promise to behave yourself."

"I'll promise anything."

He was catching fire from the flame he was partly simulating, and at tea-time he was obstreperously merry. Miss Wilkinson looked at him nervously.

"You mustn't have those shining eyes," she said to him afterwards. "What will your Aunt Louisa think?"

"I don't care what she thinks."

Miss Wilkinson gave a little laugh of pleasure. They had no sooner finished supper than he said to her:

"Are you going to keep me company while I smoke a cigarette?"

"Why don't you let Miss Wilkinson rest?" said Mrs. Carey. "You must remember she's not as young as you."

"Oh, I'd like to go out, Mrs. Carey," she said, rather acidly.

"After dinner walk a mile, after supper rest a while," said the Vicar.

"Your aunt is very nice, but she gets on my nerves sometimes," said Miss Wilkinson, as soon as they closed the side-door behind them.

Philip threw away the cigarette he had just lighted, and flung his arms round her. She tried to push him away.

"You promised you'd be good, Philip."

"You didn't think I was going to keep a promise like that?"

"Not so near the house, Philip," she said. "Supposing someone should come out suddenly?"

He led her to the kitchen garden where no one was likely to come, and this time Miss Wilkinson did not think of earwigs. He kissed her passionately. It was one of the things that puzzled him that he did not like her at all in the morning, and only moderately in the afternoon, but at night the touch of her hand thrilled him. He said things that he would never have thought himself capable of saying; he could certainly never have said them in the broad light of day; and he listened to himself with wonder and satisfaction.

"How beautifully you make love," she said.

That was what he thought himself.

"Oh, if I could only say all the things that burn my heart!" he murmured passionately.

It was splendid. It was the most thrilling game he had ever played; and the wonderful thing was that he felt almost all he said. It was only that he exaggerated a little. He was tremendously interested and excited in the effect he could see it had on her. It was obviously with an effort that at last she suggested going in.

"Oh, don't go yet," he cried.

"I must," she muttered. "I'm frightened."

He had a sudden intuition what was the right thing to do then.

"I can't go in yet. I shall stay here and think. My cheeks are burning. I want the night-air. Good-night."

He held out his hand seriously, and she took it in silence. He thought she stifled a sob. Oh, it was magnificent! When, after a decent interval during which he had been rather bored in the dark garden by himself, he went in he found that Miss Wilkinson had already gone to bed.

After that things were different between them. The next day and the day after Philip showed himself an eager lover. He was deliciously flattered to discover that Miss Wilkinson was in love with him: she told him so in English, and she told him so in French. She paid him compliments. No one had ever informed him before that his eyes were charming and that he had a sensual mouth. He had never bothered much about his personal appearance, but now, when occasion presented, he looked at himself in the glass with satisfaction. When he kissed her it was wonderful to feel the passion that seemed to thrill her soul. He kissed her a good deal, for he found it easier to do that than to say the things he instinctively felt she expected of him. It still made him feel a fool to say he worshipped her. He wished there were someone to whom he could boast a little, and he would willingly have discussed minute points of his conduct. Sometimes she said things that were enigmatic, and he was puzzled. He wished Hayward had been there so that he could ask him what he thought she meant, and what he had better do next. He could not make up his mind whether he ought to rush things or let them take their time. There were only three weeks more.

"I can't bear to think of that," she said. "It breaks my heart. And then perhaps we shall never see one another again."

"If you cared for me at all, you wouldn't be so unkind to me," he whispered.

"Oh, why can't you be content to let it go on as it is? Men are always the same. They're never satisfied."

And when he pressed her, she said:

"But don't you see it's impossible. How can we here?"

He proposed all sorts of schemes, but she would not have anything to do with them.

"I daren't take the risk. It would be too dreadful if your aunt found out."

A day or two later he had an idea which seemed brilliant.

"Look here, if you had a headache on Sunday evening and offered to stay at home and look after the house, Aunt Louisa would go to church."

Generally Mrs. Carey remained in on Sunday evening in order to allow Mary Ann to go to church, but she would welcome the opportunity of attending evensong.

Philip had not found it necessary to impart to his relations the change in his views on Christianity which had occurred in Germany; they could not be expected to understand; and it seemed less trouble to go to church quietly. But he only went in the morning. He regarded this as a graceful concession to the prejudices of society and his refusal to go a second time as an adequate assertion of free thought.

When he made the suggestion, Miss Wilkinson did not speak for a moment, then shook her head.

"No, I won't," she said.

But on Sunday at tea-time she surprised Philip.

"I don't think I'll come to church this evening," she said suddenly. "I've really got a dreadful headache."

Mrs. Carey, much concerned, insisted on giving her some 'drops' which she was herself in the habit of using. Miss Wilkinson thanked her, and immediately after tea announced that she would go to her room and lie down.

"Are you sure there's nothing you'll want?" asked Mrs. Carey anxiously.

"Quite sure, thank you."

"Because, if there isn't, I think I'll go to church. I don't often have the chance of going in the evening."

"Oh yes, do go."

"I shall be in," said Philip. "If Miss Wilkinson wants anything, she can always call me."

"You'd better leave the drawing-room door open, Philip, so that if Miss Wilkinson rings, you'll hear."

"Certainly," said Philip.

So after six o'clock Philip was left alone in the house with Miss Wilkinson. He felt sick with apprehension. He wished with all his heart that he had not suggested the plan; but it was too late now; he must take the opportunity which he had made. What would Miss Wilkinson think of him if he did not! He went into the hall and listened. There was not a sound. He wondered if Miss Wilkinson really had a headache. Perhaps she had forgotten his suggestion. His heart beat painfully. He crept up the stairs as softly as he could, and he stopped with a start when they creaked. He stood outside Miss Wilkinson's room and listened; he put his hand on the knob of the door-handle. He waited. It seemed to him that he waited for at least five minutes, trying to make up his mind; and his hand trembled. He would willingly have bolted, but he was afraid of the remorse which he knew would seize him. It was like getting on the highest diving-board in a swimming-bath; it looked nothing from below, but when you got up there and stared down at the water your heart sank; and the only thing that forced you to dive was the shame of coming down meekly by the steps you had climbed up. Philip screwed up his courage. He turned the handle softly and walked in. He seemed to himself to be trembling like a leaf.

Miss Wilkinson was standing at the dressing-table with her back to the door, and she turned round quickly when she heard it open.

"Oh, it's you. What d'you want?"

She had taken off her skirt and blouse, and was standing in her petticoat. It was short and only came down to the top of her boots;

the upper part of it was black, of some shiny material, and there was
a red flounce. She wore a camisole of white calico with short arms.
She looked grotesque. Philip's heart sank as he stared at her; she had
never seemed so unattractive; but it was too late now. He closed the
door behind him and locked it.

Six

Preparation

Doing a filthy pleasure is, and short;
And done, we straight repent us of the sport.
Let us not, then, rush blindly on unto it
Like lustful beasts, that only know to do it,
For lust will languish, and that heat decay.
But thus, thus, keeping endless holiday,
Let us together closely lie, and kiss;
There is no labor, nor no shame in this.
This hath pleased, doth please, and long will please; never
Can this decay, but is beginning ever.

DOING A FILTHY PLEASURE IS—
Ben Jonson

A PACKAGE
OF YOU KNOW WHAT

Herman Raucher

The preparation for a first sexual experience with a girl, especially if you were a contraception-conscious young man and the pill hadn't come along yet, was a drama doubtlessly replayed millions of times in those decades leading to the 1970s. Hermie's surreptitious attempt to purchase a package of rubber condoms from a perceptive but playful New England druggist reveals, to some extent, the attitudes toward sex held by those young boys who grew to manhood during the 1940s. In a curious way, the story raises a number of questions about the effects of technological "progress" on human relationships in general, and on male-female relationships in particular.

Hermie and Oscy, the young devils, sauntered up to the drugstore the next morning feeling very *très gai* and serenely confident in their plan, needing only a certain piece of rubberized madness to launch Hermie properly into the recesses of all the world's femininity. Oscy wore his usual sweat shirt, for he was to wait outside, having revealed himself to be unwilling to make the difficult purchase since he was already equipped for the night's outing. Hermie, on the other hand, having failed to get Oscy to volunteer for the hazardous condom caper, dressed himself in clothing that might work wonders in making him appear older. He was therefore not merely the only man on Packett Island wearing a tie; he was also wearing the longest tie ever to find its way to the island primarily because it was his father's, and no matter how many double Windsor knots he tied in it, it still came down three inches below his belt buckle. It was also a very loud tie, red and green leaves on a pale-yellow background, a Christmas gift to his father from a color-blind enemy. For those reasons he tucked both tails of the tie into his trousers and pulled his jacket front so close that, unless you had been with Hermie when he got dressed that morning, you had no way of knowing that he was wearing a tie.

It had all been carefully worked out. Oscy took up a position just outside the drugstore, where he casually produced his harmonica and played "Old MacDonald's Farm" in a manner that would curdle all the milk thereon. It may have seemed odd to have Oscy serve as a sentinel when no shoplifting had been planned, but it was a special request from Hermie who feared that The Mother Who Walked the Night might be dropping by, and he didn't want her to catch him buying rubbers, no, sir—ma'am. Hermie took a deep breath that brought air all the way into his toes; then, with a nod to Oscy, he nonchalantly entered the drugstore, a difficult maneuver to perform since the bell on the door announced his presence like Big Ben.

Hermie winced at the clang and began to perspire like a truck horse. But there was no danger of offensive perspiration because he had put such lumps of Mum under his arms that they kept slipping behind him when he walked, making him look as though he were about to perform a racing dive into the Erasmus pool. Unable to control his slithering arms, he plunged both his hands into his pockets, and looking as guilty as they come, he professionally cased the joint.

At the far end of the far counter was the druggist, Mr. Sanders, a crusty New Englander, thin and wiry and craggy and everything you'd expect him to be. On occasion he could even be heard saying "A-yuh" to the lady customer he was attending to. Another lady was just kind of looking around the store, plucking random items from the shelves. Other than those two ladies, Hermie was alone. He moseyed about, kind of checking out the shelves. The Band-Aids caught his eye. He knew a good deal about Band-Aids because, in any given summer, he could consume up to three or four hundred of them.

He noticed the lady at the counter pay Mr. Sanders and leave. The bell on the door chimed her exit, and as the door swung open, the sound of Oscy's miserable harmonica trailed in. It meant that Oscy was still at his post. Good man, that Oscy. The door shut. The bell rang. The harmonica was stifled in the middle of a chord they'd never find again.

Hermie moved over to the toothpaste section. A placard there announced that empty tubes should not be discarded. The other lady, the silent stroller, was still on the premises, showing no inclination to leave. It unnerved Hermie to have her around. Especially since Mr. Sanders was walking toward him and saying, "Can I help you?"

"Help *her*. She was here first." Hermie pointed to the strolling lady, who just smiled and continued to be a strolling lady. Maybe she was some kind of guard. Hermie made a mental note to tell Oscy that there was a Pinkerton woman on the premises and that the drugstore therefore was not a good place to attempt any kind of shoplifting in. Mr. Sanders returned to the far counter and hurled himself into inventory. Druggists did that a lot, took inventory. It was a way of life.

Hermie ambled along, aimlessly whistling "Jingle Bells" to keep cool. He edged his way gradually toward the door, where the irritating tones of the harmonica grew louder, sounding like a strangling chicken. Hermie opened the door. The bell chimed, and Mr. Sanders looked up to see Hermie leave without buying anything.

Oscy stopped strangling the chicken when he noticed Hermie standing alongside him, taking the sea air in big inhalations and casually inquiring, "Everything all right out here?"

"Yeah," said Oscy, wondering what the hell was going on.

"Good," said Hermie. And he studied the sky. He always made people out of clouds when he had the time. And up there was either Dick Haymes or Maria Montez or Carmen Miran—

"Did you get 'em?" Oscy knew a stall when confronted with one.

"No. Not yet."

"Well, get 'em."

"There's a lady in there."

"Oh." Oscy seemed to understand. The bell chimed as the door opened, and the strolling lady came out, on her way home. The door shut behind her, and the bell went off again only not so loud because it was inside where Hermie was supposed to be. "That her?" asked Oscy.

"Yeah."

"Any others inside?"

"Maybe. They could be bending down."

Oscy shoved him. "Go on, Hermie. For Chrissakes."

Hermie reentered the drugstore, the bell blasting in his ear, telling him there was no way back, especially since Mr. Sanders, more than just curious, was striding toward him. "Yes?"

"It's me"—Hermie smiled—"same guy as before. Just stepped outside for a little air." He kept talking like a fool. "Nice air out there. A lot of very nice sea air. This whole island has nice air. Yes, sir."

Mr. Sanders grew apprehensive at the jabbering little fool with his clothes all drawn in tight on such a warm morning. "Just what is it you're looking for? Maybe I can help you." Only he didn't look as if he wanted to help. He looked more as if he were going to make a citizen's arrest.

"Oh, I'll know when I find it." Fat chance. Rubbers were kept under lock and key. And in a back room. Or a cellar. Or a vault. Or a cave that there was no access to at high tide.

"Perhaps if you'll tell me—"

Hermie had to come up with something—and soon. "Ah, I just remembered."

"A-yuh?" And he waited to hear Hermie's request. Except it didn't look as if he were planning on waiting too long, so Hermie took a flier.

"A strawberry ice-cream cone."

There was something suspicious about that boy, thought Mr. Sanders. One thing was for certain: he was not to be left alone, out of sight. "All right," he said. "Come with me." He went behind the fountain counter, making certain that Hermie was following close by. Hermie slid up onto one of the stools, and Mr. Sanders confronted him across the marble counter. "One dip or two?" He had the ice-cream scoop ready. It looked like a microphone. Hermie wished the old son of a bitch would stop pressing him and just sing.

"Better make it a double." He tried to avoid the eyes of the weather-beaten old Yankee. With guys like that around, no wonder the British ended up with all their fucking tea in Boston Harbor.

Mr. Sanders constructed the double dip and pushed it across at Hermie. "Okay. That'll be twelve cents." Ming the Merciless. Killer Kane. The whole bunch of 'em rolled into one. Hermie had picked for himself some adversary. He wanted to bolt for the door and get out of there, but there was too much involved. It was still far off, but there was a championship at stake. He decided that the bull had to be taken by the goddamn horns. So he leaned across the counter, looking at the Yankee via his reflection in the marble countertop and said, "There a—there's something else I need."

The countertop answered, upside down. "A-yuh?" It came as a menacing growl. Sylvana, the evil scientist, had spoken, and Hermie backed off, gutless, and said, "Sprinkles."

The Yankee thrust the cone into the chrome bowl of chocolate sprinkles. Then he handed it right across to Hermie, who silently figured that he could ask for nuts and a cherry and still be within his rights. "Anything else?" snapped the druggist.

Once more into the fray, another summoning of courage, one last crack at the moon as he balanced the ice cream in his tiny hand. "I hate to bother, but—" He took a lick at the cone. Good. Strawberry. Not surprising since strawberry had been what he asked for. Still, it was a fine-caliber strawberry, rich with little chunks and tasty seeds.

"Speak up, boy!" That was a bark. A definite bark from behind clenched teeth. Not easily done.

"How about a napkin?" Hermie was surprised at how readily he could turn tail. It was a gift. But he was fast running out of deceptive tactics.

The paper napkin came flying at him; good thing it wasn't a manhole cover. "Anything else?" That was sarcasm.

"How about some rubbers?" That was quick. Hermie wasn't even sure he'd said it. Maybe it was Oscy standing behind him. Or Edgar Bergen. Or Tokyo Rose.

"Pardon?" The Yankee had a surprised look on his face. The son of a bitch was off-balance. Hermie knew he had the opening he needed. He waded in like Henry Armstrong. Hit the son of a bitch again. But with poise and carriage. Shit, it had to have some poise and carriage or else where was he? "I understand you carry them."

"Carry what?" Aha. Evasive action from the other side.

"Come on. You know what." What poise. What fucking carriage. He took another lick at his ice cream. What strawberry.

"Do you mean contraceptives?"

"Right." The old bastard caught on fast.

"You want to *buy* some?"

"Right."

"What for?"

What for? The guy had to be some kind of fuddy-duddy nincompoop. Hermie delivered a half-smile, as if he and the old codger were school chums. "Come on, you know what for." He buried his face in the ice cream because the heat of his hand was causing the strawberry shit to run down his wrist. The trick was to not look at his opponent.

The Yankee took a moment to assess the situation. Then he walked down to the far end of the marble counter and over into the drug section, the place where the hot stuff was dispensed. Kotex. Pills. Rubbers. He signaled for Hermie to come over. Hermie slid off his stool, feeling like a gangster about to pick up some protection money. He shuffled over, in no particular hurry. All was moving well. Oscy was posted outside. And *he* was about to make his purchase. The Yankee looked squarely at him but with an expressionless face. "What brand?"

What brand? That was news to Hermie. "Brand?"

"Brand and style." Mr. Sanders was sure playing it cool.

Hermie wondered if the old fart wasn't just toying with him. A diplomatic response was called for. "Oh—the usual." That should do it. Now another lick of the ice cream.

The druggist's hands disappeared from the counter. Then they reappeared. They disappeared and reappeared two, three, four times. And soon Hermie was looking at a collection of different-sized and different-colored little packages that his mother could make one helluvan afghan out of. There were enough rubbers there for the entire Second Marines. "There's a number to choose from, you know." The old man said that flatly, as if everyone in the world knew it.

Hermie was unsettled. For a moment he thought he felt his mother looking over his shoulder. He looked, but she was gone. She could do that. He looked back at the druggist. "Do you have to flash 'em around?"

There was still no expression on Mr. Sanders' face. "Which is your usual?" Hermie was standing square at the Maginot Line. In front of him was a collection of dandy little packages, all neatly sealed and wrapped and alive with raw sex. Behind him was his callow youth. He had just been asked to make his selection from the Crown Jewels of England. With so little experience in those matters, he decided to go with his favorite color. "The blue ones." He began to wonder if the color on the outside of each package was matched by the color of the rubber within. The last thing he wanted to do was frighten Aggie by confronting her with a huge blue pecker. But then, red might even be worse, not to mention green. And plaid could send a young girl screaming off into the night. He wished he'd gone with the flesh-colored package, but it was too late. The dye, as it were, had been cast. And the heat of his hand was beginning to do away with his ice cream as though a disintegrator gun were working on it. A few drops of melted strawberry plopped onto his sneakers. All of him was melting.

Mr. Sanders pushed the blue packages toward Hermie as if he were betting chips in a poker game. "How many would you like?"

Another question to boggle the mind. How many? Oh, well. Take a shot at it. "Oh, three dozen."

The druggist almost smiled, but not quite. He was playing Hermie like a trout, in a shallow stream, in a net. "Planning a big night?"

"Just the usual." It had gotten him *this* far, so why not try it again?

The druggist shoveled all the other packages under the counter and pulled out a whole carton of blue ones. Blue was obviously a big seller around those parts. The druggist counted out a seemingly endless number of them, and Hermie wondered how many Marines would have to go without because of his horny selfishness. "That'll be twelve dollars."

Twelve dollars to lay Aggie seemed pretty steep. Maybe he was being cheated. Those old Yankee traders just loved to take the city slickers. Hermie figured he'd better offer up a little resistance, or else he'd be sweeping out that drugstore for the rest of the summer, just to pay back the fucking money. "Twelve dollars?" God, his voice sounded tiny.

"And twelve cents. For the ice cream."

"I see. How much for just a dozen?"

"Four dollars."

"And how many for a dollar?"

"Three."

"I'll take two."

"They come three to a package."

"Can I owe you for the ice cream?"

Mr. Sanders became very stern. Yet he also became quite fatherly. "All right now, son, fun is fun, but how old *are* you?"

"Sixteen."

"How old?"

"Sixteen. We're inclined to be small in my family."

The druggist studied Hermie, watching him squirm and letting him. Watching the ice cream running down Hermie's wrist. Tapping the package of rubbers. "What are you going to do with these?"

"They're for my brother. He's older. But he's not much taller." He was running off at the mouth again. "None of us are very tall. There's even a couple midgets in the family." He figured he'd better cut that stuff out because he was hanging himself pretty neatly. He licked the ice cream in a spiral motion because the damn stuff was quickly leaving town.

"Why can't your brother come in and get them for himself? Too small to reach the counter?" Mr. Sanders laughed at his own dumb-assed Yankee witticism.

"He's been a little under the weather." Hermie was flying blind, but he still hadn't been thrown out. Also, he sensed that the druggist was kind of enjoying himself.

"Then what does he need them for?" asked the druggist.

"He says they make him feel better." Hermie was playing the stupid little kid. It seemed to be getting results.

"Is he going to eat them?" The old son of a bitch was really knocking himself out with all that high comedy. Meanwhile, Hermie wondered where he'd heard that question before?

"I don't know what he's going to do with them. He never tells me." Hermie figured that stupid ignorance was the best approach, especially since all else had failed.

The old man was really beaming. Two teeth were missing. Two were gold. The rest were brown. Except one, which was a fang. "Do you know what these are used for?"

"They're for servicemen, that's all I know. My brother's a Ranger. One of the smallest Rangers they have, but he still uses a lot of them." Hermie tried to look like Benjie. If he could look like Benjie, he could get away with the whole thing.

"Care to take a *guess* what they're for?"

"Well, I know what *I'd* use 'em for."

"Oh?" That stopped him.

"Yeah. I'd fill 'em with water and throw 'em off a roof." He had heard that a lot of kids did that. From a six-story building they could make quite a splat. "I think maybe the Rangers fill 'em with nitro and throw 'em at enemy tanks. My brother told me that. I think he can curve 'em." Hermie knew he had the dumbest look on his face imaginable. He had succeeded in looking like Benjie. Wait till he tried it on Oscy.

Mr. Sanders had to smile at the dumb kid. "Well, I just wanted to make sure you knew what they were for."

Hermie was getting so good at playing dumb, he couldn't resist taking it a bit further. With wide eyes he said, "Is that what they're really for? I thought maybe my brother was kidding me."

Mr. Sanders was finding a plain brown bag. "Well, different people fill 'em with different things." He chuckled. He had always figured he was a jocular type; now he knew for sure. He couldn't wait to tell the gang around the fucking cracker barrel about the dumb Brooklyn kid and the rubbers. That would be a real thigh slapper, yessiree bob.

"Be pretty wild thrown out of a B-17 at twenty thousand feet, wouldn't it?" Hermie wanted the snaggle-toothed old ferret to have a lot of real yoks around the rhubarb. Yessir-ee-rube.

The old man smiled. "Technically, son, I shouldn't be selling these to minors, but seein' as how they're for someone in service, well, I'll close my eyes to it." He rang up the cash register. "Let's call it a dollar even, okay?"

"A-yuh." Hermie handed him the dollar, which, as it turned out, was all he had; only originally he had expected some change. Still, he was glad to be done with it and lucky at that to have outcrafted the wily old druggist. And so, with the rubbers in one hand and the fast-fading ice cream cone in the other, he walked toward the door as a magnificent advertisement for adolescence. Ice cream and rubbers, there was a song in there somewhere, best sung by Bobby Breen.

Just as he reached the door, it opened and the bell tinkled, and of all people, Aggie walked in. Oscy was still at his post, blaring dissonant harmonic warnings, but Hermie had been too deep in battle to hear the blare. The door closed, and Oscy was out of it again. Aggie smiled at Hermie. Also, she spoke. That was new for her. "Hi, Hermie."

"Hi, Aggie." He clutched tightly at his bag of blue rubbers. No sense in her seeing them so early in their relationship. He put away the last vestiges of his leaky ice cream by chomping on the empty cone.

"I had a very nice time at the movie the other night."

"I did, too."

"We never really had a chance to really discuss the film, did we?"

"I guess not. How's the old arm?" He thought he'd better ask. At least to let her know that he knew it was an arm all along.

"It's fine, thank you."

"I do that a lot. I don't like to offend so, I just . . . squeeze an arm. Lets a girl know I like her and she doesn't have to panic that I'm getting fresh."

"Sure. Arms are all right." She shrugged. What the hell else could she say to such sexual theorizing?

"Yeah. Nothing wrong with arms." He was running out of sparkling chatter. "Well—there you go." He smiled like a drip.

"It was very nice of you to ask me to the marshmallow roast tonight. I'm looking forward to it."

"Me, too." He could smell the rubber burning in the paper bag. In a minute there'd be smoke, then the fire department, then his arrest. And old man Sanders could go to the hoosegow *with* him. Hermie smiled. "Well, Oscy's outside. He's bringing the marshmallows."

"And what are *you* bringing?"

"So long."

He went out through the chiming doorway, sweeping past Oscy, who fell immediately in step with him, slapping his harmonica against his palm and getting a load of spit there in a hurry. Which he then wiped on his sweat shirt, often referred to as the city dump. "Did you get 'em?"

"Yeah. They're blue." He rattled the bag as if to demonstrate the color to Oscy.

"Blue?"

"Yeah. I'm pretty sure."

"Blue's okay." What the hell did *Oscy* know? "They in the bag?"

"Yeah." He rattled the bag again. For emphasis.

"How many'd you get?"

"They come three to a pack, you know."

"I know." The hell he did. He looked very excited. "How many packages did you get?"

"I figured I'd hold it down to one." Big shot.

"Yeah." Idiot.

"Aggie's in the drugstore."

"I know."

"Think *she's* getting some, too?"

"I don't think women use 'em. It's the man's job."

"Seems we have to do everything."

"How do you think you feel, Hermie?"

"Okay."

"Think you're up to it?"

"I think so. You?"

"Sure." Oscy played his harmonica again, and the two boys went down to the grocery store to buy a couple hundred marshmallows.

PARLOR GAMES

James T. Farrell

The *Studs Lonigan* trilogy, from which this selection is taken, is a poignant study of the destructive effects of environment on an essentially good character. Set in the Irish-populated slums of Chicago, Farrell's book details the brutalizing conditions of spiritual and material poverty that change Studs Lonigan from the healthy and basically decent boy we meet in this episode to the corrupt and dissipated adult who dies before his youth is scarcely over. Even in the relatively innocent atmosphere of adolescent kissing games there intrudes the pugnaciousness, lower-class prejudice and brutal cynicism born of South Chicago streets. Yet the scene that Farrell captures here transcends cultural conditioning. It concerns the kind of sexual initiation rituals and initiation period prerequisite to maturity in societies primitive and modern. What may be particularly Western, even particularly American, however, is the awkwardness and painfulness with which these children make the sexual adjustments from childhood to self-sufficient adulthood. Lonigan's friends have been so emotionally crippled by the sense of sin instilled in them by their Catholic rearing, and by general cultural deprivation, that psychological independence and maturity is hard to come by, if it is achieved at all. Hence, we find the children scorning those parlor games that are associated with child behavior rather than adult behavior, but unable to interact harmoniously with one another on adult terms. Baffled by new social demands and by physiological changes associated with puberty, both sets of individuals, male and female, play at identities they think fit the situation. The boys clown and act brash and aggressive, and the girls feign gentility and decorum.

It was the first evening of the official maturity of the young people in the parlor, and after getting seated they wondered what to do; the boys sat stiffly on one side of the room, and gazed furtively at their long trousers; the girls faced them, acting prim and reserved. Growing up had always meant more freedom, and here they were after their graduation, afraid to do anything lest it seem kiddish; afraid, particularly, to play the kids' kissing games they used to play at parties.

"Well, what'll we do?" grumbled Weary, who sat between Studs and sallow-faced TB on the unscratched piano stool.

"Yeah, let's do something," Studs suggested.

Soft-skinned and fattish Bill Donoghue was seated under the floor lamp near them. He said:

"Now that's a bright idea!"

Studs made a face at Bill, as if to say: Go soak yer head!

"Bill's a loogin who always tries to wisecrack," Studs said.

"Studs is a little fruity!" Bill said, and they laughed.

"Such awful slang you boys use." Helen Borax said.

Studs scowled at Helen and said:

"Bill, I'm going to slap your pretty wrist!"

Helen colored slightly, and elevated her nose.

Bill got limp like a sissy, and tapped his own wrist daintily, and everybody laughed at his comics, because Bill was really very funny.

"Well, anyway, I'm glad I'm through school," said Tubby Connell, a kinky-haired, darkish boy who had plunked, uncomfortably, in the corner easy chair that Mrs. Lonigan always said must be beautiful, because it had cost over a hundred dollars.

"Ope! Look what the wind blew in!" Bill said, looking at Tubby.

"Another lost country heard from," muttered Studs.

Tubby blushed bashfully.

"Anyway, I'm darn glad to get out of that joint," Weary said.

"Frank, it isn't a joint . . . And you jus' wait. You'll be sorry and wish you were back at St. Patrick's just like Father Gilhooley said we'd all remember our days there," his sister said.

"Weary didn't hear him say that. When Gilly was talking of that, I heard him snoring," Bill said, and they laughed.

Peggy Nugent said you shouldn't speak of a priest like that, or something awful might happen to you. You should always say Father Gilhooley. She smiled, and everybody could see she thought it was thrilling to call him Gilly.

"Well, he has gills like a fish," Bill said.

"How disrespectful," Lucy Scanlan said, twinkling her blue eyes.

Weary made faces at his sister. Tubby reiterated that he was glad to get out of jail because he felt that he had to say something. He was blushing.

They laughed, and TB said he, too, was darn glad to get out of the pen, and they laughed again.

"I'll be glad to get to high school," said well-behaved Dan Donoghue, and just as he did, Bill aimed a peanut at Tubby. Connell told him to cut it out, and Bill asked what in a very innocent voice.

He and Tubby carried on a side-dialogue.

"You will, Dan? Why?" asked Fran Lonigan.

"Oh, I just will," said Dan.

"Well, I don't know if I'm glad or not," said Fran.

"What school do you think you'll go to, Studs?" asked Lucy, smiling with her sweet baby-face.

"None."

"William, you know you're going to high school," his sister said sternly, as if she were an adult scolding him.

"Yeah, I suppose I don't know what I'm gonna do," said Studs.

"You most certainly do not," said she.

"We'll see," said he, trying to save his scattering dignity.

"Father will see!" said she with finality.

He scowled, felt unmanned, felt that Weary was sneering at him as if he was a weak sister. He looked at his meaningless long trousers.

Weary said with great braggadocio he wasn't going to high school and his sister protested. Tall Jim Clayburn said he thought going to school was sensible and necessary if you wanted to get ahead. He said he thought that Sister Bertha had once told them the truth when she said you needed education and stick-to-it-iveness to get ahead in life. Lucy said Jim was so sensible, and she had a devilish look in her eyes. Dan commenced to agree with Jim, but his brother interrupted him:

"Say, did you see High Collars?"

"Yeah, I saw him walkin' with Dorothy and his wife," Tubby said, glad to get back in the conversation.

"He wouldn't let her come to the party. He told Mother that Dorothy needed her proper rest," said Fran Lonigan.

"He's an old mean thing," said Lucy.

"The poor kid! She's all right, and awfully sweet, but she can't ever do anything on account of her father. Sometimes she tells me about it, and cries," exclaimed Fran Reilley.

"I wouldn't want an old man like him," TB said.

They looked at TB, because his old man was nothing to brag about.

"Anyway, he didn't wear his silk hat tonight," Dan said.

"I wonder if he uses perfume?" TB said.

"I'll bet he wears ladies' underwear," contributed Bill Donoghue.

The guys haw-hawed, and the girls giggled modestly after stating that Bill's language was not exactly nice.

They talked on, and wondered what they would do. Bill goofed Tubby, because Connell looked like a smoke, and Bill said that now Tubby was graduated, he shouldn't find no trouble becoming a Pullman porter. TB said that every time he saw Tubby he thought it would rain because of dark clouds all around. Tubby hock-hocked in imitation of Muggsy, and the girls said Tubby was too frightful for words.

Jim Clayburn went to the baby grand, and Bill said that they would now listen to Good Old Stick-To-It-Iveness. Jim played, and they crowded around, singing, but they couldn't get any harmony because Bill bellowed and Tubby and Muggsy tried to be funny. They sang *Alexander's Rag Time Band*, *The River Shannon Flowing*, *It's a Long Way to Tipperary*, *Dear Old Girl*, *Dance and Grow Thin*, and *Bell Brandon*. Then Jim started *In My Harem*. Bill got in the center of the floor and did a shocking hula-hula that was so funny they nearly split laughing; he sang:

> *And the dance they do . . .*
> *Is enough to kill a Jew . . .*
> *Da-Da-Dadadada-Da . . .*
> *In my harem with Pat Malone.*

Jim played *When It's Apple Blossom Time in Normandy*, and just as they started the chorus Bill goosed Tubby, and Studs did the same with TB. The two victims jumped, yelling ouch. It broke up the singing and everybody laughed. Bill asked Rastus where the ghosts were, and Tubby replied by calling Bill snake Irish, so low that he crawled in the mud. Studs said that trying to decide which was the worst, an Irishman or a jigg, was like shooting craps for stage money with loaded dice; and he was proud of his crack even if they didn't laugh.

"Let's dance!" Helen said, interrupting all the tomfoolery.

The fellows who knew how foxtrotted with the girls while Lucy played. Studs, TB and Weary stood in a corner whispering dirty jokes.

When the others tired of dancing, they sat down; this time the fellows weren't all on one side of the room and the girls on the other. They talked some more, and wondered what they would do, and Bill kept the party going by his clowning. Martin wandered in, looking oh-so-darling, and the girls made a fuss trying to pet him. Tubby finally grabbed him and said:

"Let's fight, you little rascal!"

Martin biffed Tubby, and Bill said:

"The kid takes after his big brother, only he's got it on him with the dukes."

Tubby then grabbed Martin again, and the child said:

"Lemme go, you boob!"

The guys clapped, and the girls were taken by his cuteness. Fran said it was the wrong way for Martin to take after his brother.

Lucy pulled Martin toward her, tied him with her arms, said he was just too darling for words; she kissed him.

"Yeah, he's got it on his brother all around. As a Romeo, he's got Studs backed off the boards," Bill said.

Studs blushed and got exceedingly interested in the stale joke with which Tubby was laboring.

Martin fought free, and as he rushed out of the room he yelled back:

"I wish to hell you'd lemme 'lone!"

They laughed; Fran Lonigan frowned.

The conversation went on; everybody wondered what they would do. Lucy set them at ease by boldly suggesting wink. The girls blushed and giggled while they were getting into their places. But the game went off stiffly because there were too many boys. They changed to kiss-the-pillow. Everyone got into the spirit of the game, even Weary. He found it wasn't so goofy kissing girls. And Helen Borax acted like she might have a crush on him. He'd never thought much of her, except that she was the kind of a chicken who never tried to act her age and who seemed to think she was a queen. But it wasn't hard to kiss her. And Studs got gay because he was getting his chance to kiss Lucy, and he didn't have to keep his liking for her under cover. He told himself he liked her, and repeated this; he liked her around him, liked to look at her, liked her laugh, liked her near him, liked to think of doing things for her, suffering, fighting, playing football, defending her against demons and villains, and anybody.

As they played, Fran Lonigan said: "Gee, what would Sister Bernadette Marie, what would she say if she saw us now?"

"I wonder," smiled Helen Borax.

"Particularly you girls. She'd expect it of me, because she always said I was only a chicken, anyway, and not serious like Helen and you girls," Lucy said.

Helen colored.

Bill smiled broadly, and said that if Bertha knew about it she'd get jealous and wish that she'd been around to play. He said she joined the convent because she'd been disappointed in love, and maybe if she got the chance she'd get a crush on TB or Tubby.

"What do you mean she's been disappointed in love?" asked TB.

"Sure. She acts just like an old maid," Bill said.

"But what I want to know is who'd love her?" asked TB.

They laughed, and the girls thought it was horrid.

Bill kept the floor and said he knew the old battleaxe would like to play. He said he'd show just how she would play. He put on a sour pan, hunched himself a trifle, the way she was hunched, talked shrilly and goofily, and dropped the pillow in front of Muggsy. He kissed Tubby, who blushed with embarrassment, and they nearly all split their sides laughing.

The game went on. Studs dropped the pillow, by accident, in front of Helen. They looked meanly at each other, and neither moved until everybody yelled at them to play the game square, so they knelt down, each at an edge of the pillow, peck-kissed each other, and deepened their mutual hatred.

They changed to post-office. Tubby was suggested as postmaster, but Bill demanded the job, saying he was the logical person to examine all transactions. Fran Lonigan, as hostess, started the ball rolling. As she walked into the bedroom, right off the parlor entrance, Bill grabbed her, and kissed her; it was his tax. She laughed and didn't get angry. Fran called Dan. Dan kissed Bill on the way of entry. It was funny.

Dan called Fran Reilley, and kissed her. She called her brother. She stamped his toe, and ran out saying it was for a special delivery letter. He got sore, but she had gotten away too quickly. He told Bill to call Borax.

Weary kissed her flush on the mouth. He held her there, and when he finally released her, she sighed deeply.

He kissed her again, and she powerlessly tightened against him. He forced her to the bed.

"Stop touching me there. Stop!" she whispered.

When he paused, breathless, she demanded an apology.

"Shut up!" he muttered.

He bent down and kissed her.

"Unhand me, you cur. Take your hands off!" she whispered. "Take your hands off there, or I'll scream!"

He pulled her to him and kissed her. She became limp in his arms. He kissed her again, and she pressed to him. He loosed her. She called him a cur and demanded an apology.

"Shut up!"

She bit her lips, fought back tears, and said in a low, strained voice:

"Apologize!"

"Kiss me!"

She was a girl suddenly baffled by a woman's impulses.

She flung herself around him. Then he walked out.

Regaining her composure and rearranging herself, she called in Jim. In the parlor they looked at Weary, surprised and over-curious. There was a tight silence, which Bill broke by saying that Weary had received a delayed letter. They laughed, and Weary's frown broke into a smile.

Jim, in the meantime, had called in Lucy; and she called Studs. She pursed her lips before she kissed him. It was so sudden, and her lips had such a sweet, candy taste that he was pleasantly surprised and stood there, not knowing what to do or say. He had never kissed sweet lips like that before. He faced her, and she was something beautiful and fair, with her white dress vivid in the dark room. She looked beautiful, like a flame. She pursed her lips, moved closer to him, flung her arms around him, kissed him, and said:

"I like you!"

She kissed away his surprise, looked dreamily into his eyes, kissed him again, long, and then dashed out.

Jesus Christ! he said to himself.

The game went on. Studs and Lucy, Helen and Weary kept calling each other into the post office. All the guys except TB and Tubby got their share of kisses. Tubby was called a few times for charity's sake, but TB was left out in the cold. He sat in a corner, wisecracking as if he didn't mind. He knew he didn't belong there anyway. Probably he did have the con, as everybody said and believed.